Scotland's
Greatest Games

David Potter

Know The Score Books Limited
118 Alcester Road
Studley, Warwickshire B80 7NT
01527 454482
info@knowthescorebooks.com
www.knowthescorebooks.com

A CIP catalogue record is available for this book from the British Library
ISBN: 978-1-84818-200-4

Printed and bound in Great Britain
by TJ International

CONTENTS

FOREWORD

SANDWICHED DELIGHTFULLY between years of supporting Scotland as a member of the famous Tartan Army came a period when I was unbelievably privileged to sit on the bench during 136 full internationals and have an influence, to a greater or lesser degree, on the outcome of the match.

As a boy I regularly occupied the schoolboy enclosure at home matches at Hampden. This was a packed standing area at the front of the South Stand. Now my frequent visits to the famous stadium reawaken all sorts of familiar memories – pipe bands marching, a booming broadcast system, the impeccably turned out players with their faces set in grim determination as they walk out to respect the National Anthems. Being small, I saw very little. But I was there!

The fans were, and still are, there too. With fervent, almost manic, dedication, they work, live, and save up to go to watch Scotland. Their devotion is total. Football is in their hearts. It gives meaning to their existence. This is learned from an early age and never forgotten. In spite of the worldwide credit crunch, rising unemployment, falling house prices and recession, the members of the famous Tartan Army find a way to follow their team. Never a rebellious support, they have a passionate, romantic belief in the superiority of all things Scottish, especially Scottish Football. They are not alone because one thing for which foreigners have always given us credit is for the quality of our football players.

Proof of this 'phenomenon' is easy for me. To have seen so many legends such as Bill Brown, Dave Mackay, Joe Jordan, Davy Wilson, Danny McGrain, Denis Law, Jimmy Johnstone, Jim Baxter, Eric Caldow and Billy McNeill, then to be honoured to be on the same training pitch with greats like Alan Rough, Jim Leighton, Andy Goram, Kenny Dalglish, Willie Miller, Alex McLeish, Murdo Macleod, Gordon Strachan, Paul McStay, Paul Sturrock, Steve Archibald, Graeme Souness, Mo Johnstone, Murdo Macleod, Steve Nicol, Tom Boyd, Ally McCoist, Kevin Gallacher, Paul Lambert, Colin Hendry, Colin Calderwood, David Weir, etc, etc... This far from exhaustive, incomplete, list continues with the likes of Craig Gordon, Darren Fletcher and James McFadden of the modern era.

The story of Scotland's national football team is an ever-changing tale of drama, heart-stopping moments of occasional euphoria, but too frequently tears and recriminations. Having enjoyed the experience of coaching at three World Cups (1986, 1990, 1998) and two European Championships (1992 and 1996 – the only two in which Scotland have participated), I am biased, but I feel this was the halcyon period for Scottish international football.

In that 12 year period not only did the full international team enjoy success, the Scotland U21 side twice reached the semi-final of the European Championship, being officially placed 3rd in 1992 and 1996. The U20 side reached the quarter-finals of the World Youth Championship in Chile in 1987 and was officially 6th in the world FIFA rankings. In 1989, in the final of the FIFA World U16 Championship, our side finished runners-up to Saudi Arabia, achieving 2nd place in the FIFA rankings. As I coached Scotland on all those occasions, I am proud of all these achievements, not only at senior level.

Prior to this 12 year period of unprecedented success, I witnessed Archie Gemmill's masterpiece against the Netherlands in Argentina in 1978, I delighted in us 'winning the

World Cup' by beating holders, England, at Wembley in 1967, I saw Joe Jordan score that great goal against Czechoslovakia, and held my breath when the late, great Davie Cooper slotted that penalty against Wales ... wonderful memories!

Informed and gifted writer David Potter has chosen his 50 most momentous games from Scottish history. It would be hard to disagree with his selection. When I was with the team for 5 of Sir Alex Ferguson's 10 games in charge, 60 of Andy Roxburgh's 61 games (except for a friendly in Saudi Arabia when I was with our U21 side playing England in the UEFA semi-final first leg at City Ground, Nottingham) and the 71 games when I was in charge, there were many highlights. Clearly, the four of these fixtures chosen for this publication are vivid in my memory.

One which looms large in my memory, although not only for on-the-pitch reasons, was when French manager Michel Platini brought a team of superstars to Glasgow on a wet evening in 1989 only to be humbled by Mo Johnston's two great goals. However the real drama came prior to the game. Everyone speaks about the importance of proper preparation for a match. Normally this is the case, but on the way from our hotel at Gleneagles to Hampden for this match against France our coach was caught up in the busier than normal match traffic. Amazingly, only one mobile phone existed among our squad, so Roy Aitken's 'half brick' was used to summon an escort from Cumbernauld. Even with the excellent police provision we arrived at the National Stadium just before 7.30pm for the 8 o'clock kick-off, with no time for a proper warm up. Compensating for that was the collective and heroic application normally associated with Scottish teams. The result? A resounding 2–0 victory and a place in the FIFA World Cup finals in Italy at the expense of our visitors.

Among David's selection is the UEFA European Championships in Sweden where, not surprisingly, our fans were given the award for being the best in the tournament. Inspired by those wonderful fans off the pitch and Pat Nevin, Brian McClair and Paul McStay on it, we trounced the CIS 3–0.

Qualification for Euro 96 was obtained by yet another outstanding Jim Leighton performance (one of his 45 clean sheets in his 91 international appearances) and by dint of a fine solo goal by John McGinlay against Sweden at Ibrox. With the National Stadium being refurbished we had to play our bigger home matches at Ibrox and Celtic Park. Both venues proved to be successful as the fine victory over Austria at Celtic Park, also included, will testify.

Having qualified for two successive tournaments, Euro 96 and France 98, a third hinged on a play-off tie against England in late 1999. My contention is that had Paul Lambert not sustained a facial injury in the Old Firm game the week before the first leg at Hampden, Paul Scholes would not have scored the two goals which effectively eliminated us from the tie. In the second leg, once again tremendous resolution and character enabled us to get back into the game through a fine Don Hutchison goal before half-time. The fates undoubtedly conspired against us when we dominated the second 45 but just couldn't score to take the game to extra time. During the interval, while I was in the visiting dressing room (we were given the 'home' one against England in Euro 96 as we were the 'home' side then), my two Tartan Army sons, Hugh and John, assured me that players and staff missed out on a never-to-be-forgotten singing interlude by the incorrigible Scotland fans. Although the narrow, and undeserved, defeat deprived us of a third consecutive qualification, it did not deprive any of the fans of exciting memories ... and there are many more in this outstanding publication.

CRAIG BROWN CBE

INTRODUCTION

I N RECENT YEARS it has often been the case that Scotland's results have been received with a certain amount of levity; even hilarity and ridicule. It has to be owned that Scotland have been conspicuously absent from recent feasts of World and European finals. A full decade has passed without Scotland being seen on the major stage. For a nation which is obsessed with football and has more people per head of the population involved in football (playing, refereeing, spectating) than most other nations, this is an intolerable situation.

Yet it was not always so! This book is an attempt to show that there have been times in history when Scotland were the best in the world – I refer to the 1880s, the 1920s and possibly the early 1900s – and that at other times, they were very respectable opponents indeed. 50 games have been chosen to show Scotland at its best, and an attempt has been made to set Scotland games against national and world events; Empire, wars, depression, Welfare State and industrial unrest not excluded.

The tragic years of 1914 to 1919 for example have been highlighted by the Scotland v England games at each end of the conflict. For similar reasons, the Victory international of 1946 (the only unofficial international of the 50) has been included to indicate the sheer passion for Scottish football which had been perforce compelled to lie dormant among the sands of the African Desert, the jungles of Burma or the waves of the Atlantic Ocean.

An attempt has also been made to show the gradual development of the game from the benign amateurism of the 1870s and 1880s to the obsessive and money-centred professionalism of the present day. This has also been paralleled by the expansion of 'Scotland' from the area of Glasgow and Dunbartonshire to first Edin-burgh then north to Dundee and Aberdeen before becoming in the 21st century a global concept. Yet in all ages, the desire to win for Scotland has been paramount.

A large proportion of the games selected have been against England. This is inevitable. England – one hesitates to say the 'Auld Enemy', for enemies are people that you want to kill, whereas Scotland and England have shared a marvellously symbiotic rivalry as Jimmy Quinn, Hughie Gallacher and Alan Gilzean took over from William Wallace, Robert the Bruce and Bonnie Prince Charlie – remain Scotland's oldest rival, and the games against England were always the highlight and even the defining point of the season, attracting crowds of well over 100,000 on a regular basis, and possibly being a greater rivalry than Celtic v Rangers.

Not all the games chosen have been victories, although the vast majority are. The criterion: 'Did this game make Scotland feel good about itself?' For this reason some of the high profile grizzly horrors of World Cup games have been omitted. For example, the 2-0 victory over Zaire in 1974 was Scotland's first ever victory in World Cup Finals. It was significant, but could it honestly be described as one of the greatest?

INTRODUCTION

Unusual things abound. A black man played for Scotland in the 1880s and no-one seemed to care or even mention it, a game was played in Edinburgh in a snowstorm and the miniscule crowd pleaded with the referee to let them go home, the Gordon Highlanders were summoned from their Barracks and kept in readiness lest a crowd got out of hand, a Scottish footballer was freely compared to Charles Stewart Parnell in Ireland, an English goalkeeper who had a shocker against Scotland entertained visitors to his pub by telling them about it for decades, a Raith Rovers player captained Scotland to a treble against the other British counties, a Morton goal-keeper saved the day at Wembley, the SFA refused to play in the World Cup unless they were British Champions first, Scotland players were 'prayed for' in Churches for playing a World Cup qualifier on a Sunday, a Celtic player needed reassurance that IRA terrorists would not shoot HIM, a Scotland manager died tragically on the bench at the end of a game, and one of Scotland's best ever performances in Europe was against a team that did not exist a year before and did not exist a year later either!

Supporting Scotland can, of course, be a painful experience. It certainly has been so recently, but it can also be pleasant, as for example in the aftermath of the two great victories over France in 2006 and 2007. This book is an attempt to recreate some of this, and includes a wish and a prayer that such days can return.

My thanks are due, in the first instance, to the scribes of *The Scotsman*, *The Glasgow Herald*, *The Courier*, *The Sunday Post* and many other newspapers which faithfully reported Scotland games since 1872, and to the unfailing courtesy and help shown to me by librarians in the National Library of Scotland in Edinburgh, the Wellgate Library in Dundee and the Mitchell Library in Glasgow where such news-papers and journals are stored.

People who have given me help and encouragement include Tom Campbell, Drew Balfour, David McGregor, Richard Grant, Dave McKenzie and many others. Scotland's one time Manager, Craig Brown, apart from writing the Foreword has proved very helpful in talking about a few of the games in which he has involved. For the English perspective (always very valuable when the emotion is likely to get out of hand!), I am indebted to Simon Lowe, Phil H. Jones and John McCue. Posthumous thanks are due to the late John Jolly, Colin McNab, my father Angus Potter, grandfa-ther William Pringle and my uncle Willie Young who did not depart this scene without sharing a few of the memories and passions involved in supporting Scotland. My wife Rosemary, son Andrew, daughters Alison and Susan and their respective husbands David Weir and Dougie Simpson are also due a note of thanks for their benign and supportive tolerance of my obsession. Hamish Leifer was also very helpful in proof reading. But my main acknowledgement must go to those who have played for Scotland over the years, and the untold millions who have supported them. Supporting Scotland remains an incurable disease – endogenous, addictive, all consuming and occasionally close to life threatening! To them all, I am much indebted.

David Potter

v ENGLAND 0-0
Hamilton Crescent; Att: 3,500
30 November 1872

Scotland:	England:
Gardner (Queen's Park)	Welch (Wanderers)
Thomson (Queen's Park)	Greenhalgh (Notts County)
Ker (Queen's Park)	Barker (Hertfordshire Rangers)
Taylor (Queen's Park)	Maddison (Oxford University)
J. Smith (Queen's Park)	Maynard (1st Surrey Rifles)
Leckie (Queen's Park)	Brockbank (Cambridge University)
Rhind (Queen's Park)	Clegg (Sheffield Wednesday)
R.Smith (Queen's Park)	Smith (Oxford University)
McKinnon (Queen's Park)	Ottoway (Oxford University)
Wotherspoon (Queen's Park)	Chenery (Oxford University)
Weir (Queen's Park)	Morice (Barnes)

Referee: Mr Keay, Scotland

T WAS CURIOSITY more than anything else that impelled 3,500 people to go to Hamilton Crescent on 30 November 1872 to see what was billed as an 'INTERNA-TIONAL FOOT-BALL MATCH'. To see Englishmen actually coming to Scotland to play a game of football would have seemed bizarre and eccentric in 1872. And what sort of football would it be?

Football had been played for many centuries in Scotland. James II and IV had both tried to ban it in the fifteenth century, and Churches had moaned about it 'disrupting the Sabbath' for many years. It was noisy, rough and the only thing that could be said in its favour was that it at least kept young men away from the darker pleasures of drink, and women and (worse!) the subversive practices of Chartism and Trade Unionism.

But there was change in the air. In England, the laws of the game had been codified; referees and umpires had been appointed and spectators were coming to watch matches, even occasionally paying an admission fee to get in to watch teams like Notts County and Sheffield Wednesday. In Scotland, in 1867 the Queen's Park club had been formed, and they were totally respectable. In fact they were quite exclusive, making sure that the riff-raff and the hoi polloi were not welcome. There was also a team in Kilmarnock and several in Dunbartonshire.

But it was in England where it was all happening. Impressed by the numbers of Scotsmen living in the London area, the authorities had arranged a few games calling themselves England v Scotland. 'Scotland' were often supplemented by a few Englishmen, and England had generally won these games, but enough interest had been generated to make people wonder whether it would be possible to play an 'international' fixture. Rugby had seen a Scotland v England game at Raeburn Place in 1871, and a football game like that seemed a good idea.

It also seemed a good idea to take the game out of London. This was, of course, a great age for exploration and exportation of ideas. Already cricket teams had visited Australia and Canada, and it seemed a good idea to ask the Scottish Queen's Park team if they would like to play a game of football. The railways would facilitate travel to Scotland, and with the overnight sleepers it was possible to travel up on a Friday night and return by the Sunday.

Accordingly a letter was sent, on the initiative of Mr C.W. Alcock, to Queen's Park, who immediately saw possibilities in this idea. They hired, at considerable financial risk, the cricket ground of West of Scotland at Hamilton Crescent. Their own ground at Hampden was small and might not have been able to hold a large crowd, and they decided for the purpose of this game to call themselves not 'Queen's Park' but 'Scotland'. They might thus attract a few more spectators who would identify with their country. The ramifications of this decision were enormous, for therein lay the birth of international football. Things might have been different for the subsequent development of world football if they had just called themselves 'Queen's Park' playing 'an England XI'. 'Scotland v England' added far more spice. The other significant decision that they made came after the game, and that was when they arranged a return fixture in London the following March, for thus the game became an annual event. They could never have guessed what they were starting.

It is probably true to say that there was not any great political movement for Scottish Home Rule or Independence for Scotland in the Victorian age. The Union was clearly working, and although there was dissatisfaction at poor working and living conditions, this was not seen as the fault of the English (as it was in Ireland, for example). The Queen herself was very fond of Scotland with her Balmoral Castle and the Scottish ghillie John Brown, who may or may not have been her lover but who certainly helped to get her out of her prolonged sulk after the death of her husband Prince Albert.

The Prime Minister was William Ewart Gladstone, a Liberal who in some ways represented the conscience of Victorian Britain. That year had seen the Education Act (Scotland) a measure which would in time wipe out illiteracy and give control of schooling to politicians rather than the Church of Scotland. He had also tried to restrict the sale of alcohol – a well-meaning attempt to solve a serious social problem but one which rebounded on him when it seemed to be an attack on people's freedoms. A Bishop in the House of Lords for example, said that it was better to see "England free than England sober". But Gladstone's greatest achievement had been to keep Britian out of the Franco-Prussian War of 1870-71. Earlier Prime Minsters like Palmerston or later ones like Churchill or Thatcher might have found it more difficult to resist the siren voices of martial glory.

On the surface, there was no strong antipathy between Scotland and England, no rancour for the dreadful things that happened after Culloden and no blame for the Highland Clearances which had been responsible for the sudden rise of this new city called Glasgow. But the Scots are a tribal nation, and although very critical of their country in some respects, defend it when challenged. It would be nice, people felt, to get the better of England now and again, especially at something like football where no-one got killed.

These were the nascent nationalist feelings that Queen's Park tapped into that fateful day of 30 November 1872. No-one seems to have made much comment on the fact that this was St. Andrew's Day, a special day for Scotland. The date seems to have been chosen at random. The 3,500 spectators who decided to attend this game was a huge amount of people and the authorities may well have feared some political disturbance, with such a large number of people present, but football fans in 1872 were benign, middle-class people, motivated by curiosity rather than anything else. They would also have had to have been fairly wealthy for one shilling, the admission price, was an enormous sum of money in 1872.

It was raining heavily (as often happens in Glasgow in November) but the pitch was adjudged to be firm enough to go ahead. But the bad weather did have one effect that posterity will regret. A photographer had been engaged to take a group picture of both teams, but as this would have involved the players having to stand for some considerable time in the rain (for there was not enough room in the pavilion), the players turned awkward and refused. In any case, there was no guarantee of the photograph turning out well on such a dark day, and the players refused to pay a deposit against a copy of the picture. The photographer thus returned home empty handed, and without taking the photographs that history demanded.

Wattie Arnot, who a decade later would be a great player for Queen's Park and Scotland tells the story of how he and his friends, middle-class, privileged Glasgow boys, arrived to see the game but were shocked at the price of the one shilling entrance fee. They did not have this sort of money, so were reduced to asking the owner of a hansom cab who was waiting (presumably while his customer watched the game so that he could convey him home again), if they could stand on the top of his cab to watch the game. Rather improbably, the cabbie agreed – but perhaps he had negotiated a reduced fee with the boys.

The cartoon of the game in the *The Graphic* magazine shows a funny elliptical ball, players wearing long trousers like knickerbockers and some of them wearing cowls on their heads. The game seems to have been rougher than we know it now, but then again we are at the mercy of the cartoonist who will obviously highlight what he thinks are the most interesting aspects of the game. But it is recognisably Scotland v England in that Scotland are wearing navy blue and England white. The spectators look middle-class, middle-aged and are all well dressed.

The 0-0 draw would suggest 'nae goals, nae fitba' as it was later described, but in the week up to the game it had been impossible for either team to practise because of the bad weather, and in any case, some reports praise the standard of play. The *North British Daily Mail* implies that Scotland were unlucky not to win, for just before half-time Bob Leckie of Scotland had a 'good kick' which caused 'tremendous cheering from all parts of the ground' but sadly from the point of view of the Scottish spectators, the referee Mr Keay, in consultation with his two Umpires, Mr Alcock of England and Mr Smith of Scotland, ruled that it should be 'given no goal, the ball having passed hardly an inch over the tape'.

Press reports also emphasise the difference in the approach of both nations, a factor that would become more marked in future years. 'The Southrons (i.e. England) did not play to each other so well as their opponents who seemed to be adept at passing the ball', but on the other hand 'England, especially forward, astonished the spectators by some pretty dribbling, an art both novel and curious'. For many decades after this, Scotland would be famous for the passing game, while England excelled in the dribbling game.

At this time the pitch would be bereft of all lines, apart from the boundaries. Penalty boxes, centre circles, corner arcs and such fripperies would come later. The goalkeeper wore the same as anyone else, and was allowed to handle the ball 'near his own goal'. Umpires took half the field each, waving flags to indicate suggestions to the referee and as in cricket, players had to appeal to an umpire or the referee for a decision.

Newspaper coverage in papers like *The Scotsman* for example was minimal, and it was also clear that some sections of the newspaper industry did not appreciate the difference between football and rugby! Some football matches at the time are mentioned as having 'put-downs', for example, but football was still very much in its infancy. The baby would now grow however at a prodigious rate.

At full-time, Scotland's goalkeeper and captain Robert Gardner ran out to the centre of the field and invited the crowd to join him in three cheers for England. England then reciprocated, everyone shook hands and then went off to Carrick's Royal Hotel for a dinner and then a soiree in which everyone was invited to do a song, a recitation or some other piece of entertainment. It was a friendly occasion, and happily (and crucially for the future) a date was arranged for the return match in March at Kennington Oval, home of Surrey Cricket Club. Queen's Park had made over £33, and this would help pay for the railway fares to London.

No-one realised exactly what they were starting, but this was the birth of international football. The World Cup, the European Championships and other major trophies were all actually born on that rainy, misty day in Partick, Glasgow in 1872. From small acorns great oaks do indeed grow.

v ENGLAND 2-1

Hamilton Crescent; Att: 7,000
7 March 1874

Scotland:	England:
Gardner (Clydesdale)	Welch (Harrow Chequers)
Hunter (Third Lanark)	Ogilvie (Clapham Rovers)
Taylor (Queen's Park)	Stratford (Wanderers)
Campbell (Queen's Park)	Birley (Oxford University)
Thomson (Queen's Park)	Ottaway (Oxford University)
Weir (Queen's Park)	Owen (Sheffield)
Ferguson (Vale of Leven)	Wollaston (Wanderers)
McNeil (Queen's Park)	Heron (Uxbridge)
MacKinnon (Queen's Park)	Edwards (Shropshire Wanderers)
McKinnon (Queen's Park)	Kingsford (Wanderers)
Anderson (Clydesdale)	Chenery (Crystal Palace)

Referee: Mr Rae, Scotland

THE 7,000 WHO assembled at Hamilton Crescent to see the second international played in Scotland and the third overall were probably a lot more than the ground authorities budgeted for. Certainly the kick-off was delayed to allow everyone into the ground, and the attendance was at least twice what it had been eighteen months ago. The weather was also a great deal better than it had been a year past November.

The interest in the game was mirrored by the attention that the press paid to it. *The Scotsman*, based in Edinburgh but priding itself on being Scotland's national newspaper devoted a whole column to the game, majoring on the crowd and the general atmosphere. The kick-off had been fixed for 3.30pm, 'to the considerable advantage of the exchequer', but long before that, the road to Partick had been thronged by every kind of vehicle with both the roads and the carriages proving inadequate to the purpose. The official attendance was 7,000 but *The Scotsman* thinks that the total attendance might have been a staggering 10,000, for 'the many coigns of vantage round the ground were largely taken advantage of by the non-paying portion of the community', while every window in Hamilton Crescent seemed to be 'teeming with life' and quite a lot of ladies were seen to be looking out of their windows.

There were several reasons for this sudden explosion of interest. In the first place it was a pleasant spring day, give or take the occasional shower and a strong wind, but it was a fine day to play the game in. The second reason was that it was Scotland against England. England had won last year at the Kennington Oval, but only with two goals late in the game. Revenge was therefore required. And the third reason was that the game had enjoyed a great deal of publicity since the first visit of England. Not only had a body been formed with the pompous name of the Scottish Football Association, but there was now something called the Scottish Football Association Cup. This was a piece of silver which would be awarded to the best team in the country. It would be organised along the lines of one team playing another, and then the winners would subsequently play the team which emerged as victors of another game, and so on, until there was only one team left. The two remaining teams were Queen's Park and Clydesdale and they would play each other in two weeks' time. The winner would then take away a silver trophy, made in the shape of a goblet or a cup, and therefore called the 'Scotch Cup' or 'Scottish Cup' to distinguish it from the English Cup or the FA Cup which had now been contested for two years.

Yes, there was little doubt that this international match had caught the imagination. There was nothing new about football, of course, as it had been played on the streets of Scotland for centuries, but this was done officially and you could charge people to come in to watch it, and people did go along and support a particular team (whether it was Queen's Park or anyone else), and there were even teams outwith Glasgow in Dumbarton, for example, and even as far away as distant Kilmarnock in Ayrshire – all of them thriving concerns! And of course there was England to beat. England had played the game first (at least in an organised form with referees, umpires and rules) but Scotland were developing the game fast, and what a boost it would be if only Scotland could beat them! Wars between the two countries were, thank heavens, a thing of the past, but beating England at anything was vital to a Scotsman.

Things had recently changed on the political front. In the General Election held a few weeks previously (until 1918 General Elections were normally held over a period of weeks), Disraeli and the Conservatives had defeated Gladstone and the Liberals. It had been a strange election, for voters (and there were still only a restricted few men amongst the electorate) now registered their vote inside a small tent and then put their paper in a box, so that no-one could see who they voted for! In Ireland, this had had a tremendous effect because the landlords no longer knew who voters voted for, so that a tenant could vote for political agitator Charles Stewart Parnell, for example, without the danger of being thrown off his land for doing so.

Scotland had tended to stay loyal to Gladstone and the Liberals, but England had voted for that Jewish charmer Disraeli with his flamboyant style of dress and of speechmaking, which the Queen so obviously approved of. Yet Gladstone had done a good job, trying his best to limit the sale of the demon drink and also making it compulsory for every town and parish to provide some education. Would this mean that in a generation's time, everybody, even the ship builders and the Irish navvies would be able to vote?

Football remained a middle-class sport in both Scotland and England. It required money to pay for strips and the ball, and a team had to find a piece of grass to play on, and that was sometimes very expensive. In any case it was wise, was it not, given the passions that the game seemed to raise, to restrict it to those who could behave like gentlemen?

Queen's Park supplied seven members of the Scotland team, and there were two from Clydesdale and one each from Third Lanark and Vale of Leven (added on the Thursday night to add variety). It was nice to see John Ferguson of Vale of Leven there for this added interest from outside Glasgow. The game was spreading and who could deny it? There might one day be some teams from as far afield as Edinburgh or even Dundee.

Any large crowd would always worry the authorities, even though they had full confidence in their police forces to keep law and order. But large concourses could lead to mischief and political demonstrations, and as politics had recently been in the air with the General Election, there was always some danger or trouble. But this ground was well laid out with loads of room, and a clear two or three yards between the actual pitch and where the crowd were situated behind the rope.

The writer of *The Scotsman* is clearly at once both a poet and a lecher, for he penned this beautiful sentence to set the atmosphere: 'The majority of the ladies, as if by prescriptive right, had monopolised the green slopes at the top of the ground, where row upon row of many coloured toilettes met the eye, while the background of trees and shrubs, with the villas dotted here and there on Partick hill, presented a *coup d'oeuil* seldom surpassed.'

He was able, however, to tear his eyes from that sight and tell us that England started kicking off down hill and with the wind. The play on both sides was 'really brilliant' and much appreciated by the crowd who cheered the good play of both sides, particularly that of Francis Birley and the England captain with the unlikely name of Cuthbert Ottaway, who had endeared himself to the Scottish crowd by praising the arrangements for the game and telling everyone how much he loved Scotland.

From the start of the game, the previously identified trend became apparent – namely that England were good at dribbling and Scotland were more adept at passing. In this they had the great advantage of the seven players of Queen's Park knowing and understanding each other. But England had the better of the first half, 'earning much clapping' and actually scored but had the goal disallowed, or as *The Scotsman* puts it: 'the ball got under the tape, but as the ball was said to be handed (sic) nothing came of it.' England did score just before half-time, however, when goalkeeper Gardner of Clydesdale could not hold a shot, the ball cannoned of his chest and KINGSFORD of the Wanderers scored the rebound.

In these days the teams changed ends after a goal was scored, and half-time merely meant a brief respite, not the changing of ends. Scotland now had the advantage of playing down the hill. But England might have scored again when Heron missed an easy chance, before Scotland, ashamed at the thought of losing before such a large crowd redoubled their efforts.

'Cometh the hour, cometh the man.' In the *Iliad* of Homer, each hero has his 'aristeia' – his hour of glory. Today belonged to Henry McNeil, variously spelt as McNeill and McNiel. From Rhu in Dunbartonshire, Henry and his brother Moses were playing an important part in the founding of the Rangers club, but at the moment he was still a Queen's Park player. He would win four Scottish Cup medals with them, but he never played as well as he did today. Not only did Henry pass well but he dribbled excellently and at speed and it was he who was mainly responsible for bringing the ball down into the England goal area for his Queen's Park team mate JAMES WEIR to score Scotland's first ever home goal. The writer of *The Scotsman* hints at partisanship among the Hamilton Crescent crowd when he states that, 'the spectators gave vent to their feelings now in a much more unmistakeable manner than on the occasion of the first (English) goal.' This forerunner of the Hampden Roar (the Hamilton Crescent Howl, perhaps?) grew in intensity, even though it meant that Scotland were now once again kicking uphill. Then just three minutes after the first goal, the Scottish forwards, prompted by the ubiquitous McNeil, ran the ball up the hill, passing to each other with perfection until ANGUS MacKINNON shot home between the goalkeeper's legs and under the tape.

That this goal caused great rejoicing is obvious from *The Scotsman's* account: 'the scene which ensued baffled description, the vast multitude cheering and waving handkerchiefs for several minutes with the wildest excitement', for Scotland were now ahead and playing down the hill again. Another observer wrote that it was, 'a scene that will never be forgotten as long as internationals are played.' 30 minutes remained, and England battled hard. Both teams almost scored, but eventually, Mr Rae, the referee who was also the secretary of the SFA signalled 'no side' and the game finished to prolonged applause, three cheers for both sides and Henry McNeil being carried off on the shoulders of enthusiastic spectators.

That evening both teams repaired to the George Hotel where the England party were staying and enjoyed a banquet. Mr Ottaway was gracious and magnanimous, saying that, "in life one seldom gets one's deserts, but Scotland got theirs today." The Scottish captain James Thomson was similarly wholesome in his praise of the Englishmen as they each toasted each other, before listening to a few recitations and songs. Curiously someone proposed a toast to "the rugby game" but by that they in fact meant football, for Rugby School was where football was played long before rugby!

The news of this victory spread like wildfire throughout Glasgow. On the Saturday night, passengers on trains to Aberdeen, Inverness and Dundee passed it on, and not since the ending of the Crimean War in 1856 was news received with such excitement. Scotland had beaten England for the first time! The game of football was now played by everyone and a few enterprising saddlers and leather merchants began to order leather footballs to sell to their eager public. There was clearly a future in this game!

v ENGLAND 6-1
Kennington Oval; Att: 8,500
12 March 1881

Scotland:
Gillespie (Rangers)
Watson (Queen's Park)
Vallance (Rangers)
Campbell (Campbell)
Davidson (Queen's Park)
Hill (Rangers)
McGuire (Beith)
Ker (Queen's Park)
Lindsay (Dumbarton)
McNeil (Queen's Park)
Smith (Edinburgh University)

Referee: Major Marindin, England

England:
Hawtrey (Old Etonians)
Field (Clapham Rovers)
Wilson (Oxford University)
Bailey (Clapham Rovers)
Hunter (Sheffield Heeley)
Holden (Wednesbury Old Athletic)
Rostron (Darwen)
MacAuley (Cambridge University)
Mitchell (Upton Park)
Hargreaves (Blackburn Rovers)
Bambridge (Swifts)

ONE OFTEN WONDERS why this game is not more commemorated in the footballing culture of both Scotland and England, for it was a momentous Scottish performance and one which deserves to be mentioned in the same breath at least as the Wembley Wizards. Not again until 1953 would any side score six goals against England, and it needed the breathtaking Hungarians to do that (the following year they made it seven), and although Scotland would once or twice put more goals past mediocre opposition, they would never come near to emulating that performance against England.

In fact high scoring games were quite common in the early days. Three years previously Scotland had beaten England 7-2 at First Hampden, and the last two games had been thrilling affairs both ending 5-4, with England victors in 1879 and Scotland in 1880. The game was changing, and with thrilling matches like that, it was not surprising that the popularity of the game was increasing, as were the amount of people willing to pay good money to come and watch it.

Attendances in Scotland had been higher than the 8,500 who came to the Oval on that day, but such a large crowd was a clear sign that London was beginning to develop a fondness for the game. It was speculated that this was probably the largest ever attendance at a sporting fixture in the capital – certainly far more than Surrey would attract for a cricket match, even when the Australians were playing – and the authorities, as always in Victorian England, were more than a little uneasy about the possible threat to public order at such a large gathering.

The Chartists, who had wanted to reform Parliament, and the Anti-Corn League of half a century previously had frequently threatened public order, something which the authorities always had at the back of their minds. Still fresh were thoughts of what had happened in France in 1789 when things got out of hand, and now of course there was the added dimension of Irish terrorism. The Fenians were quite capable of bomb outrages in England (they had done so in 1867, for example), and it would be a very easy matter to smuggle an explosive into such a large crowd as 8,500.

The authorities need not have worried. The audience were all respectable, middle-class people with a genuine love of sport. The riff-raff would be deterred by the fact that a tariff had to be paid for entrance, and in any case London's Police Force, the lasting memorial to Robert Peel, would be there in strength to deal with any problems.

The one serious threat to the match was actually provided by fog. The Spanish writer Pio Baroja would later describe London as 'La Ciudad de la Niebla' – The City of Fog – for there always seemed to be fog hanging over the city from the river Thames. Certainly other Victorian writers like Charles Dickens and Conan Doyle would seem to agree on this point, and the authorities hated fog. More accidents would happen, more crimes would be committed and the horrible air was undeniably bad for chesty conditions which affected such a large percentage of the population.

Football in 1881 was still an amateur and a middle-class pursuit. The English team had Christian names like Edgar, Thurston, Claude and Reginald and played for Oxford and Cambridge Universities, Clapham Rovers and Old Etonians, whereas the Scottish team had five men from Queen's Park, three from the new Glasgow team which had made such an impact over the past few years called Rangers, one from Dumbarton, one from Beith and a fellow from Ayrshire who was currently studying at Edinburgh University. The Scottish team was therefore exclusively from west-central Scotland, whereas in the England team, industrial towns in the north like Blackburn and Sheffield were represented.

There was something a little unusual however about Scotland's right-back, a chap making his international debut called Andrew Watson. He was black. The curious thing about this was that nobody seemed to care or even notice at the time. Newspaper reports are devoid of comment about the colour of his skin, from which we perhaps should conclude that race in the 1880s was not as big an issue in Great Britain as it was in the United States of America or Southern Africa, for example.

Andrew Watson was born in British Guyana in 1857 to a black plantation worker called Rose Watson. His father was the owner of the plantation, a Scotsman called Peter Miller. Unlike many in similar situations, Miller did the right thing for his concubine and her son by bringing the boy to the United Kingdom and giving him an education at Halifax Grammar, Harrow and Glasgow University. The boy started to play football in Glasgow for a team called Parkgrove before proving good enough to be asked to join Queen's Park. From there it was a short step to playing for Scotland, as indeed he had every right to do. Little is known about what happened to his parents but one hopes they were able to enjoy the footballing prowess of their son.

Scotland's captain was Charlie Campbell, the captain of Queen's Park who in later years would become a referee, before becoming president of the SFA. He had led Queen's to many successes and would eventually win eight Scottish Cup medals with them. There was also Henry McNeil, brother of Moses McNeil who played a large part in the founding of the Rangers team, and John Smith, a prodigious all-round sportsman who came from Mauchline (one time haunt of Robbie Burns) and ended up being a doctor in Kirkcaldy. He was to play a large part in the game.

Scotland did not lack support that foggy day at the Oval, but very few would have made the journey south. Train travel was possible in 1881, and not even outrageously expensive for those with a reasonable income, but the days of travelling long distances to see football games were still a long way off for most of the population who would work in their ship-yards, mines and factories until midday on a Saturday. But quite a few Scottish people who now lived and worked in London (a fair amount, particularly in banking and commerce) would have made the effort to see the team representing the land of their birth.

The team were in fact 'on tour', for they travelled from Glasgow on the Friday, stayed in London on Friday and Saturday night, and then on the way home, as it were, called in to Wrexham to play Wales on the Monday. Wrexham had the honour of hosting quite a few of the early internationals for Wales, simply because the Racecourse Ground was close to the main railway line between England and Scotland.

The game at the Oval kicked off at 3.15pm with the crowd still pouring into the ground and 'jostling to get a good view of proceedings'. England started the stronger team but it was Scotland who scored first. This happened when Willie McGuire from the Ayrshire village of Beith released fellow Ayrshireman JOHN SMITH who ran through and scored to 'wild applause'. England now fought hard but Scotland's defence held firm and it was they who scored a second goal before half-time – or so they thought. The English defence 'appealed for offside' (as one did in Victorian football, for the referee, like an Umpire in cricket, would only give offside on appeal) and Major Marindin upheld it.

Scotland were thus only one goal up at half-time, but something happened early in the second half to illustrate another point of law. Scotland were awarded a free-kick after 'an Englishman, a non-goalkeeper, handled the sphere in the vicinity of the goal'. Scotland's McNeil took the free-kick – and scored! But this was not allowed, for there was no such thing as a 'direct' free-kick. Once again, England appealed and no goal was awarded.

But Scotland would not be denied for long. The fog was now lifting as a slight breeze picked up, and Scotland's passing game could be seen by the London citizens to have a great effect. It was DAVIE HILL of Rangers who scored the second goal after a rebound from the goalkeeper, before Smith again netted – only to see once again an appeal for offside upheld by the referee after he had consulted his Umpire (as linesmen were then known).

Scotland had more reason to feel aggrieved for England then ran up and scored through EDWARD BAMBRIDGE who put one over the head of the goalkeeper. But Scotland, ignoring any doubts about the referee, who did seem to favour the home side and also appeared to be affected by advice from the crowd, pressed forward and for the rest of the game passed the ball about at speed, eliciting reluctant applause from an appreciative English crowd and 'wild enthusiasm from the Scottish minority'. In the last 20 minutes before the referee eventually put an end to the suffering of the Englishmen, Scotland scored four times, twice through John Smith and twice through the industrious George Ker.

A pass from Campbell set up SMITH, then KER beat the goalkeeper with a lob which a defender could only help into his own net. SMITH then charged through on his own to score Scotland's fifth and his own third, before KER found the net again at the end. In fact there could have been more goals, for McGuire and McNeil both came close as well. Everyone agreed at the final whistle that this had been an inspired Scotland side who deserved all the applause that they got, and all the drinks that admirers bought them at their hotel that night.

John Smith's hat-trick was not the first in international football, for John McDougal had achieved the feat in 1878, as had George Ker in 1880, but he was the first to do it in England. The likelihood is that he would have been presented with a new hat at the team's soiree after dinner at the hotel. The origin of this custom came from cricket of course, and possibly explains why it would be a bowler hat that he would receive.

This had been the tenth fixture between the two countries. There had been two draws and two wins for England, but Scotland had won the other six. This statistic would explain why football now developed at a phenomenal rate in Scotland, for here was a pursuit in which the Scotsmen could regularly beat the English. The 1881 international would also be the second of a run of five victories in a row up to and including 1884. No Scottish team has subsequently equalled that run.

The game on the way home at Wrexham was played with a slightly different team, with John McPherson of Vale of Leven coming in for Charlie Campbell, but with a similar result of 5-1 for Scotland with Wales delighted that they had restricted the Scots to five and had not conceded six goals like the English! In 1881 news travelled fast via telegraph and it was small wonder that a crowd was waiting at Glasgow Station to meet the triumphant Scottish party, now without any sort of doubt the champions of Great Britain. No wonder the Queen enjoyed coming to Scotland and Balmoral Castle – she wanted to learn how to play football!

v **ENGLAND** 1-0
Old Cathkin Park; Att: 10,000
15 March 1884

Scotland:	England:
McAulay (Dumbarton)	Rose (Swifts)
Arnott (Queen's Park)	Dobson (Notts County)
Forbes (Vale of Leven)	Beverley (Blackburn Rovers)
Campbell (Queen's Park)	Bailey (Clapham Rovers)
McPherson (Vale of Leven)	Macrae (Notts County)
Shaw (Pollockshields Athletic)	Wilson (Hendon)
Anderson (Queen's Park)	Bromley-Davenport (Oxford University)
Lindsay (Dumbarton)	Gunn (Notts County)
Smith (Queen's Park)	Bambridge (Swifts)
Christie (Queen's Park)	Vaughton (Aston Villa)
McKinnon (Dumbarton)	Holden (Wednesbury Old Athletic)

Referee: Mr Sinclair, Ireland

O FFICIALS MAY HAVE been slightly disappointed by the turn-out of 10,000 (not quite the highest ever crowd), but it was an impressive sight anyway at old Cathkin Park in Govanhill, Glasgow. Possibly if the rain had eased an hour or two earlier instead of persisting until 1pm there might have been a bigger crowd, certainly from the outlying areas of Dumbarton and Alexandria. But there were some fans from even further afield than that – from Edinburgh and Dundee, it was claimed – and the hope was expressed that the game itself might develop further into those areas.

That morning before the game, the officials of both nations and those of Wales and Ireland had met at the Bath Hotel in Glasgow. After the routine business of arranging the fixtures for the next season (the dates caused confusion because of 1884 being a leap year), a motion was passed deploring professionalism and outlawing it in every form of the game.

Professionalism was a growing issue in the game, for rumours spread round Glasgow of players being paid by certain clubs, sometimes in the more subtle guise of 'travelling expenses', other times a few coins being put into the shoes of players in the dressing room. Sometimes, players would even demand a 'signing-on' fee before playing for a club. But the British Associations were all insistent that this could not be officially recognised, otherwise football might go the same way as cricket with 'Gentlemen' and 'Players'.

The day was fast approaching (in fact it was probably already there) when football would overtake cricket in both Scotland and England as the main sport. In fact judging by the 10,000 people who assembled despite the overcast and damp conditions, one could not possibly disagree. In Scotland in particular, the sheer fact that if they were to win today, they would have beaten England five times in a row, meant that the sport was rapidly gaining ground. Scotland was eminent in such matters. Why even Queen Victoria, it was rumoured, preferred Scotland to England these days.

Wales now played football as well – in fact they would be at Cathkin in a couple of weeks – and this year football had even travelled overseas, for Scotland, even with a weak team, had been to Ireland to beat the enthusiastic but overwhelmed Irishmen 5-0 in Belfast. But it was clear that the game which mattered more than any other international match, more than any Queen's Park v Dumbarton or Vale of Leven game, more than any Scottish Cup final, was this fixture. Everyone wanted to play in it, and every fan wanted to be there to watch it.

There were signs that football was beginning to be played seriously by the labouring or the working classes. They had always played football in a rough and ready sort of way in the streets and even in kirkyards ('making enough noise to waken the dead'), but now as more and more employers were stopping work at midday on a Saturday, the proletariat could begin to play the game more seriously. After all, it was a lot healthier for them than the alehouses.

The road to Cathkin in the Govanhill area of the ever-expanding city of Glasgow was packed with spectators and vehicles of every description – trams, cabs, even vehicles looking like post-chaises and (incredibly) hearses had been pressed into service, and there was also a huge collection of horses tethered in a nearby field and guarded by enterprising 'horse minders' for a small fee while their owners went to see the football. Inside the ground, as well as the normal stand, two other temporary (and slightly unsteady-looking) ones had been erected in the corner of the pitch, and the occasion was graced, to a greater extent than ever before, by ladies. This had compelled the allocation of an area for a 'Ladies Rest Room'. One hopes that the 'groundlings' moderated their language in the ladies' presence!

The Press were there in greater numbers than previously, for the nation would wish to read of the game on Sunday or Monday. The score would be almost instantly known across the nation, as telegraphs could now be sent to the other Scottish cities, but newspapers sold more copies on days after there had been big sporting events, and the game would be well covered in *The Scotsman* and the *Glasgow Herald* on Monday.

The big political talking point, apart from the perennial ones of Ireland and Africa, was Gladstone's Third Reform Act which would enfranchise all male householders, and lodgers who paid more than £10 per year. This meant that about six million people could now vote – but not yet the really poor and there was no mention of women. Some thought this was a great idea, others were less impressed – the concern being that it might encourage all the radicals and agitators who caused trouble at work.

A huge cheer greeted the teams as they came out, Scotland resplendent in their blue shirts with the Scottish lion crest, and England in their normal white. Scotland had won 8 of the previous 12 games and this was believed to be because they played the 'passing' game. However they had also now mastered the English skill of dribbling, and speed had also been one of the skills that had been cultivated in the past few years in Scotland. They lined up in the traditional formation of two full-backs, two half-backs and six forwards – the 2-2-6, whereas England were slightly more defensive with a 2-3-5 set up.

The team had five men from Queen's Park. This was hardly surprising, for the Hampden team had now won the Scottish Cup seven times out of eleven since its inception in 1874. This year however had seen somewhat exceptional circumstances as Vale of Leven had failed to turn up for the final on 23 February, alleging some dispute about the date, and Queen's Park had been awarded the Cup by default. There remained a certain amount of ill feeling about this, especially among Vale supporters, but the decision had been made.

In two weeks' time, Queen's Park would be in London to play in the final of the Football Association Cup, referred to in derogatory terms as the 'English Cup'. They were due to play Blackburn Rovers, for whom Joseph Beverley, the England defender on duty today, played. Queen's Park would therefore be able to assess just how good he was.

Queen's Park provided three stars of the era in Wattie Arnott, Charlie Campbell and John Smith, the multi-talented Mauchline doctor and famous goalscorer. For England the star man was William Gunn, better known as a cricketer with Nottinghamshire. Curiously enough, although an amateur at football (nominally, if not in actuality) he was a professional cricketer, and the time was fast approaching when he would be invited to play for the England team against Australia, perhaps even to go there and play some day.

Gunn was a huge man, at least six feet three inches tall, and with a tremendous physique and pace. He was also a character, having established for himself a reputation of being his own man, on one occasion making himself very unpopular with his fellow professional cricketers for refusing to join their 'strike' for better conditions in 1881. But the Nottingham crowd loved him, as did the fans of Notts County football club, for whom he starred.

The game was under the control of Mr Sinclair from Ireland, and he was supported by an Umpire from each country – Major Marindin of England and Mr Lawrie of Scotland. These two men had flags, but unlike 'linesmen' or 'assistant referees' did not stay on the line but wandered around their half of the field waving flags to attract the referee's attention, and responding to appeals for offside or fouls. The Umpires were men of the utmost integrity, and any suggestion that they favoured their own side would be treated with derision.

The game was fast, but it was immediately obvious that the heavy, strong men like Willie Gunn of England and John Smith of Scotland would be at an advantage for they could deal with the wet conditions better than the smaller men. In fact, the sun was now beginning to shine through, but this did not alter the ground as it would take a long time for it to dry out.

It was also obvious from the cries that Scotland were being encouraged far more than England were when the game was played in London, and that there were a great deal more than 10,000 watching the game. Trees, hillocks and the top floors of houses were being used as vantage points, with some enterprising youths collecting firewood, concrete, lumps of earth and other things to make a mound so that they could see the game. All the cabs now had people sitting or even standing precariously (it would be disastrous if the horses were to bolt) on top of them, and for those who could not see in any of these ways, a few stentorian-voiced friends inside the ground provided a primitive radio commentary for their benefit!

Play flowed from end to end, but it was Scotland who took an early lead. Wattie Arnott picked up a loose ball in the central area of the field, punted the ball forward and it was headed on by a Scottish forward, probably Robert Christie, to Doctor JOHN SMITH who ran on and scored with a rising shot which grazed the crossbar. In this Doctor John was rather fortunate, as before crossbars were introduced (they were not yet compulsory in games other than internationals) a rope was used or the matter was left to the judgement of the Umpire. Smith's shot might well have kept soaring; as it was it hit the crossbar and bounced inside the goal.

The cheering went on for some time, but England now fought back with Gunn and Bromley-Davenport prominent in their attacks. However Scotland's goalkeeper, James McAulay of Dumbarton was in top form, saving well and marshalling the rest of the defenders. England's shooting was less effective than the rest of their play but a great deal of credit for that had to be given to Wattie Arnott, of whom it was said that 'better back play has probably never been seen'. Another man who was singled out for praise was William Rose, the English goalkeeper whose ability to clasp the ball and then 'fling it back into play' was much praised by the press.

The second half saw England press ever further, but Scotland's defence held firm, and as the English defence was equally competent, there was no further scoring. Mr Sinclair consulted the chronometers of himself and both Umpires and agreed that it was time for 'recession'. Scotland then gave three cheers for England, and England, beaten but not bowed, returned the compliment. The Cathkin pavilion had the amenities of running water and sinks, so that both sets of players were able to have a much needed wash to get rid of most of the mud before their cabs took them back to the Bath Hotel for the post match banquet.

Scotland had now defeated England five years in a row. Unlike some of the previous wins, this one had been close and the Scottish authorities were careful to point this out, for the last thing that one wanted was a feeling of complacency, that Scotland were bound to win anyway. The takings had not yet been counted, but it was clear that they would be substantial. The game in Scotland was in rare good health, as was evidenced by the way that everyone, even the porters and the bellboys at the Bath Hotel talked about little other than the football match. Everyone was already looking forward to next year's game, and speculation was rife about whether it would be at Bramall Lane again as in 1883, or whether it would return to the Oval. Talking of which, in another month or so, the weather might be good enough to start playing cricket again.

v WALES 6-1
Tynecastle; Att: 1,200
26 March 1892

Scotland:	Wales:
Downie (Third Lanark)	Trainer (Bolton Wanderers)
Adams (Hearts)	Arridge (Bootle)
Orr (Kilmarnock)	Powell (West Bromwich Albion)
Begbie (Hearts)	Hughes (Bootle)
Campbell (Kilmarnock)	Jenkyns (Small Heath)
Hill (Hearts)	Roberts (Preston North End)
Taylor (Dumbarton)	Wilding (Wrexham)
Thomson (Dumbarton)	Owen (Chirk)
Hamilton (Queen's Park)	W. Lewis (Chester)
McPherson (Rangers)	Egan (Chirk)
Baird (Hearts)	B. Lewis (Wrexham)
Referee: Mr Reid, Ireland	

IT WAS a commendable policy on the part of the SFA to move internationals around, and this was the first time that Tynecastle had been asked to host one. It was not the first in Edinburgh, for Easter Road had hosted the equivalent fixture in 1888, but Heart of Midlothian were now considered to be big enough to be invited. They had of course done themselves no harm by winning the Scottish Cup in 1891, and it was now clear that in football terms, Edinburgh was a city to be reckoned with, although not yet as huge as Glasgow. Edinburgh possibly had a wider diversity of sporting interests, being very strong in rugby, football, cricket and tennis.

Football in 1892 was now, however, the major sport in Scotland. It was not yet professional, at least not officially, but those with eyes to see could figure out that the larger city teams like Hearts, Celtic and Rangers were probably offering 'under the counter' payments to their better players to dissuade them from going to England to ply their trade there. The following year 1893 would see such hypocrisy abolished and professionalism legalised.

The only international that really mattered in the late Victorian era was the England v Scotland game which could well have been entitled the championship of the world. Internationals were played against Ireland and Wales, but they were usually mismatches. Wales were not without their successes against England, but to date had not won any of the sixteen games played since 1876 against Scotland. They had held Scotland to a draw in Wrexham in 1889, and only a late Scottish goal had granted victory in 1891, but the men from the Principality had never even been close to causing an upset on Scottish soil.

Their day would come of course, but Scotland now treated the games against Wales and Ireland as trial matches in which promising players were blooded, and also consideration was given in team selection to the venue and the potential of crowd pulling. We are not surprised to discover for example that four Hearts players would represent Scotland at Tynecastle against the Welsh.

A totally different team had represented Scotland the week before in Belfast against Ireland. This game did not lack controversy, for the Irish, clearly desirous of their first ever win or even draw against the Scots, invaded the field at the end to remonstrate with the referee Mr Taylor of Wales who had awarded Scotland a goal when the ball had seemed to go over the bar and enter the (clearly imperfectly made) net from above. A 'storm of execrations' had arisen and Mr Taylor had required the support of all the players and a few of the local constabulary to get himself rescued at the end of the game from an angry mob. Only one man was arrested but the Scottish press had a great deal of pungent remarks to make about the name of the ground. It was the home of Cliftonville and rejoiced in the unlikely name of 'Solitude'. 'It is to be hoped that the perpetrator of the assault on the official soon experiences several years of "solitude" – of a different kind' says the *Glasgow Herald*.

Life would be totally different at Tynecastle the following week. The Scottish team contained men like James 'Bummer' Campbell and John 'Kitey' McPherson who might just force their way into the team for the 'big' match against England the following week, and a big crowd was expected. Hearts went out of their way to encourage their supporters to come along, with posters and advertisements in the local papers. Indeed they made improvements to their ground, aware of what had happened at the Scottish Cup final at Ibrox a couple of weeks previously when the game had had to be played as a friendly because of repeated 'crowd encroachment'. Therefore barriers were strengthened to prevent this happening again.

Hearts were not having as successful a season as the previous year. They had gone out of the Scottish Cup at the quarter-final stage to Renton after two replays, and were to finish (although there were still a few more games to play) third in the Scottish League behind Dumbarton and Celtic, but ahead of Rangers and Leith Athletic, who had appeared as their city rivals now that Hibs had temporarily gone out of existence. Hibs had shot themselves in the foot by their sectarian 'Catholics Only' policy, and had lost out badly when the new Irish team, 'the Celtic' had appeared with plenty of money, support and success in Glasgow. Hearts were determined to become the 'establishment' team of Scotland, and to wrest the initiative of football's development in Scotland from Glasgow to Edinburgh. For this reason it was important to make a success of this international.

The Welshmen arrived at the Princes Street station on the Friday night. It would probably be the first time that some of them had been in Scotland, and they would be shown sights like the Castle and Holyrood Palace on the morning before the game. The Scottish crowd who gathered to see them was small in numbers – it would have been different if it had been England – but they were interested to see the men who played for teams like Chirk, Bootle and Wrexham and who rejoiced in such unlikely names as Job Wilding, Caesar Jenkyns, Seth Powell and Smart Arridge.

The weather was cold on the Saturday morning, and then ominously around midday turned a little milder as black clouds appeared from the north-east. Snow had been forecast, even though on 26 March the equinox had been passed and *The Scotsman* was advertising 'Spring Outfits For the Lady of the Household'. The snow fell slowly and gently at first, but then as the wind picked up, it began to drift and to lie.

In Victorian times, snow caused less travel disruption than in the present day, for horses were better able to cope with wintry conditions than motorised transport, and in any case, the pace of life was slower. But even so, when the teams arrived at Tynecastle, it was clear that there would be a problem. The ground was covered with snow and play seemed unlikely with Mr Reid, the referee, far from enthusiastic about the possibility of starting. But both teams were keen, and there was the pragmatic point that if the game were postponed, it would be difficult and expensive for the Welsh team to come back. Hearts, having spent money on the ground, wanted the game to go ahead, and the decision was taken that the match would kick-off on time. One should not be too hard on the officials here. Victorian football was tough, and the players themselves would not have been too upset about the game being played. They were amateurs (at least in theory), which of course meant that they loved the game and were only there to play for the pure love of sport and of victory. The Scottish players also welcomed the chance to show everyone that they deserved a chance to play in the big game against England next week.

But this could not stop rumours from spreading not only through Edinburgh but in the surrounding districts as well, particularly and crucially at railway stations where fans would meet before going to the game. 'Oh, they'll never play in this!', 'It's getting heavier' and 'It's too dangerous' very soon became 'The match is off' and 'They'll try again next week!'. No radio or television existed to officially dispel such rumours, and the result was that when Johnny Hill ran out with his Scottish team, he found a virtually empty enclosure.

The Welsh captain was their goalkeeper by the name of James Trainer. He had made an attempt to ask the referee to limit the game to 30 minutes each way, but the referee and the Scotland authorities felt that this would be defrauding the brave souls who had appeared and paid their money. Reports of the actual attendance vary from 600 to 1,200 with the latter number possibly being closer to the mark. It was clear, however, that this was to be a financial disaster for all concerned. Takings in fact were about £25 once the referee had been paid and all other expenditure covered.

Ironically enough, the blizzard was now intermittent and play, although difficult, was possible. It certainly was difficult for the poor Welshmen whose boots seemed to lack studs and who, even in the best of circumstances would have been outclassed by a good Scottish team. By half-time, the score was 4-0 for the Scotsmen with goals from WILLIAM THOMSON, JAMES HAMILTON and a couple of 'fliers' from JOHN 'KITEY' McPHERSON.

These goals were greeted by the minuscule crowd 'pinned against the enclosure wall' to escape the force of the blizzard. The brave Scottish supporters did not lack enthusiasm or humour. Those lucky enough to be wearing large Tam O' Shanter bonnets were well protected from the elements and *The Scotsman* declared that a few cries of 'Good Old

Scotland' were heard as well as the odd made-up song asking the referee to take pity on them and to let them go home. The *Glasgow Herald*, clearly enjoying Edinburgh's discomfiture, pointed out that the mounted police detailed to control the crowd more or less outnumbered the spectators and joked that they hoped the horses survived their ordeal.

Scotland scored a couple more goals through DAVIE BAIRD of Hearts (this one raised a particularly loud cheer) and JAMES HAMILTON of Queen's Park, before BEN LEWIS scored for Wales. Then Mr Reid the referee blew for time up, in the opinion of a few newspaper writers 'a considerable time before it was due – but he can hardly be excoriated for that'. Scotland had won 6-1, the Welsh had scored only their fifth ever goal on Scottish soil and the minuscule crowd went home to tell their incredulous friends what had happened. Very soon after the final whistle, the snow turned to rain and eventually stopped.

For Hearts this fixture was a disaster in terms of lost revenue and lost credibility. It was not their fault but everyone seemed to find it funny. The serious effect that it had was that Hearts shelved any plans to build themselves a new stadium, thus surrendering the hegemony of Scottish football to Glasgow where a magnificent new stadium was being built at Celtic Park to match the one at Ibrox. Within 12 years there would be another one at Hampden. Hearts would host other international games in future years, but they must have felt themselves cursed in the aftermath of that next game. It was also against Wales and was a disaster for different reasons. It was in March 1906 and was Wales's first ever win in Scotland!

For Scotland in 1892, there was a dismal aftermath. The following week a totally different Scottish team took to the field against England at Ibrox. Thus Scotland had fielded three different teams in three separate weeks – and this time it was the 'real' Scotland team with men like Dan Doyle, Wattie Arnott and the two alliterative Queen's Parkers – Sellar and Sillars. 33 men playing for Scotland in three weeks might have seemed like a sign of the strength of Scottish football in 1892, but sadly in the game against England, Scotland were on the wrong end of a 4-1 drubbing.

v ENGLAND 2-1
Celtic Park; Att: 56,500
4 April 1896

Scotland:
Doig (Sunderland)
Drummond (Rangers)
Brandon (Blackburn Rovers)
Hogg (Hearts)
Cowan (Aston Villa)
Gibson (Rangers)
King (Hearts)
Lambie (Queen's Park)
Hyslop (Stoke City)
Blessington (Celtic)
Bell (Everton)
Referee: Mr Jones, Wales

England:
Raikes (Oxford University)
Lodge (Corinthians)
Oakley (Oxford University)
Henfrey (Corinthians)
Crawshaw (Sheffield Wednesday)
Crabtree (Aston Villa)
Bassett (West Bromwich Albion)
Goodall (Derby County)
Smith (Oxford University)
Wood (Wolverhampton Wanderers)
Burnup (Cambridge University)

THE SCOTLAND v England international of 1896 was a landmark. It was the first time that Scotland had ever allowed the use of 'Anglos', i.e. men who were Scottish by birth, but who played for an English club. For a long time Scotland had resisted this move, believing that if a player chose to further his profession south of the Scottish border, he had thereby forfeited his right to represent his country. Indeed, there was even a body of opinion in England which maintained that such players should actually be available to play for England, for that was now their 'footballing nation'. Opinions on this issue had filled newspaper columns and been argued with ferocity, but it is hard not to believe that Scotland's repeated defeats by England – 1888, 1891, 1892, 1893 and a particular shocker at Goodison Park in 1895 – did not sway opinion in this proud footballing nation and suggest that the 'purity of the Scottish game might to advantage yield to the necessity of beating the Southrons'. Anglos were to be chosen for the 1896 England game, although Home Scots could do the job against Wales and Ireland.

In the event five Anglo-Scots were chosen, and the remainder of the Scottish team consisted of two each from Rangers and Hearts and one each from Celtic and Queen's Park. Professionalism had now been legalised for three years, so that was no longer an issue, although the purists did point out that Scotland had only one amateur – Willie Lambie of Queen's Park – while England had several who either played for Corinthians (as rigidly amateur in England as Queen's Park were in Scotland) or one of the other two Universities.

Celtic Park was the venue. Celtic, the team of upstart Irishmen founded in the winter of 1887/88 and instantly successful, had amazed Glasgow by building a huge stadium in 1892. They may even have ruffled a few Establishment feathers by inviting a Fenian and one time friend of Charles Stewart Parnell called Michael Davitt to plant shamrocks on the centre line, but the building of the stadium was for no other purpose than to secure for the club the staging of the Scotland v England game every two years. Attendances at domestic games in the early 1890s would seldom be more than 10,000 – it was the international that everyone would want to attend. Celtic had indeed already staged the international in 1894, (a 2-2 draw) and when they were asked to do the same in 1896, they took the precaution of extending their ground and building a huge embankment at the east end of the ground in realistic expectation of a huge crowd.

The *Glasgow Herald* had stirred up its readers all week, and ended up by stating roundly that: 'latterly nothing but the result of this tussle was talked about' throughout the land. The football season had been an exciting one with Celtic winning the Scottish League, and for the first and only time the Scottish Cup final had been played outside Glasgow at Logie Green, Edinburgh and won by Hearts against their city rivals Hibs, a team who had been in abeyance for some time a few years previously but who were now back up and running.

An example of the spread of the game could be seen in the enormous amount of trains that disgorged passengers into Glasgow on the day of England's visit from such far away places as Dundee, Aberdeen and Inverness. It was now clear that this was in a real sense the 'Scotland' team. Ned Doig the goalkeeper, for example, now played for Sunderland in the 'team of all the talents' as they were called, but had cut his teeth playing for Arbroath, and many people from that part of the world came to see their hero, taking advantage of the now well-developed railway system. Even ten years previously 'Scotland' had tended to mean little more than Glasgow, Dumbarton, Vale of Leven and a few more places, but this was now a Scotland team for the whole nation to identify with.

And sport was now a big thing in the world, with even Churches slowly coming round to the conclusion that young men playing competitive sports was at least better than drinking and fornication. And what was this that was about to happen to the world on Monday? The Olympic Games were to be held in Athens! This seemed to be an attempt to recreate ancient Olympic Games and Great Britain had sent some athletes to compete. So too, incredibly, had the United States of America! The world would watch with interest, but it was surely a one off rather than an idea that would catch on.

Glasgow in 1896 was quite rightly described as 'The Second City Of The Empire', for it thrived and prospered. Everything hustled and bustled from the shipbuilding yards on the Clyde, to the university in Kelvinside, to the innumerable tea-rooms where the genteel ladies would meet to discuss world and family affairs. The Victorian era had seen some tremendous development and the population and area of Glasgow had expanded to engulf neighbouring villages, and now dwarfed even Edinburgh.

But there was some dreadful poverty as well. A man who had a job could probably support his family – if he could stay off 'the drink'. But that was a very big 'if', for there was so much in terms of poor housing, insanitary conditions and ill health that a man would want to forget – and drink certainly did provide such temporary oblivion. So, of course and far more innocently, did football.

SCOTLAND'S GREATEST GAMES

The weather was dry and it was clear from an early stage that there was to be a huge crowd, without much doubt another world record and far more than the 40,000 who had been there two years previously. The gates opened at 12 noon for a 3.30pm kick-off and as soon as this happened, 'many people who had been in the vicinity since the early morning' rushed int to grab a comfortable space on the embankment or the stands. Celtic Park had two stands and two huge embankments – the word 'terracing' did not yet apply, for the embankment was simply a mound of earth sprinkled with cinders to give people a stance from which they would not slip. 'Pay boxes were busy places' for a long time, as indeed were the food stalls and the tables of those who sold Scottish flags, rosettes, posters and favours.

After about 2pm things took a more sinister turn as another element of the crowd arrived. These were the 'refreshed', i.e. those who had been in one of the many public houses which were springing up in the east end of Glasgow almost as quickly as the dwelling houses. These were worse behaved, with foul habits and profane language and they were determined to see the game, even although it meant pushing others out of the way. The result was dangerous overcrowding on the eastern embankment, and a few overspills onto the cycling track which ran round the ground. The Glasgow police tried to push them back, but when this met with little success, the authorities took the unusual step of summoning a detachment of Gordon Highlanders from Maryhill Barracks to supplement their ability to control the crowd who had now taken to pelting policemen with cinders. But the crowd also used the cinders for a more constructive purpose, namely hurling them at the encroachers who were endangering the chances of the game beginning on time. This actually worked and the trespassers eventually squeezed their way back onto the overcrowded embankment.

It was just before 4pm when the game eventually started, Scotland taking the field in dark blue to a huge cheer, and England to a more sedate but still polite round of applause. The crowd had now settled down, although with 56,500 inside the ground, there was still a great deal of overcrowding and some frightening swaying, with horse-drawn ambulances called upon now and again to take away an injured spectator, or someone who had fainted with the heat of so many people.

Mercifully a west wind had sprung up to cool down those in danger of asphyxiation on the east embankment, and Scotland's captain, Jock Drummond of Rangers, decided to play with the slight breeze. From the start it was obvious that Scotland were on song with Willie Lambie of Queen's Park coming close on several occasions. It was Neil Gibson of Rangers who earned most of the plaudits from the Celtic Park crowd (the partisan behaviour of fans booing those of another team had not yet become the sad feature of Scottish life that it would in the twentieth century) for his hard tackling and splendid passing created all sorts of opportunities for Jimmy Blessington and Jack Bell, as England, clearly overawed with the massive Scottish crowd, struggled to cope.

It was WILLIE LAMBIE who put Scotland ahead in the 20th minute, when he charged through on goal, shot and then was on hand to net the rebound after goalkeeper Raikes could not hold the fierce drive. Ten minutes later, JACK BELL scored a second following some fine work by Hyslop and Blessington. At this point, Scotland looked as if they could add several more, and England were visibly relieved to hear the half-time whistle and to go in to the old Celtic Park pavilion on the north west corner of the ground only two goals down.

It was different in the second half, as England now played with the advantage of the strengthening breeze and piled pressure on Scotland. Ned Doig was from time to time called upon to perform a few heroics in the Scotland goal, but Scotland's defence were up to it with Tommy Brandon of Blackburn Rovers, a virtual unknown before the game, proving his mettle with timely clearances and interventions.

But England eventually scored in the 80th minute, just after Doig had begun to look unbeatable. It was WILLIAM BASSETT of West Bromwich Albion who scored from close range after some fine work down England's left wing. The goal was given a polite round of applause and a cheer from the few Englishmen in the crowd, and then the huge Scottish support was forced to hold its breath as England attacked and attacked. Everyone was aware that Scotland had not beaten England since 1889, and that a win here would be especially sweet after recent disasters. Surely victory would not be dashed from Scotland's lips now?

Anyone who doubted that Ned Doig was the world's best goalkeeper would now be convinced otherwise, as the man from Letham, the tiny village near Forfar in Angus, made save after save; tipping the ball round the post, diving this way and that, and showing the greatest courage and concentration in all that he did. Jimmy Cowan, the centre-half of Aston Villa (who would win the English League that year) was also outstanding, but the man of the match remained Neilly Gibson who had hardly put a foot wrong all game.

'Scotland's hearts were as high as some of the bonnets' at full-time as the Welsh referee 'pointed homewards'. Fortunately everyone was able to leave the ground with no further injuries in spite of some tremendous crushing as everyone tried to get out at the same time. The roars of acclamation were deafening, as Scotland shook hands with the referee and their English opponents. But the SFA had another reason to be happy as well. The receipts for this game were listed as £3,744 – a phenomenal amount of money and an eloquent testimony to just how popular this game of football was. Yes, there certainly was a future for this sport – and a victory over England is always sweet.

v ENGLAND 2-1
Crystal Palace; Att: 35,000
3 April 1897

Scotland:	England:
Patrick (St.Mirren)	Robinson (Derby County)
Smith (Rangers)	Oakley (Corinthians)
Doyle (Celtic)	Spencer (Aston Villa)
Gibson (Rangers)	Reynolds (Aston Villa)
Cowan (Aston Villa)	Crawshaw (Sheffield Wednesday)
Wilson (Sunderland)	Needham (Sheffield United)
Bell (Everton)	Athersmith (Aston Villa)
Millar (Rangers)	Bloomer (Derby County)
Allan (Liverpool)	Smith (Old Carthusians)
Hyslop (Rangers)	Chadwick (Everton)
Lambie (Queen's Park)	Milward (Everton)

Referee: Mr R.T. Gough, Wales

THIS GAME WAS generally regarded to have been one of the closest between the two sides with the *Glasgow Herald* saying that the difference was 'infinitesimal'. Nevertheless, it was the Scots who emerged on top, and the triumph, as always in Victorian days, was much celebrated.

Scotland had won the encounter last season at Celtic Park, but it was in 1889 that they had last won in England, and the previous visit south of the border, to Goodison Park, Liverpool in 1895 had been a particularly unfortunate one in that Dan Doyle had gone AWOL overnight, had returned to the hotel in time to be (incredibly) allowed to play, but only for Scotland to go down to a spectacular 0-3 thrashing which should in fact have been a lot more. Such occurrences did not go down at all well in Victorian Scotland, where the annual game against the Auld Enemy was now much discussed, speculated upon, worried about and subsequently dissected.

The team for the England game was chosen the week before, immediately after the game at Ibrox in which Scotland, in dreadful weather of sleet and snow, beat Ireland 5-1. The 'Selecting Seven' (a body of Chairmen, Directors and Officials charged with the job of choosing the national team) then 'repaired' (as the Victorians would say) to the Bath Hotel in the centre of Glasgow, followed by an eager throng of newspaper reporters and fans, not slow, presumably, to offer advice about who should be and who should not be in the team. After a 'sederunt of an hour and a half' (the actual length of a football game, someone pointed out) during which time the mob outside increased in size and in nervous anticipation, someone appeared to announce that telegrams, advising of selection, had been sent to the players concerned.

The first thing noticed was that the team again contained Anglo-Scots (i.e. Scotsmen who played for English clubs). They had been allowed for the first time the previous year against England but had not featured this season against either Wales or Ireland. This was a major issue in the Scottish game at this time, for Home Scots objected when they were called upon to play against Ireland or Wales, but not for the 'big' international against England. But what mattered the most (and in 1897 this was paramount) was the necessity to beat the Auld Enemy, a necessity that was all the more pressing because England were now beginning to catch up in terms of internationals won. This would be the 26th meeting of the two nations, and England were now only five victories behind.

But the perils of choosing Anglo-Scots were highlighted when one of the players was declared unavailable by his club. This was, of course, just the first of a long line of such instances, and it featured goalkeeper John 'Ned' Doig of Sunderland, generally regarded to be the best goalkeeper in the business. Ned was already a cult hero when he joined Sunderland from Arbroath in 1890. He very soon won three League Championships in the excellent Wearsiders' team of that era, and he was recognised as a vital and indispensable cog in their success. Moreover, he had been absolutely outstanding in the previous year's victory over England at Celtic Park.

Sunderland now turned a little awkward by refusing to allow Doig to go to Crystal Palace to play for Scotland. Doig himself was very keen on the idea, and Sunderland illogically and irrationally allowed left-half Hugh Wilson, who had also been selected, to play, but not Doig. Legally at that time, Sunderland were well within in their rights as there was no organisation like FIFA to assert global rules such as they do today, and indeed quite a few Scottish fans and journalists detected a hint of conspiracy here, claiming Sunderand were endeavouring to ensure that England would beat Scotland if the latter had an inferior goalkeeper playing. That 'inferior goalkeeper' was John Patrick of St. Mirren, a modest and likeable young man who went around telling everyone how lucky he was and how Ned Doig was a far better goalkeeper than he was.

The Home Scots of the Scotland team left St. Enoch's Station in Glasgow at about lunch time of Friday 2 April to travel to the first ever international at Crystal Palace, so called because of the great glass house built there for the Great Exhibition of 1851. Such was the fanaticism about football and about this international match in 1897, that thousands thronged to the station to see the team off and to wish them well. Youngsters, hoping to catch a glimpse of the charismatic Dan Doyle, the ferocious Nick Smith or the unassuming captain Willie Lambie, caused such serious congestion to the players trying to fight their way through the platform that the train had to be delayed. Once the horseshoes, white heather and good luck charms had been put on the train, the players, with a few lucky and wealthy supporters, sped south, under no doubt, presumably, of exactly what this game meant for their nation.

1897 saw Great Britain at the height of her powers. In a few months' time old Queen Victoria would celebrate 60 years on the throne. It was rumoured that the grand old dame wasn't keeping too well these days (she still would stay around until 1901) but there seemed little doubt that during her reign 'progress' had been the word with schools, hospitals, libraries, cemeteries, prisons, museums, railways, dams and reservoirs all constructed. The Empire, albeit now challenged by the Germans and the new power across the Atlantic of the USA, was supreme and it was indeed true that the sun never set on some parts of this vast institution. People like Fenians, Suffragettes, Anarchists and Socialists might have beeen unhappy, but peace and progress were the main features of Victoria's reign.

But were they? Slums, illness, malnutrition, poverty, drunkenness abounded in the dreadful streets of the larger cities – but we could worry about that some other time. Tomorrow would see a football match, *the* football match that mattered more than anything else!

The team arrived in London late on the Friday night, having enjoyed the wisecracks and banter of the likes of Jimmy Millar and Dan Doyle. Rangers had won the Scottish Cup that year and Hearts the Scottish League, whereas Celtic had had a poor season. But much was made of the fact that Willie Maley, one time player with Celtic, was now to be appointed as full-time secretary/manager of the club. Millar and Smith of Rangers sagely warned Dan Doyle that Maley 'would sort him out' – in fact, they said that was why he had been appointed! Dan smiled, for he knew that his indiscretions were frequent and well known.

En route some of the Anglos had joined the train – Jack Bell of Everton and George Allan of Liverpool at Manchester, and then Jimmy Cowan of Aston Villa at Birmingham. When Hugh Wilson of Sunderland teamed up with them in London, he was asked if he had brought Doig with him. When he said 'no', John Patrick pretended to faint and said that he would have to play before that huge crowd after all.

And a huge crowd it was, variously given as 35,000 or even more, a massive attendance for London which had been a tad slower than the midland or northern cities like Birmingham, Sheffield, Liverpool, Newcastle and Sunderland to catch the football bug which had spread like wildfire throughout the British Isles in those last 30 years. The kick-off at the Crystal Palace was 4pm, but the press was surprised to discover that soon after midday people began to appear, including an intriguing number of ladies. Much was the talk of the Boat Race, won by Oxford for the eighth successive year that day, but after about 3 o'clock 'an excited buzz ran round the crowd' for the teams had arrived at the ground. The appearance of the occasional gentleman in the crowd wearing a kilt or some other Scottish garb caused 'much animation' as well.

The weather was not favourable, being cold and with the ever-present threat of rain, but the pitch was firm, there was a gentle breeze, and cries of 'Come on England' and 'Good Old Scotland' were heard in good natured rivalry. Both teams were well received when they appeared, led by their respective amateur captains – Willie Lambie of Queen's Park and Gilbert Smith of Old Carthusians. England won the toss, but there was little advantage to be had for the breeze was blowing across the pitch. At 4pm exactly, referee Mr Gough signalled the start of proceedings.

It was England who scored first. Indeed they had dominated the early play with Dan Doyle having to clear his lines with the goalkeeper beaten, and on several other occasions the England forwards squandering good opportunities by shooting inaccurately and wildly. But in 20 minutes it was STEVE BLOOMER who opened the scoring with a fine volley after a good move involving both wingers Athersmith and Milward. Bloomer was the personality goalscorer of his day, yet the Derby County man looked anything but a football player. Thin, white-faced and consumptive looking, and occasionally called the 'ghost' or the 'phantom', Bloomer would score 352 career goals to set a British record which would last until Jimmy McGrory beat it in 1935. Bloomer had scored against Scotland in 1895, would do so again in 1898 and looked as if he might rival Edward I for the title of the 'Hammer of the Scots'.

However the applause had hardly died down before Scotland were back in the game. As frequently happens, success breeds complacency among defenders and a series of errors led to a goalmouth scramble in which Rangers' TOMMY HYSLOP stabbed home an equalizer to a roar 'less emphatic than the English one, but only because there were fewer Scots to contribute to it'.

The rest of the first half was played out by two teams on equal footing, and half-time arrived with little to separate the two teams.

The second half saw a ding-dong battle with both sides going all out for the winner. Patrick in the Scotland goal 'was awkward in some of his saving', and Scottish fans began to fear that the loss of Ned Doig might yet have been vital, but after 20 minutes of the half, Scotland, with superb play from Gibson and Cowan, began to take command of the game. The vital goal came well within the last ten minutes, and occurred when Tommy Hyslop picked up a ball from Cowan and shot so hard that Robinson could only parry the ball to JIMMY MILLAR, 'who lying close at hand, rushed in, outmanoeuvred the goalkeeper and placed to the credit of Scotland the point that was to win the match', as *The Scotsman* quaintly put it.

But at least five minutes remained and England now threw everything into the attack, and Scotland were indebted to their full-backs Nick Smith and Dan Doyle for keeping the Englishmen at bay. Full-time came when Mr Gough consulted his chronometer, and bedlam was raised by the Scottish fans in the ground as 'three cheers' were called for. The joyous scenes at the ground would in a matter of minutes be replicated in Scotland itself after the despatching of telegrams to the main newspaper offices in Glasgow, Edinburgh, Dundee and Aberdeen. From there every Post Office would be informed, often to the joy of crowds of people who had been waiting for the last half an hour in eager anticipation.

Celebrations would go on for some time, and the players were given the whole of Sunday off to enjoy the sights of London before they caught the 10.45pm overnight train back to Scotland where they were given breakfast in a Glasgow hotel after they had fought their way through the deliriously happy fans and wellwishers who welcomed the arrival of the victorious team.

'Scotland is more than ever the home of football,' declared the *Dundee Courier*. And at the turn of that century that was absolutely true.

v ENGLAND 4-1

Celtic Park; Att: 65,000

7 April 1900

THIS YEAR, 1900, defined the end of the era of the British Empire. The reign of Queen Victoria was not yet at an end, although she was seldom seen these days and rumoured to be failing, and the power of the British Empire was as yet unchallenged. There were worries about the new Germany and indeed the new power across the Atlantic, which Great Britain had done so much to create – the United States of America. In far away South Africa, the soldiers of the Empire were engaged in a seemingly pointless struggle against the Dutch farmers – but this was the price one paid for trying to civilize the world.

The combination of Scotland and England had clearly been an unbeatable one as far as Empire building was concerned. This is not to say that there was not a great deal of rivalry between the two nations – and for the past 30 years this had expressed itself on the football field, with Scotland being able to claim to have had more success than England. Football was therefore a key way for Scotland to express its identity within the British Empire.

Such thoughts had occurred to Lord Rosebery, Prime Minister of Great Britain for a brief and unhappy period between 1894 and 1895, and still in 1900 an influential Liberal politician well known for his team of race horses and, latterly, his interest in Scotland's football team. He was called their patron (nowadays he would be called a sponsor). There is a parallel with the present day Princess Royal who is a tremendous (and apparently genuine) supporter of the Scottish rugby team. Back in 1900, for the international between Scotland and England, Celtic Park, particularly the old cricket style pavilion in the north-west corner of the ground, was bedecked in the Rosebery racing colours of yellow and pink. Scotland would also that day be wearing the colours that Rosebery's jockeys normally sported. It would be a fair assumption that Rosebery had paid a considerable sum of money into the SFA coffers for this privilege.

Celtic Park was the only ground in the country with any hope of holding the expected 80,000 crowd that would be likely to turn up. This stadium, built by the ambitious Irishmen of Celtic FC for no other purpose than to stage the 'England game', looked very impressive with its new grandstand, cycle track and lush turf. Flags flew – the harp of Ireland, the saltire of St. Andrew and the Union Flag of the British Empire – alongside, of course, the flag of Lord Rosebery. It was to be hoped that the ground could hold the crowd, since there had been problems in 1896 and 1898.

There were now clear signs that the Scottish establishment had accepted football, and even professionalism in football. A few hands were still raised in horror at professional sport and certainly the religious wing of the Liberal Party was very unhappy about Lord Rosebery's connections with horse racing and gambling, but it was clear that professional football was not going to go away. It had reached down to the lower orders and provided them with their 'circuses', while the industry of Empire, most of the time, provided the bread.

The last two internationals against England had been lost, and the country had been plunged into mourning and self-recrimination with everyone offering their opinion about what had gone wrong. But now that the century had turned, Scotland seemed to be doing better. Wales and Ireland had both been comfortably disposed of, and the previous week at the Crystal Palace the Scottish League had earned a respectable draw against their English counterparts, even though they had needed a late own goal to do so.

The Scottish crowd had every reason to be optimistic as they trudged, some of them sadly and obviously the worse for drink, along the Gallowgate and London Road to the game, singing Scottish songs and a new anthem that was beginning to be heard all over the Empire called 'Goodbye Dolly Gray'. It was nothing to do with football, but it had a nice beat to it, and was about a lovelorn soldier saying goodbye to his lady friend as he set out for the Boer War. Near the ground, as well as the normal beggars, pickpockets and prostitutes that one would meet anywhere in urban Victorian Britain, there were more respectable stalls with drawings of Scotland players like Neilly Gibson and Jack Bell on sale, along with sweets like toffees, caramels and 'black balls', and rattles with tartan stripes on them for cheering on the Scots. A few speakers stood on boxes to address the multitude on all things from religious revivalism, to opposition to the war in South Africa, the demon drink, and even a couple of brave ladies wanting the Vote for Women. They were all looked upon with benign but disinterested tolerance by the Scottish crowd who were far more interested in the prospects of their football team.

The Scotland team was a strong one with the defence built on the Rangers quartet of Nick Smith, Neilly Gibson, Jock Drummond and Jock (sometimes called Jack) Robertson. They were supplemented by Liverpool's Alex Raisbeck, reputed to be the best defender in the English League. They would be much required as England boasted in their forward line Steve Bloomer, the anaemic-looking forward who had won the game for them in 1898.

Scotland's forward line contained the young Bobby Walker of Hearts, already talked about as one of the best dribblers in the game, and the line was led by Bob McColl of

Queen's Park, a man who in later years would be known as R.S. McColl, the confectioner. Already his sweet shop earned him the nickname of 'Toffee Bob'. Today was destined to be his finest hour.

McColl was different from the rest of the Scottish team in that he was, nominally at least, an amateur who played for Queen's Park. Oakley, Smith and Wilson of the England team were of similar status and played for the Corinthians. One would have to be rather naïve, even in 1900, to be totally convinced that such men truly played for nothing – they would perhaps be given gifts like clocks or new suits of clothes – and in any case it was a distinction that was fast disappearing, although Queen's Park to this day remain ostensibly amateur.

The crowd cheered loudly as Lord Rosebery took his seat on the balcony of the Celtic Park pavilion alongside Celtic manager Willie Maley and other SFA dignitaries. They also showed their approval vocally when England took the field, but the cheering absolutely 'rent the heavens' as Jock Robertson led out Scotland in their bright and impressive Rosebery colours. 65,000 were said to be there (in fact there would have been a lot more) all straining to catch a glimpse of the fair hair of Alec Raisbeck, the rugged features of Jock Drummond, the tall angular deportment of Jack Bell or the almost self-effacing gait of Bob McColl.

It was BOB McCOLL who scored first, less than a minute after Mr Torrans of Ireland had blown the whistle. A charge down the left wing had seen Alec Smith cross to McColl who netted with a low, crisp drive which gave Robinson no chance. The crowd applauded such brilliance, but the jumping up and down with delirium caused a certain swaying on the packed East embankment, something that caused a little alarm to the Glasgow police.

As England were trying to recover from this setback, they suffered another two, as they turned out, fatal blows. It was the wizard Bobby Walker of Hearts who created it all. He made space on the right wing and cut inside. England goalkeeper John Robinson and full-back Bill Oakley rushed out to deal with him. In those days, players did not shun physical contact; there was an almighty collision, all three players were knocked onto the ground and the ball trickled to JACK BELL who had the easiest of tasks to poke the ball into the net for Scotland's second.

Barely five minutes had elapsed, and Scotland were now two ahead. It was immediately obvious however that although Robinson and Walker got up from the collision, Oakley needed medical attention. In fact he was seriously hurt with a broken nose and concussion, and although he made a brave effort to carry on for a spell, he eventually had to retire from the fray and was taken to hospital where he had to be detained overnight. Most of the sympathetic crowd gave Oakley a round of applause, but the actions and shouts of a minority were 'despicable in the extreme' when he eventually left the field for good.

He was actually still on the field but clearly dazed and disorientated when BOB McCOLL put the rampant Scotland even further ahead. This time it was Johnny Campbell of Celtic (there was another John Campbell of Rangers and they would both play against Ireland the following year) who made the goal with some fine play before sending a perfect pass on to McColl.

The Scottish crowd had seldom seen anything like this before, for their team were indeed playing like champions, but they were temporarily silenced just before half-time when England pulled one back, inevitably, through STEVE BLOOMER, the only England forward who looked vaguely like troubling the water-tight defence. Bloomer took advantage of a very rare moment of slackness from Jock Drummond, scored and must have been amazed at the cheer that he got from the Scottish crowd who clearly felt that this could only be a consolation goal.

Their confidence was totally justified when BOB McCOLL notched his hat-trick and his side's fourth just as Mr Torrans was about to blow for half-time. This one was a lovely drive from far out, and the resulting cheers were heard all over the east end of the city, drowning out the brave efforts by the military band to entertain the crowd at half-time. A gymnastics demonstration was also put on to amuse the vast throng, but they were still talking about Bob McColl and his first half hat-trick!

4-1 up and with England reduced to ten men, Scotland, with no great desire to further humiliate their chivalrous foes, clearly eased up in the second half, and no further goals ensued. But this was in the opinion of observers the best Scottish team there had ever been, with their precision passing and their ability to read each other's intentions. Bob McColl would later pay tribute to his team by saying that he could not imagine 'a set of eleven combine more effectively'.

In fact the most impressive player on the field that day was England's goalkeeper John Robinson, who saved his side's blushes again and again with terrific stops, tipping the ball over the bar or round the post, palming and punching, and brilliantly dodging and evading the shoulder charges of the Scottish forwards. But the Southampton man's brilliance was all wasted, for the other Englishmen were absolutely outclassed, and even when the Scottish crowd gave them a few cheers and encouraged them to 'make a game out of it, England!', they could not respond.

At full-time, Lord Rosebery rose to address the multitude from the pavilion gallery. Most of the crowd had gone home, but a minority wandered to the pavilion with police blessing (but firm control with ropes as well) to hear him talk. A few, supporters of the nascent Labour party, booed but were quickly silenced, but most listened with respect to the Lord who tried manfully to roll his Rs and introduce a few Scotticisms like 'aye' and 'och' into his obviously patrician English accent. He expressed his concern and best wishes for Mr Oakley's welfare, praised Scotland and Bob McColl in particular and hoped that 'no worse civil war will ever occur between us' than football.

Historically, this in fact this was a fairly profound remark, and was a clear indication that Scotland no longer needed men like William Wallace or Bonnie Prince Charlie to put the English in their place, for they now had R.S. McColl!

v ENGLAND 2-1
Hampden Park; Att: 102,741
7 April 1906

Scotland:
McBride (Preston North End)
McLeod (Celtic)
Dunlop (Liverpool)
Aitken (Newcastle United)
Raisbeck (Liverpool)
McWilliam (Newcastle United)
Stewart (Hibs)
Howie (Newcastle United)
Menzies (Hearts)
Livingston (Manchester City)
Smith (Rangers)
Referee: Mr Nunnerley, Wales

England:
Ashcroft (Woolwich Arsenal)
Crompton (Blackburn Rovers)
Burgess (Manchester City)
Warren (Derby County)
Veitch (Newcastle United)
Makepeace (Everton)
Bond (Preston North End)
Day (Old Malvernians)
Shepherd (Bolton Wanderers)
Harris (Old Westminsters)
Conlin (Bradford City)

THIS WAS HAMPDEN'S first big international day. The new ground had been opened on 31 October 1903 and had already staged Scottish Cup finals, notably the one in 1904 when Jimmy Quinn scored his famous hat-trick for Celtic, but it had not yet staged a Scotland v England game. Queen's Park had built the ground for that very purpose, deliberately making it bigger and better than Celtic Park where there had been dreadful overcrowding in recent games and knowing that, following the disaster of 1902, Ibrox would be out of contention for some time.

The crowd was given as 102,741 making it the first ever six figure crowd in world history and one which astonished the Englishmen. Even the writer of *The Scotsman,* from his safe vantage point in the stand said, 'yes, it was indeed just a trifle awe-inspiring to look at the great mass of humanity which had already taken up its place all round the amphitheatre and to see the roads and streets outside literally black with thousands upon thousands eagerly hurrying towards the turnstiles'. Such was the crowd that the gates were closed early, leaving several more thousands outside. Queen's Park's directors could thus congratulate themselves on their vision in building such a huge ground, although they, ever mindful of the dreadful events at Ibrox four years ago, may well have been worried at the crush inside. Mercifully, no-one seems to have been injured, and in any case a gates receipt of £4,300 was gigantic for 1906.

Scotland had been going through a bad spell. Two weeks previously the Scottish League team had gone down to an embarrassing 2-6 defeat at Stamford Bridge, and three weeks before that they had managed to lose to Wales at Tynecastle in the Welshmen's first ever victory on Scottish soil. An unimpressive 1-0 win in Dublin had been little compensation.

In addition to this, the pressure was now building on Scotland for they had lost to England in both 1904 and 1905, and only once before had England recorded a hat-trick of wins against Scotland.

When announced the Scotland team was greeted with almost universal dismay because of the profusion of Anglo-Scots, and even the inclusion of one Celt (Donnie McLeod), one Ranger (Alex Smith), one Heart (Alex Menzies) and one Hib (George Stewart) looked like an amateurishly token attempt to appease the supporters of the four big city teams. There was no Bobby Walker, the dazzling inside man of Hearts, and no Jimmy Quinn, the bustling Celtic centre-forward – both blamed for poor performances earlier in the spring. Celtic supporters in particular were entitled to feel aggrieved for the lack of representation of their brilliant Championship winning team that year.

But the Selectors knew what they were doing. They picked three men from the superb Newcastle United team of that era – Andrew 'the Daddler' Aitken at right-half, Peter 'The Great' McWilliam at left-half, and up front Jimmy Howie, the man from Galston with the strange run which made it look like he was going more slowly than in fact he was. Liverpool won the English League that year, and they were represented by the great centre-half Alec Raisbeck and a debutant at left-back called William Dunlop.

Also making his debut at inside-left was George Livingston of Manchester City, an interesting character who had already played for Hearts, Celtic, Sunderland and Liverpool, and would join Rangers six months later, but not before he had been suspended by the English FA for his part in a bribery scandal. He had actually played for Scotland once before in the Ibrox Disaster game of 1902, but that was deemed to be unofficial. He had a reputation of being a great entertainer, but the Scottish crowd had a few reservations about him.

Little was known about goalkeeper Peter McBride. He came from Ayr, and now played for Preston North End, where he seemed to lead a competent and unspectacular life. That was a great thing, reckoned the Scottish fans, because he must be good to be included ahead of men like Harry Rennie, Davie Adams and Jimmy Raeside. McBride was generally considered to be the safest goalkeeper in England and despite having little to do that day, he 'radiated security' in the opinion of the *Dundee Advertiser*.

The weather was good, and there was optimism in the air. The very sight of the new stadium in itself probably attracted more folk, and as the railway companies offered excursions from stations all over Scotland there was a huge influx into Glasgow from early morning. There was another cause for optimism in early 1906, for the Liberals had just won the General Election and had taken office under the Premiership of the benign Glaswegian Henry Campbell-Bannerman. This government, itself under pressure from the infant Labour Party, had pledged to make improvements to the living conditions of the poor. Yet if one lived in Cathcart, or Mount Florida or King's Park on the south side of the city, one would be forgiven for thinking that poverty did not exist, such was the affluence and prosperity all around, with more than a few 'horseless carriages' or motor cars, as they were now called, in evidence.

But a walk through the Gorbals or Cowcaddens would have given a totally different impression of ill-clad, ill-cared for children, of women offering themselves for a few pence, and everywhere, everywhere the 'Demon Drink'. The Church made some protest about this, but everyone knew that the Church was financed by the rich, some of whom had done very well out of the licensing trade in the same way as they had done well out of the slave trade a century before, so their protest was targeted at the consumers of alcohol, rather than at the obscene profits made by the licensing trade.

But there was also something very progressive and confident about Glasgow. The Second City of the Empire, famous for its shops and tea-rooms, had now left Edinburgh far behind as the most important city in Scotland. Foreigners on business filled Glasgow's hotels and boarding houses and the feeling was expressed that some day, such was the strength of the ship-building industry, Glasgow might outstrip even London.

Football typified this. Glasgow was undeniably the football capital of the world with three great teams – Queen's Park, proudly amateur and aristocratic, Celtic, the phenomenally successful team of the Glasgow Irish, and Rangers, the team supported by workers in the nearby shipyards. Glasgow was not yet tainted with the stain of violence and sectarianism that would make them the shame of Scotland for many decades later in the century. As well as the three other Glasgow teams of Clyde, Third Lanark and Partick Thistle, there was also a host of teams from the immediately adjacent areas of Renfrewshire, Dunbartonshire and Lanarkshire. The only real challenge came from distant Edinburgh, from Hearts who would win the Scottish Cup that year, but such was the contempt for Edinburgh that it was widely believed that the only reason Scotland had lost to Wales that year was because the game had been played at Tynecastle!

The English players travelling to the ground in their horse-drawn omnibus were visibly shaken by the sheer amount of people heading towards the the game. Oddly enough, they were not overtly hostile, although a few of them indicated with fingers that the score would be 5-0 today, but they were curious to see the players of whom they had only heard or read – Makepeace, Shepherd, Crompton and Conlin – the men who had thrashed the Scottish League two weeks previously.

The English Press would claim that the game hinged on the injury to left-half Harry Makepeace within ten minutes. Makepeace, himself a late replacement for the injured Houlker of Southampton, was an interesting character who would go on to play Test Match cricket for England after the Great War, but today he sustained a bad injury when he fell over Menzies and strained the muscles of his back. He could not resume today, but would recover enough to win an English Cup medal in a fortnight's time when Everton beat Newcastle United at the Crystal Palace.

There were no substitutes in those days, so England were compelled to defend and also to employ skillfully the offside trap, which in 1906 included catching Scotland offside in their own half! This was frustrating for the Scots crowd, but they had cause to be happy with the performance of their team with the two Newcastle half-backs, Aitken and McWilliam, being particularly impressive. Behind them bustled Donnie McLeod of Celtic. Donnie was fated to die in Flanders in 1917, but this was his finest hour, as Scotland took control.

Just before half-time Scotland broke the deadlock. When this happened – such were the wonders of new technology – the journalists would immediately phone, using the primitive apparatus proudly assembled by Queen's Park for this occasion, to their offices who would then pass on the tidings to the assembled crowds in the street. Thus, within a few minutes of it happening, Edinburgh, Dundee, Aberdeen, London, Manchester and Newcastle would all know that JIMMY HOWIE had scored for Scotland. It was a bizarre goal as well, for Howie's shot looked as if it had been saved by goalkeeper Ashcroft, but Ashcroft had been so keen to avoid the charges of Scotland's forwards that he had stepped over the line without realising it and the ball had crossed the line too. Scotland appealed to Welsh referee Mr Nunnerley and the goal was given. No account of any English protest is recorded, but *The Scotsman* adds the now familiar description that 'there was a tremendous amount of cheering'.

Thus it was a happy half-time for the Scots, and ten minutes into the second half there was even more cause for rejoicing when HOWIE scored again. This time the goal came from Alex Smith the Rangers left winger, who made space, crossed for Menzies who miskicked altogether, but Howie was coming up behind to do the necessary.

It was now all one way traffic with England two goals and a man down, accepting the inevitable, it seemed, until they got a break near the end. Jimmy Conlin of Bradford City was fouled unnecessarily outside the penalty area. ALBERT SHEPHERD of Bolton Wanderers took the free-kick and scored to give England a lifeline inside the last ten minutes. But that was all that it was. With Scotland now totally dominant and the half-back line of Aitken, Raisbeck and McWilliam totally in command, Scotland finished the game well on top, the huge crowd indulging themselves with songs in praise of 'Bonnie Mary' and a few less complimentary ones along the lines of 'Goodbye England we have beat you...'.

The departure of the crowd was likened somewhat improbably to 'lava erupting out of Mount Vesuvius' (the Italian volcano being in the news at the time), and everyone headed home to celebrate a great Scottish victory. The Home International Championship would be shared between England and Scotland, for England had beaten Wales, who had then drawn 4-4 with Ireland, but it was felt that Scotland had won a great moral victory here, especially at their new ground. What caused more eyebrows to be raised than anything else was the size of the crowd, and it was suspected that for propaganda reasons, Scotland had 'massaged' the figures with the idea of reaching the six figure mark. Certainly for Hampden, not being as large as it would become in later years with extensions to the East and North terracings, 102,741 does seem rather excessive.

Against that, the Queen's Park accounts are well audited and well preserved, earning words like 'meticulous', so any 'massaging' would have been skilfully done. In subsequent years, that figure of 102,741 would even increase. What was certain is that in 1906 Scotland had a stadium and now a team to be proud of.

v IRELAND 5-0
Dalymount Park, Dublin; 10,000
14 March 1908

Scotland:	Ireland:
Rennie (Hibs)	Scott (Everton)
Mitchell (Kilmarnock)	Craig (Rangers)
Agnew (Kilmarnock)	McCartney (Belfast Celtic)
May (Rangers)	Harris (Shelbourne)
Thomson (Hearts)	Connor (Belfast Celtic)
Galt (Rangers)	McConnell (Sunderland)
Templeton (Kilmarnock)	Blair (Cliftonville)
Walker (Hearts)	Hannon (Bohemians)
Quinn (Celtic)	Andrews (Glentoran)
McColl (Queen's Park)	O'Hagan (Aberdeen)
Lennie (Aberdeen)	Young (Linfield)
Referee: Mr Ibbotson, England	

I

T IS PROBABLY true to say that Irish football was slower to get started than its English or Scottish counterparts, but by the early years of the twentieth century, football was slowly becoming big in Ireland. They had joined the Home International Championship in 1884, and after a decade or two of being on the wrong end of some horrendous thrashings, were slowly earning the respect of the other nations. They had twice drawn with Scotland, and on 21 March 1903 had shocked the Scots by beating them 2-0 at Celtic Park, a result that the nation found very hard to accept. Scotland had played so badly, apparently, that some of the 17,000 crowd began to cheer for Ireland!

This, however, was really only a blip as far as Scotland was concerned, and they continued with their policy of using the Irish and the Welsh games as trials for the big match against England. No great effort was made to secure the release of Anglo-Scots from their English clubs, and as a result many good-to-ordinary Home-Scots would earn the one and only cap of their career against the Irishmen.

But the Irish trip was looked upon as a perk. Sailing from the Broomielaw normally on the Thursday, then there followed a day in Dublin with only some light training, with the game itself on the Saturday followed by socialising (even in 1908 Dublin had a deserved reputation for good food and drink), then a free Sunday before returning to Scotland on the Monday. For the past three years, the game against Scotland had been played in Dublin rather than Belfast in a conscious and praiseworthy attempt by the Irish authorities to spread football to the south of the island.

It is very easy to forget that in 1908, Ireland was one country and part of the British Empire. Northern Ireland only came into being in 1922 as the Protestant majority in the north of the country did not want to have any part of Home Rule which they saw as 'Rome Rule'. There were other differences apart from religion, but the big concern in Ireland was the constant haemorrhaging of population after the dreadful potato famine of the 1840s and the consequent Irish diaspora which now extended to all parts of the world, not least Scotland.

Football had been more popular in the industrial north of Ireland than in the agricultural south. It would be a gross over-simplification to see any sort of sectarianism in all this, but that was possibly a factor in that the northern Protestants would tend to copy the cultural trends of Great Britain, whereas the southern Irish would stick with their more traditional pursuits like hurling and Gaelic football. In 1878 two Scottish teams – Queen's Park (always keen to be missionaries in spreading football) and a team called the Caledonians (presumably a team of Scotsmen now living in Ireland) played a game in Belfast, and a couple of years after that the Irish Football Association was formed.

In 1882 they played international matches against England and Wales, and in 1884 against Scotland. Domestically, the Irish Cup was first played for in 1881, but we find a huge Scottish influence in teams like the Gordon Highlanders and the Black Watch playing in the final. Clearly the British military (particularly the Scottish regiments) had a great influence on the development of the game.

Dublin in 1908 was far from being an introverted centre of narrow Irish nationalism. It was cosmopolitan with a very large English population, as the lovely Georgian architecture would testify. It was certainly the most British of the cities of southern Ireland, certainly far more so than Cork in the west. One would not have immediately identified Dublin in 1908 as the city which would 'host' the bloody rebellion of 1916.

The political tension of the Charles Stewart Parnell era seemed to have settled down with the Irish Nationalists quietly supporting the Liberal Government of the ailing Henry Campbell-Bannerman. The Fenians, men dedicated to freeing Ireland by violent means if necessary, were for the moment in abeyance, but the British authorities of Dublin Castle would take the visit of the Scottish football team very seriously. As in 1904 and 1906 there would be a large, if discreet, police presence backed up with troops in readiness just in case of anything untoward.

Scotland had defeated Wales narrowly at Dens Park the previous week. A few changes had been made to the team, notably the recall of the man on the tip of everyone's tongues – Jimmy Quinn of Celtic, the controversial 'charger and barger' but also the scorer of many goals. He had been out injured since shortly after the New Year, but his presence in the forward line would make such a huge difference. It was not, however, as if that forward line was in any way lacking talent, for there was the 'will o' the wisp' Bobby Templeton (ex-Celtic and now Kilmarnock), another man who was seldom out of the news, Bobby Walker, the marvellous inside forward of Hearts and Queen's Park's Robert McColl.

Charlie Thomson of Hearts was the centre-half and captain and he was flanked by Johnny May and Jimmy Galt of Rangers. Galt had a reputation of being tough – he was referred to, even by his own supporters, as 'dirty Galt', and Thomson must have wondered how he would get on with his team mates, notably Celtic's Jimmy Quinn. He need not have worried. Quinn and Galt, sworn enemies on the field when Celtic played Rangers, were friends and allies when playing for Scotland.

The team had three Kilmarnock men – Templeton, and the two full-backs Jimmy Mitchell and Willie Agnew, and the goalkeeper was Harry Rennie of Hibs, generally reckoned to be the best in the business. Two Aberdeen men joined the party as well – one was left winger Willie Lennie, but the other was Charlie O'Hagan, a brilliant purveyor of the ball – but sadly, for Scotland, an Irishman who would therefore be playing, along with Alec Craig of Rangers, for Ireland.

Craig and Jimmy Quinn had a history, but it was an honourable one. It went back to the Scottish Cup semi-final of 1905 when Quinn was sent off by an officious referee for kicking Craig. What had happened was that Craig had fallen on the wet turf, had grabbed Quinn's leg to break his fall and Quinn had shaken his leg to rid himself of this accidental attention. He had not kicked Craig but the referee saw it this way in spite of the fact that the honest Craig intervened on Jimmy's behalf both on the field of play and at the disciplinary hearing some time later.

Dublin was far from being a city like Glasgow where no-one spoke of anything other than football, but there was still a sizeable crowd at the docks as the ship sailed in bearing the Scotsmen with their officials and a very small band of supporters, some of whom attracted some attention by wearing the kilt or a tartan Tam O' Shanter, now called a 'tammy'. Everyone strained to see the great Quinn, whose parents were of course Irish and who played for the team that that Scots-Irish supported – the Celtic or as they were pronounced in Ireland sometimes, the Keltic. The players were smartly dressed, although well wrapped up in gabardines against the Irish rain as they climbed into their horse drawn charabanc which would take them to their hotel.

The rain would continue all Friday (the 13th!) although this did not stop Scotland practising, and even into the Saturday. The pitch at Dalymount Park would be wet and heavy, therefore, but this was no handicap to the Scotsmen, particularly men like Quinn who had experienced wet conditions and who revelled in the heavy ground. The tricky Bobby Walker on the other hand, being a very skilful ball player, preferred a drier and harder pitch but he was the first to say that a really good footballer should be able to play in all conditions.

10,000 made their way to Dalymount Park, many of them curious and wishing to see this great Scotland team and to learn more about this game which had taken over the mainland of Great Britain so dramatically over the past 30 years, but which had not yet taken such a hold in Ireland. Dublin itself boasted of a few teams, notably the Bohemians, Shelbourne and the Freebooters, but the game was anything but the obsession that it now was in Scotland. Bohemians would win the Irish Cup that year, as Shelbourne had done in 1906. Noticeably both these teams had a player in the Irish team that day; there were five players from the north of the country, two who now played for Scottish clubs and two who now plied their trade in England.

The rain which had continued unabated suddenly stopped in such a way that the *Dundee Advertiser* in its report of the game waxed poetically that, *'Old Sol* [the sun] *must have been a lover of Scotland and Quinn, for it had rained incessantly up to kick-off, but it ceased miraculously whenever the referee blew his whistle so that the sun and the stars could admire Jimmy's goals.'*

Indeed there was a great deal to admire in Scotland's play as the Irishmen were simply swept aside. Templeton and Lennie rampaged down the wings and supplied McColl and Walker who in turn set up Quinn. QUINN scored four – a brilliant shot from the edge of the penalty box, a 'charge through' and two where he simply did what all strikers do and read the situation well enough to be in the right place at the right time. JIMMY GALT scored the other goal in the 5-0 rout, and there is a certain amount of newspaper evidence to suggest that Scotland took it easy to avoid totally humiliating the dispirited Irishmen who took their beating manfully and sportingly.

The Irish crowd, as crowds do sometimes, began to cheer for Scotland, claiming, not entirely unreasonably that Jimmy Quinn was one of their own, and stating that the Scotland team was far better than the English team which had beaten Ireland in Belfast a month earlier. Scotland were cheered off the park and that night the talk in Dublin was of 'Quinn, Quinn and nothing but Quinn' according to one newspaper whereas another is even more hyperbolic when it says that 'not since days of Charles Stewart Parnell has a man been talked about so much in the city as Jimmy Quinn!'

The irony was that the hero himself was an intensely shy man. Unlike some celebrities who pretend to be shy, thereby gathering even more glory, Jimmy was genuine, worrying about his wife and children (including a recent baby) in faraway Croy, worrying about whether he was fit enough for the rest of the season and worrying about whether he would be seasick on the way home. It was often said of Quinn that he was 'just like an ordinary man'. He certainly seemed like that in the hotel as he chatted to the porters and the bellboys (visibly in awe of the demigod), ate his meal and drank his beer. On the Sunday morning, he went to Mass.

But this was more than just Jimmy Quinn. The whole team had cause to be happy, for they had now defeated both Wales and Ireland, something that they had not done since 1902, and they knew that they had done their chances of selection for the 'big' game against England at Hampden no harm at all.

v ENGLAND 2-0
Hampden Park; Att: 106,205
2 April 1910

Scotland:	England:
Brownlie (Third Lanark)	Hardy (Liverpool)
Law (Rangers)	Crompton (Blackburn Rovers)
Hay (Celtic)	Pennington (West Bromwich Albion)
Aitken (Leicester Fosse)	Ducat (Woolwich Arsenal)
Thomson (Sunderland)	Wedlock (Bristol City)
McWilliam (Newcastle United)	Makepeace (Everton)
Bennett (Rangers)	Bond (Bradford City)
McMenemy (Celtic)	Hibbert (Bury)
Quinn (Celtic)	Parkinson (Liverpool)
Templeton (Kilmarnock)	Hardinge (Sheffield United)
Higgins (Newcastle United)	Wall (Manchester United)
Referee: Mr Mason, Burslem	

HAMPDEN HAD CAUSE to fear the approach of the Scotland v England game in 1910. Four years previously, the world had been astounded when a crowd of over 100,000 appeared to see the same fixture. This had been bettered in 1908 when over 121,000 were there, and it was widely expected that even more would pay their shilling entrance fee to see this game. And Hampden was still injured, still licking her wounds received last year at the Scottish Cup final when Celtic and Rangers fans had rioted – not at each other, but at the authorities for denying them extra time after two drawn Scottish Cup finals. It was suspected that the Cup final was being unnecessarily prolonged for the purpose of another huge gate.

To say that Glasgow was the world capital of football in 1910 is to state the obvious. Celtic and Rangers both had huge stadia, and Hampden had been built in 1903 to stage Scotland matches. The damage done to the stadium during the previous year's disturbances had been considerable, but it had been repaired by the enthusiastic Queen's Park club, determined not to lose their opportunity to continue to host the Scotland v England game every two years. Additions had been added to the ground to accommodate even more spectators and many people asked if there was any end to this insatiable love of football which seemed to afflict every Scotsman.

The England game was the highlight of the season, dwarfing at this stage of the year any interest in the domestic scene. Celtic had won the League Championship for the past five years and would win it again this season, although they had slipped up against Clyde in the Scottish Cup semi-final. Clyde would take on Dundee the following week in what was termed a 'virgin' final, neither of these teams having partaken of the feast previously. All this was fine, but what really mattered for the well being of the nation was beating England.

The Scotland team had horrified their supporters by going down to Ireland at Belfast a couple of weeks previously. These things did not happen in Edwardian Britain and it was only the second time in history that defeat to the Irish had occurred. The Irish team, a plucky, determined but talentless bunch had got the better of Scotland by concentrating their defenders on Jimmy Quinn, Celtic's centre-forward, reckoning that he was Scotland's only threat. Scotland supporters in their trains, cabbies and tramcars going to the game at Hampden feared that England might do the same thing.

Jimmy Quinn was the most famous man in Scotland. If King Edward VII had ever come to Glasgow to meet him, people would have asked who that was with 'Jimmie'. He was not universally liked, and he had been involved in two very high-profile incidents against Rangers in 1905 and 1907 which had riven Edwardian Scotland into two distinct factions. There could be little doubt, however, that he was the mainstay of the success of Willie Maley's Celtic team which was on the point of breaking its own record by winning the League Championship six years in a row. Ironically, Quinn could be seen after training each day sitting quietly in the corner of his train home to Croy (a tiny East Dunbartonshire mining village) every night as people nudged each other and said 'that's him'.

In 1910 the nation was facing a constitutional crisis. Since 1906, the Liberal Government of Glaswegian Henry Campbell-Bannerman and then, after he died, Henry Herbert Asquith, had passed some much needed social reforms in education, unemployment benefit and trade unions. This had been resented by the Establishment and things came to a head when the House of Lords refused to pass the Budget proposals of the Liberal Government in 1909. This was unusual but still constitutional. The Asquith Government had then tried to curtail the powers of the House of Lords, and had been prepared to call a General Election in January 1910 to ask for a mandate. Unfortunately the nation had been almost equally split between the Liberals and the Conservatives, although the Liberals were still in office with the support of Labour and the Irish Nationalists.

The country was thus in stalemate and things were not helped by the obviously failing health of King Edward VII. The old rogue, man of many mistresses and scandals in the past, was probably well meaning, but no-one knew what he would do if another General Election (probably to be held at the end of the year) produced a similarly 'hung' parliament. As it turned out, Edward would die in May and it would be his son George who had to make the decision.

All this was of less than immediate concern to the many 'trippers' from both Scotland and England who made their way to Hampden that fine spring day. 1906, 1908 and now 1910 had all produced good days for the game against England, and it was confidently believed that the record crowd of two years previously would be surpassed. Railway companies had laid on 'Football Specials' at cheap rates to take fans from all over Great Britain to Glasgow, and from early on it was obvious that there was some special event in the city as the crowds thronged the streets with their tartan bonnets and rosettes. It was a noticeably family occasion with plenty of wives there accompanying their husbands, not necessarily to go to the football, but to sample the atmosphere of Glasgow and to visit one of the 'tea rooms' for which the city was now famous.

After about midday, everyone began to head 'Hampdenwards', some even walking, for the weather was fine, and all talking in excited animation about Jimmy Quinn and Jimmy McMenemy, about 'Peter the Great' (as Peter McWilliam of Newcastle was called), about goalkeeper Jimmy Brownlie of Third Lanark, about the great Charlie Thomson, once of Hearts but now captaining Sunderland, who would skipper this Scotland side at centre-half, and the charismatic Bobby Templeton on the left wing, who had once entered a lion's cage after being challenged to do so. On the other hand, there was the English team of men with strange names like Pennington and Makepeace and who played for exotic teams with names like Woolwich Arsenal and West Bromwich Albion.

Public houses had opened early – too early for some who would thus never see the game and who would be relying on the good offices of others to see them home – and the road to the ground was jam packed with sellers of sausages, doughnuts and other delicacies including, for youngsters, black balls. It was noisy, with some singing a Scottish ditty of Robert Burns, and there was also the sound of thousands of rattles with tartan ribbons and 'Come On, Scotland. Hurry Up' written on them. All was good humoured, but the police were there in strength – 284 of them, with some of them detailed to be on horseback to escort the English charabanc through the streets from the St. Enoch's Hotel.

The crowd looked as if it might have been more than two years previously, but it was somewhat down on that figure, and in any case Hampden was large enough to allow everyone in without having to lock the gates. The new stand, rebuilt after the fire at last year's riot, now boasted of a better developed 'telegraph and telephone station', so that the half and full-time scores might reach the eager populace of the British Isles so much quicker, and so that the evening newspapers could give a detailed account of the game.

The vast crowd was entertained by the pipes and drums of the Argyll and Sutherland Highlanders, and in between times amused themselves by some community singing of their own, with for example the Victorian music hall, 'Oh My Darling Clementine' but with alterations to the words so that it was 'Oh My Darling Jimmy Quinn'. The game, scheduled for 3pm started on time and for the first few minutes it was England who looked the nippier team with Jimmy Hay, in what was not his best position at left-back obviously struggling against the thrusts of Bond and Hibbert. Once or twice Jimmy Brownlie earned a round of applause with some confident handling before, in the 20th minute, Scotland struck.

The move stemmed from Bobby Templeton, the man who had been blamed for inadvertently causing the Ibrox Disaster of 1902 as everyone had moved forward at once to see him receive a pass. This time, he beat several men with an intelligent dribble, and just as he was tackled, passed the ball through to Quinn. Unfortunately, it was just marginally ahead of Jimmy and seemed to be heading for goalkeeper Hardy. But Quinn did not give up and clattered onwards like an express train, managing to slip the ball to McMenemy before Hardy got there. Quinn's Celtic colleague, JIMMY McMENEMY, who rejoiced in the nickname 'Napoleon' was on the spot to slip the ball home, despite an English defender's attempts to punch the ball clear on the line. Over 100,000 throats roared their welcome for that goal which owed so much to the trickery of Templeton, the courage of Quinn and the cool head of McMenemy, and little more than ten minutes later, the game was virtually over, as Scotland scored again.

This time it was all about JIMMY QUINN, scoring a goal which these days might have been chalked off but which was considered perfectly legal then. Jimmy's ex-Celtic colleague, Alec Bennett, sent in a cross and Jimmy simply charged into the net with the ball, knocking over full-back Jesse Pennington and goalkeeper Sam Hardy at the same time, and leaving them on the ground looking at each other, while he accepted the acclaim of a nation. 'Flags and handkerchiefs could be seen waving, whistles were shrilling and bells were ringing' on the vast Hampden terracings as the crowd went berserk.

England were already a beaten side, and in the second half only heroic work from Sam Hardy in the England goal prevented a rout. Long before full-time, the huge crowd was cheering, singing, slapping each other on the back, throwing bonnets and hats in the air and doing all the things that an Edwardian football crowd did when their team was winning. The toast was, of course, Jimmy Quinn, but there were other good Scottish players on view as well, notably Bobby Templeton and Jimmy McMenemy in the forward line, while Peter McWilliam (who would soon win an English Cup medal with Newcastle) had justified his nickname of 'The Great'.

As for Quinn, it was a day on which the bigots could forget his ethnic origins (his father was an illiterate Irishman) and rejoice in Scotland's triumph. But it was not only Scotsmen who enthused about Jimmy. The London based *Evening Dispatch* posed the rhetorical question: 'Is there a better centre-forward in the kingdom than James Quinn? If so, who is he?' and the *Daily Mail* said categorically: 'In Quinn, they [Scotland] have undoubtedly the finest centre in the four countries – strong, resolute and dashing, sometimes opening the game up for his wings and on other occasions going through by himself, but nearly always doing the best thing possible in the circumstances.'

Quinn would be embarrassed by all this adulation, especially when the horse-drawn coach trips from Glasgow to Edinburgh to the Trossachs in the summer would re-route themselves just to pass through Croy in the hope of seeing the great but painfully shy man. Already the darling of the Celtic community, this particular day had made him the hero of Scotland as well.

For Scotland, this day was good enough, for beating England was the be-all and end-all of existence, but even more good news came from Wrexham some nine days after that, for Wales beat Ireland 4-1 thereby cancelling out Ireland's victory over Scotland and making Scotland the British Champions for the tenth time outright since 1884. There was indeed little doubt in 1910 where the capital of world football was.

v ENGLAND 3-1
Hampden Park; Att: 105,000
4 April 1914

Scotland:	England:
Brownlie (Third Lanark)	Hardy (Aston Villa)
McNair (Celtic)	Crompton (Blackburn Rovers)
Dodds (Celtic)	Pennnigton (West Bromwich Albion)
Gordon (Rangers)	Sturgess (Sheffield United)
Thomson (Sunderland)	McCall (Preston North End)
Hay (Newcastle United)	McNeal (West Bromwich Albion)
Donaldson (Bolton Wanderers)	Walden (Tottenham Hotspur)
McMenemy (Celtic)	Fleming (Swindon Town)
Reid (Rangers)	Hampton (Aston Villa)
Croal (Falkirk)	Smith (Bolton Wanderers)
Donnachie (Oldham Athletic)	Mosscrop (Burnley)
Referee: Mr Bamlett, England	

THE ATTENDANCE FOR this game was officially given as 105,000, some 16,000 short of the record attendance in 1908 for the Scotland v England international of that year. In fact, it is probable that more people saw the game than in 1908, as there were break-ins and people climbing over walls in such numbers that the police could not stop them. Well before kick-off time, with thousands queuing up outside, the authorities, acting on police advice, closed the gates. This very act lead to scenes of violence, and the police were taxed to the limit to disperse the crowd.

But the Scottish football fan will always find ways of getting in to a football match. Someone 'fainted' and required police and medical attention. He recovered immediately, but not before the policeman's attention had been distracted so that 20 or so fans had climbed over the wall. There was also a mound outside the ground on the North side, from there at least half of the ground could be seen. Some 300 people climbed up there, taking turns to stand on each other's shoulders and to shout information about the game to the less fortunate. Not that anyone would be in any doubt if Scotland scored, for the roar would be unmistakable. It was also possible to detect howls of outrage at a foul on a Scottish player, claims for a corner as distinct from a goal kick, and of course a penalty would be indicated by a loud cry, then a deathly silence as it was being taken, and finally a roar of acclamation or disappointment as appropriate.

The world outside of football was of little concern to the average Scottish football fan. The Suffragette movement was still a subject of jest rather than anger, even though the ladies seemed to be going to more and more extreme lengths to draw attention to their cause. Ireland was more serious, for the Northern counties seemed more and more determined to resist what the British Government was offering them. But in April 1914, Europe was at peace...

The letter columns of the *Glasgow Herald, The Scotsman* and other establishment journals were seriously concerned about football, and the huge crowds that it attracted. Some of the crowd in 1914 in the environs of the ground indulged in 'behaviour likely to shock any right-thinking Christian', (presumably urinating in someone's garden or simply being drunk), and this was complained about in the same way as women wanting the right to vote 'when they had children to nurture' – clear indications of what upset the Glasgow bourgeoisie in April 1914.

But in addition to this snooty attitude to the game, one also finds genuine concerns about people being crushed to death in the huge crowds, and the SFA being urged to do something to limit the attendance on future occasions. Praise is also given to the police for the way that they managed to control the huge crowds, considering the amount of 'trippers' from places like Aberdeen, Oban and Sheffield who had attended the match.

Scotland approached this match with a mixture of confidence and realism. On the one hand, they usually did well in Scotland. Ten years had passed since England had last won north of the border, and England had never won at the new stadium of Hampden, Scotland having won in 1906 and 1910 and drawn (unluckily) in 1908 and 1912. In addition to that, the Scottish League had defeated their English counterparts 3-2 at Turf Moor two weeks previously in a heartening performance. Against that, Scotland had played two dreadfully insipid draws against Wales and Ireland, the game against Wales at Celtic Park which ended in a 0-0 draw being generally described as one of the dullest internationals of all time.

But there were some exciting players in Scotland's ranks. Celtic were having a good season and seemed to be heading for a League and Cup double. Unfortunately for Scotland, their best player was an Irishman, Patsy Gallacher, but he had been ably supported by Jimmy McMenemy. McMenemy, now well past his 30th birthday and rejoicing in the unlikely nickname of 'Napoleon', was a master strategist with a brilliant shot and ability to pass. The full-backs were Alec McNair and Joe Dodds – Dodds the more attack-minded, while 'Eck' McNair was known as the 'Icicle' for his ability to remain cool under pressure. An ex-Celt was in the team as well in James Hay, now with Newcastle United, and much was expected in the goalscoring department from Jimmy Croal of Falkirk and Willie Reid of Rangers. Croal had been outstanding in the League international at Turf Moor and it had been Reid's goalscoring ability that had done so much to win the League Championships for the past three seasons for Rangers. But Rangers' best player was Jimmy Gordon, the talented right-half, and at centre-half there was Charlie Thomson, Sunderland's captain. If there were any weaknesses in the team, they were possibly the wingers – Donaldson and Donnachie, neither of whom had any great experience at this level and they would be facing the ruthless Bob Crompton and the more cultured, elegant and gentlemanly Jesse Pennington.

The crowd contained more English supporters than had been seen hitherto, with one or two pockets of the crowd where the white rosettes prevailed. They were welcomed by the Scottish supporters and much handshaking was in evidence, for some of them had come from as far away as Surrey and Hampshire. Also in the crowd in the official party of Mr Stevenson, the Lord Provost of Glasgow, were the French consul and his wife, clearly overwhelmed by the size of the crowd and the passions that this very British game engendered. He could understand this game, though, he said, but he would be less successful in sorting out the complexities of a game of cricket!

The first half was even and enjoyed by the huge crowd which swayed on the terracing as the game moved to and fro. From an early stage it was clear that Gordon and Hay, Scotland's wing halves, had established a grip over the midfield and there was a steady supply of balls to the forwards. England had an early opportunity in the first minute, but then Scotland forced two corners in quick succession. From the second of these, the ball was headed out of the goalmouth by an England defender. It was a good strong header, but landed at the feet of CHARLIE THOMSON, some 30 yards from goal. The English defence momentarily hesitated, for they did not think he would shoot from there. In this they were mistaken, for Thomson shot hard past all the players and into the net past the unsighted Hardy in the England goal. And all this in the first five minutes!

England now fought back and Jimmy Brownlie of Third Lanark in the Scotland goal was hard pressed. Jimmy was generally reckoned to be Scotland's best goalkeeper since Ned Doig at the turn of the century, but on several occasions in the first half, he was very lucky – once he had to use his knee to turn the ball back to Joe Dodds, and several times the English forwards missed good chances, but England did equalise when Bob Crompton's free-kick was knocked on by Joe Smith for HAROLD FLEMING to do the necessary and give those with white rosettes and rattles in the crowd something to cheer about.

Half-time thus came with the scores level, but Scotland felt that they were the better team, and if they just remained patient, they would win. They were superior in the key positions of wing-half and inside-forward and the longer the game went on, the more they would take over. There was also the other factor that the crowd might 'roar them to victory' with their encouragement. It certainly was a huge crowd and one or two players expressed concerns about their safety, due to the crowd's swaying on the terracing. The Ibrox Disaster of 1902 which had occurred in this very fixture was never far away from anybody's thoughts.

On the resumption Jimmy McMenemy took charge of the game. He was lucky in that he could use both feet to equally devastating effect. He had played originally at inside-right for Celtic, but then had moved to inside-left to accommodate Patsy Gallacher, and now he was back at inside-right for the sake of Jimmy Croal. McMenemy knew how to hold the ball, when to release it, the exact weight to put on a pass, when to speed up and when to slow down. He was a quiet, thoughtful man by nature, and his tactics were usually spot on. The second half had been in progress for five minutes when McMENEMY won Scotland a corner kick. He then lost his marker as the corner came across, met the ball on the volley and Scotland had regained the lead.

From now on, McMenemy orchestrated the game. But the beauty of this Scotland team was that they understood each other, and even if McMenemy could have been marked out of the game, there were others around, notably Croal, who could take over. McMenemy also brought the Scottish wingers Alec Donaldson and Joe Donnachie more into the game by his superb passing, and the result was that England were soon almost totally overwhelmed.

Halfway through the second half Scotland went further ahead. McMenemy found himself on the edge of the box, and having beaten his man with a deft flick, had enough space to shoot – but he also had enough common sense to realise that a blast for goal might miss, and so instead of opting for power he gently lobbed the ball over the goalkeeper. To his chagrin, the ball hit the bar, but WILLIE REID came running in and tapped the ball home.

Scotland were now 3-1 up and in total charge of the game. England did have one chance but Fleming miskicked, and the general opinion was that Scotland should have been even more ahead. It so happened that the fans who were on the mound at the back of the North Terracing were able to see Scotland's second half goals, and the result was that Highland flings were being danced on the streets round Hampden. Normally the ground authorities would open the exit gates about ten minutes from the end of the game to allow the crowd to go home. They did not dare do that on this occasion, for they feared a massive influx from those outside, and that there would actually be more rushing in than going out. In any case, such was the atmosphere inside the ground that very few would wish to leave, as all the old Scottish songs of Robbie Burns and a few of the current ones of Harry Lauder began to be sung.

When the final whistle sounded and the players sportingly shook hands with each other, the crowd did then make their way home singing the praises of Gordon, Croal, Thomson and particularly Jimmy McMenemy. "Why do they call him Napoleon?" asked an English fan, and indeed it was odd that he was given and rejoiced in being named after the leader of an enemy in a war of 100 years ago. But that was a bygone age when we fought the French. All that had stopped now. Even these silly little disputes in the Crimea and South Africa were things of the past. This was 1914! All the wars could be fought and won on the football field now! There was no need for any other kind of war...

v ENGLAND 4-5
Hillsborough; Att: 35,000
10 April 1920

Scotland:	England:
Campbell (Partick Thistle)	Hardy (Aston Villa)
McNair (Celtic)	Longworth (Liverpool)
Blair (Sheffield Wednesday)	Pennington (West Bromwich Albion)
Bowie (Rangers)	Ducat (Aston Villa)
Low (Newcastle United)	McCall (Preston North End)
Gordon (Rangers)	Grimsdell (Tottenham Hotspur)
Donaldson (Bolton Wanderers)	Wallace (Aston Villa)
Miller (Liverpool)	Kelly (Burnley)
Wilson (Dunfermline Athletic)	Cock (Chelsea)
Paterson (Leicester City)	Morris (West Bromwich Albion)
Troup (Dundee)	Quantrill (Derby County)

Referee: T. Dougray, Scotland

THE GREAT WAR took a long time to come to its interminable conclusion. Theoretically over on 11 November 1918, it in fact lasted longer than that for several reasons. One was that it spawned further conflicts in Ireland and Russia where new nations were being born, another was that it took a long time for soldiers to be demobilised from far flung theatres of war and yet another factor was that the war never really ended in the eyes and minds of those many people who had lost loved ones.

Football had actually had a good war in the sense that many matches were played by regimental sides, and the game had actually continued in some form or other in both England and Scotland, providing some much needed light relief and entertainment for troops on leave and for those at home in the munitions and food supply industries. No internationals had been played however, and even in season 1918/19, the Victory internationals at the end of the season had been deemed unofficial ones in that neither country could claim to have its best available side because of the slow process of demobilisation and the still chaotic state of life at home, particularly in areas like transport.

So 1919/20 was the first real post-war season. Scotland had started with a creditable draw in Wales then a convincing win over Ireland at Parkhead before the 'big' international against England, to be played that year at Hillsborough in Sheffield, a northern venue chosen no doubt to make it easier for Scottish fans to get there. In the circumstances of 1920, the team to play England had been much discussed for months previously by fans eager for the return of the action, and the general opinion of Scotsmen travelling south in the special trains to see the game was that although the defence was sound, the forward line contained several weak links. John Paterson of Leicester City, for example, had played for

Dundee, but without any great success, and Andy Wilson played for Dunfermline Athletic, a team who were not even in the Scottish League! Then Alan Morton, the talented left winger of Queen's Park who was rumoured to be attracting the attention of Rangers, had been injured and forced to cry off on the Thursday, compelling the inclusion of wee Alec Troup of Dundee, a tricky player but not really proven at this level.

The fear was of a real thumping. Three weeks earlier, at Celtic Park, the Scottish League had taken on their English counterparts and the general opinion had been that the Scottish League were never really in the game at all and had even been lucky to get away with a 0-4 defeat, such had been the dominance of the English, with men like Bob Kelly and the unfortunately-named Jack Cock totally dominant over their Scottish counterparts.

But the defence had been fortified by several Anglo-Scots, not least Wilfred Low of Newcastle at centre-half who was known as the 'Laughing Cavalier', and Jimmy Blair of Sheffield Wednesday at left-back. Kenny Campbell in the goal was in the throes of a transfer from Liverpool back to Partick Thistle. He had not enjoyed life on Merseyside, but was a great goalkeeper who clearly hoped for better things in Scotland. Captain of the side was the vastly experienced Alec McNair who had now played for Celtic for approaching 17 years. He had been associated with much of the Celt's success during that period. Nick-named 'The Icicle' because of his coolness and unflappability, 'Eck' was the ideal choice for captain.

It was often said that the success of a team lay in the wing-halves, the midfield men whose job was to take a grip of proceedings in midfield and to turn defence into attack with the spraying of passes. For this game, Scotland turned to the Rangers pairing of Jimmy Bowie and Jimmy Gordon, fine players both and largely responsible for Rangers' success that year in the Scottish League championship.

The Scottish team, immaculately attired in dark suits, ties and with even the occasional bowler hat, left Glasgow Central Station at 10am on Friday 9 April with best wishes from supporters, but the topic that would have dominated conversation as they travelled south was not Russia, not Ireland, not what to do with the Kaiser and the 'Hun arch criminals' for whom the press stridently and hysterically demanded the death penalty – but the weather. Heavy rain had fallen for days and continued to fall, appearing to get even heavier in Sheffield where the team were staying at the Royal Victoria Hotel.

Saturday morning brought little change in the conditions, and when the Scottish party arrived at Hillsborough, they saw a gluepot of a pitch, very heavy and flooded in places. The possibility of a postponement was discussed. The referee was Tom Dougray from Bellshill in Scotland, for the convention in the 1920s, (at least in games between Scotland and England), was for the away country to supply the referee. Dougray must have dabbled with the idea of calling the game off, but practical considerations swayed him. For one thing, it was an international game, very expensive to arrange and the Scots and their supporters (a sizeable contingent of about 5,000) had travelled a long way. And when could the game be re-arranged for?

Encouragingly, the rain began to abate, and enthusiastic Sheffield Wednesday reserves and a few supporters went out with brushes and spikes and began to work on the pitch with

Dougray himself, to his credit, among them saying laudable things like, "I've come a long way, and I want to see a fitba' match". Eventually the pitch was pronounced playable by Mr Dougray.

It was not an opinion shared by everyone, but many are of the persuasion that the best football is played (certainly by Scottish teams) in wet conditions. It is also a fine excuse if things go badly! The players themselves were keen to play, for considerations of money and international 'caps' – (Scotland had three international debutants that day in Miller, Troup and Paterson) – came into it, and eventually the game went ahead with a slightly delayed kick-off.

From the start it was clear that defenders were likely to find conditions more difficult, and Scotland, although being twice behind, found themselves in the dressing room at half-time 4-2 ahead. Within ten minutes, Charlie Wallace of Aston Villa had made space down the right wing and crossed for JACK COCK to head home. Indeed it was wing play that was significant, for the extremities of the surface tended to be marginally drier and for Scotland, Alec Donaldson and Alec Troup, in particular were outstanding. Troup crossed for TOMMY MILLER to equalise, then after ALF QUANTRILL had put England ahead again almost immediately, Troup once again made ground on the left and this time crossed for ANDY WILSON to score.

The crowd were in permanent fervour after this first pulsating 20 minutes, and with the rain now virtually off, felt that they had had their money's worth already. The admission charge had been more than double the price for a normal League game at two shillings, (a florin as it was then called or 10p in modern money), but very few felt that they had been cheated, and the Scots in particular had no reason to regret what they had spent on their train fare when Scotland scored another twice before the interval.

It was ALEC DONALDSON of Bolton Wanderers, a man who had never played in Scottish domestic football, who was responsible for both goals. Scotland's third goal was a wonderful cross field move with Troup beating Longworth yet again on the left and sending a cross over to Wilson who this time saw a challenge coming from two England defenders and promptly hit the ball to the other wing for Donaldson to run in and smash home a tremendous drive.

The acclaim for this goal included cheers from the English crowd who could appreciate good football when they saw it, and then just before half-time, Donaldson once again got the better of the legendary Jesse Pennington, reputedly the best player in England. He crossed for TOMMY MILLER to do the needful and put Scotland 4-2 up. As the teams left the field at half-time, Scotland were treated to a rapturous ovation from their fans, including the many in the Disabled Enclosure in front of the main stand, some wearing Glengarry bonnets as they sat in their wheelchairs.

But this wonderful Scottish play had been achieved at a cost – the cost of exhaustion. England's players were more burly than the slight Scottish ones, and one or two Scotsmen, notably the influential Bowie, were nursing slight injuries. As the pace of this game never slackened, this would turn out to be a significant factor. There was also a certain element of the Scottish character in all this. 'Shutting up shop' and 'What we have we hold' has never really been a factor of Scottish football, and explains why to this day, Scottish clubs do badly in Europe, often going out on the 'away goals' rule. It is quite simply something that is alien to Scotland with only a few teams, notably Jim McLean's Dundee United of the 1980s, being exceptions to the rule. The Scotland team of 1920 however was no such exception. BOB KELLY pulled one back, then FRED MORRIS scored from the edge of the penalty area after some fine work from Quantrill, and then with the Scottish team still reeling BOB KELLY scored again, colliding in the process with Scotland's hitherto inspired goalkeeper Kenny Campbell.

Yet 20 minutes remained and the cause was not yet lost, even though Scotland were now down to ten men as Campbell was taken off after England's winning goal, clearly stunned by his accidental impact with Bob Kelly. Left-half Jimmy Gordon had to go in goal, and although he did well there, his influence on the centre of the field was much missed.

But with the return of Campbell for the last ten minutes, Scotland rallied as England in turn tired and wilted against a Scottish onslaught, focussed on the wingers, Donaldson and Troup. The crowd was once again in a fervour, and England's goalkeeper Sam Hardy was compelled to make save after save as Scotland kept forcing corners, and Andy Wilson came close on several occasions. Once Hardy had to save from point blank range, and then just on the whistle (Dougray allowed a few extra minutes which the English thought was deliberate, but in fact was because of the long delay after the injury to Campbell), Alec Troup shot from the edge of the box through a ruck of players and the ball struck the post. Some times they go in, some times they don't and Alec was unlucky this time as the ball rebounded to Arthur Grimsdell of Spurs, who booted clear.

So Scotland lost, but the fans of both nations were unanimous in saying that this was a great game of football with hyperboles like, 'after all the years at the front, this was British football at its best and it showed what we'd been fighting for'. The unusual scoreline of 5-4 had in fact happened twice before in 1879 and 1880 with the advantage going to the home side now in all three cases.

The Scottish side were taken to the Peak District and given tours of caves on the Sunday before they went home, and when English people saw them, they were given a round of applause.

Scotland had lost this particular game, but won a great deal of affection. They had little to reproach themselves for, and this match became regarded as one of the best internationals of all time. In future years, Scotland would have a great deal more success against England, but seldom would they play so well as they had done in 1920.

v ENGLAND 3-0
Hampden Park; Att: 85,000
9 April 1921

Scotland:	England:
Ewart (Bradford City)	Gough (Sheffield United)
Marshall (Middlesbrough)	Smart (Aston Villa)
Blair (Cardiff City)	Silcock (Manchester United)
Davidson (Midlesbrough)	Smith (Tottenham Hotspur)
Brewster (Everton)	Wilson (Sheffield Wednesday)
McMullan (Partick Thistle)	Grimsdell (Tottenham Hotspur)
McNab (Morton)	Chedgzoy (Everton)
Miller (Manchester United)	Kelly (Burnley)
Wilson (Dunfermline Athletic)	Chambers (Liverpool)
Cunningham (Rangers)	Bliss (Tottenham Hotspur)
Morton (Rangers)	Dimmock (Tottenham Hotspur)
Referee: Mr Ward, England	

SCOTLAND'S FIRST OFFICIAL home international against England since the end of the Great War was much looked forward to, but was deprived of spectators because of two problems. One was the sad truth that so many men who would have gone to the game were under the soil in France or whiling away what remained of their lives in a convalescent or mental hospital. The second hinted at the labour problems that would bedevil the 'land fit for heroes to live in' for the next decade – a rail strike. As in 1912 with a similar problem, the strike was patchy and incomplete, but it did effectively prevent many people from far away from attending, although *The Scotsman* talks about charabancs from Tweedmouth and North of the Tay managing to convey passengers to Hampden, and of other spectators arriving in all other kinds of vehicles including one that we would wish to know more about, namely 'the most dilapidated growler', presumably a motor bicycle which had seen better days.

A particular blow was struck inside Glasgow when the railway company announced that there would only be a restricted service that day and that for the Cathcart Line which served Mount Florida station, only season ticket holders would be allowed. This in fact meant that 'the oldest form of locomotion' or 'Shank's pony' had to be employed. Thousands had to 'hoof it' from the city centre to Hampden, starting from very early morning and becoming a 'veritable torrent' from midday onwards.

The fans would have had a great deal to be excited about as they made their way to the ground. The weather was dry but cold and there was a stiff breeze which might affect the game. Scotland had had a great season, beating both Ireland and Wales with Andy Wilson of Dunfermline Athletic scoring in both games. Andy would be in the centre again today, his direct opponent being another Wilson, George of Sheffield Wednesday. Andy was really a Middlesbrough player, having registered with them before the war, but had opted to play for Dunfermline, and as they were not playing in the official Scottish League, but in an unofficial one called the Central League, Middlesbrough had no legal redress.

Andy Wilson was an interesting character. His arm had been badly damaged in the War at Aras while serving with the 6th Highland Light Infantry, and he had been convalescing in Stobhill Hospital in 1919. In March he and some friends went to see the Scotland v Ireland Victory international at Ibrox. Outside the ground, while wearing the traditional hospital blue of a wounded soldier, he was approached by an SFA official and asked if he were Andy Wilson of Hearts. He said he was, for he had played a few games for the Tynecastle club earlier in the War. The SFA official then offered him a game, as Scotland were several men short – McNair and McMullen had been delayed by late-running trains and McMenemy had cried off injured. Wilson grabbed his chance and scored twice for Scotland, once with a penalty and the other with a (then legal) shoulder charge on the goalkeeper.

Wilson was the hero of that gane, but the crowd were also very impressed with left-winger Alan Morton, who had now played one season for Rangers after joining them from Queen's Park. Morton was fast, nippy and had a devastating cross, but so too did his England counterpart, Jimmy Dimmock of Tottenham Hotspur. Other players were less well known to the Scottish crowd, for this team contained six Anglo-Scots, a move forced upon the Scottish Selectors after a very poor performance by the Scottish League team against their English counterparts a month ago.

If there had been any doubt in anyone's mind that they were living through the aftermath of a War, it was dispelled when they got nearer the ground. The sheer amount of beggars – some hideously deformed – women and children pathetically dressed with placards saying where their breadwinner had met his death – Loos, Somme, Ypres (spelt and pronounced Wipers) – were hard to ignore and more sinisterly, there was the constant threat of pickpockets. Evangelists preaching about Armageddon and how the War had been caused by immorality, sexual licence and drunkenness vied to gain the attention of the crowd with Socialist preachers who argued, rather more probably, that it was the wickedness of the capitalist classes who had caused it all, and that thousands had died in the mud 'to make the world a safer place for Henry Ford and Pierpont Morgan'. A few were still wanting to hang the Kaiser and to crush Germany forever before she rose again, and some braved the ire of the crowd by arguing for independence for Ireland.

But football was more important to the thousands hurrying to the game. Some English supporters appeared, full of good humour and saying things like 'Hi, Jock' and singing one of the War songs:

'Wash me in the water,
Where you wash your dirty daughter
And all will be whiter than the whitewash on the wall.'

This song, originally a reference to the power of propaganda to minimise casualties caused by the follies of generals whose daughters apparently could 'entertain' the troops, had now been adopted by England supporters because they wore white. They were jeered at and scoffed at by the Scots, but there was no real hatred or violence, for both countries had been comrades in arms and had suffered so terribly and so recently.

Further evidence of the War and its devastation came when the blind were brought in to their special enclosure in front of the Stand where they would 'see' the game thanks to the help of a few stentorian-voiced volunteers who would provide a running commentary. It was probably through this phenomenon that the BBC in later years would decide that one could do a running commentary over the 'wireless'. That, however, was way in the future, for the BBC had not yet been founded. The blind were given a special cheer and handshake, even a group of them with white England rosettes. They would always be the real heroes.

The military band of the 9th Highland Light Infantry provided the music before the start, but the writer of *The Scotsman* was impressed by the way that the crowd were handled. 3 shillings and 6 pence was the price for admission to the stand or the 'pavilion opposite the stand', and 2 shillings for behind the goal. These were heavy charges for 1921 but it did not seem to deter the crowd. Rather prematurely, the gates were closed ten minutes before kick-off when there seemed to be still room for more.

From the start, Scotland, facing the stiff breeze, attacked the Mount Florida goal, but it was clear that this was going to be no easy game against the determined Englishmen. For a long time the play was even, although the Scottish fans took heart with the thought that if they could hold the game at 0-0 until half-time, they would then have the advantage of the wind in the second half. But on 20 minutes, Scotland took the lead. It came from the brilliant Alan Morton who charged down his left wing but was tackled before he could cross and the ball went out for a corner. Morton himself took the corner, the ball did funny things in the wind and Harold Gough in the England goal missed his punch. The ball came through to ANDY WILSON, who evaded two desperate lunges and shot home from close range. He raised his right hand to acknowledge the cheers of the crowd as his team-mates congratulated him, but this merely emphasised the sight of his damaged left arm hanging uselessly and impotently by his side.

England now pressed furiously, conscious that they had to as long as they had the advantage of the wind, but the Scottish half-back line of Davidson, Brewster and McMullan stood up to all that they could offer, while right-back and captain Jock Marshall of Middlesbrough kept the dangerous Jimmy Dimmock quiet. Just on half-time, Scotland counterattacked and Harold Gough made up for his earlier blunder with a fine save from a Wilson drive.

But it was the same luckless Harold Gough who gave away the second goal immediately after the restart. Once again, he could blame the Hampden swirl to an extent, but it was a harmless-looking cross from ALAN MORTON which simply went through his hands. In a masterpiece of meiosis, *The Scotsman* said, 'there was a gasp from the spectators'. One imagines that there was a great deal more than that from the 85,000 Scottish voices who now delighted in their team being two goals ahead and playing with the wind, which if anything seemed to be strengthening.

In another ten minutes, the game was all over and once again poor Harold Gough, his confidence totally shattered in his one and only international, was at fault. Alex McNab of Morton on the right wing sent over a perfect cross for ANDY CUNNINGHAM to head downwards and the ball bounced over Gough's diving body. Harold, who had won an English Cup winners' medal with Sheffield United in the 'Khaki Cup Final' of 1915, would never be the same again, but unlike many footballers he lived long, cheerfully told stories about his horrible Hampden in 1921 to the customers in his Chesterfield pub and died in June 1970 at the age of 80.

England redoubled their efforts in sheer desperation, but could make little of a now supremely confident Scotland defence. Goalkeeping errors apart, this was a good England team, but they were up against a superb Scottish one, and although the Scottish Press virtually unanimously said that 3-0 was more than a little generous to the Scots, they were convinced that Scotland deserved their victory and, having now beaten all three British teams (the Triple Crown, as it became known in rugby), their first Home International Championship since the end of the War.

At full-time, while the Scottish fans celebrated noisily and their players congratulated each other as they walked off, Jock Ewart, Scotland's goalkeeper was seen to sprint up to the opposite goal to commiserate with his English counterpart. Ewart knew that this could have happened to him as well in that Hampden breeze, and as a goalkeeper he could empathise, especially when the ignorant would say things like 'Gough the Goof' in the weeks to come.

Scotland's fans were triumphant. The continuing absence of public transport meant that thousands marched back to central Glasgow, 'not unlike the aftermath of Bannockburn,' in the somewhat hyperbolic words of a Scottish newspaper, with much singing and waving of tartan rosettes.

'We'll crown Andy Wilson King of Scotland...
and Alan Morton the Prince of Wales.'

was the song that they sang again and again.

Rangers fans in particular had a good day, for as well as singing the praises of Cunningham and Morton, the evening papers told them that Raith Rovers had beaten Celtic in Kirkcaldy, meaning that Rangers were virtually certain to win the Scottish League. The following Saturday would be a less happy event for them because in the Scottish Cup Final, Partick Thistle shocked them by winning 1-0 at Celtic Park.

But the victory over England was much needed and much deserved. It would be nice to say things like 'they all lived happily ever after'. That would not be true, however, for the 1920s were a dreadful decade for the Scottish working class whose sufferings were almost permanent. But perhaps fortunately for the British establishment, the Scots did not resort to violence and revolution as the Russians did in 1917. No, a victory over the Auld Enemy at the national game was enough!

v ENGLAND 2-0
Hampden Park; Att: 92,000
4 April 1925

Scotland:	England:
Harper (Hibs)	Pym (Bolton Wanderers)
McStay (Celtic)	Ashurst (Notts County)
McCloy (Ayr United)	Wadsworth (Huddersfield Town)
Meiklejohn (Rangers)	Magee (West Bromwich Albion)
Morris (Raith Rovers)	Townrow (Clapton Orient)
McMullan (Partick Thistle)	Graham (Millwall)
Jackson (Aberdeen)	Kelly (Burnley)
Russell (Airdrie)	Seed (Tottenham Hotspur)
Gallacher (Airdrie)	Roberts (Manchester City)
Cairns (Rangers)	Walker (Aston Villa)
Morton (Rangers)	Tunstall (Sheffield United)
Referee: Mr Ward, England	

THIS WAS ONE of Scotland's best ever wins over England, and meant that as in 1884, 1887, 1900 and 1921, they had beaten all three British countries in the annual Home International tournament. The man of the moment was undeniably the handsome, unassuming captain, Dave Morris of Raith Rovers who had led his own Kirkcaldy side to one of the very few glory periods of their history, and had not flinched from doing so with the national side as well, earning the respect of mighty men like Willie McStay of Celtic and Davie Meiklejohn, Tommy Cairns and Alan Morton of Rangers, whilst harnessing the prodigious talents of Hughie Gallacher of Airdrie. It was indeed Gallacher who scored the two goals.

The team was made up entirely of Home-Scots. There were two reasons for this: one was that there had been problems in obtaining the release of Anglo-Scots from their English clubs in the past, but the other reason was, quite simply, that the game in Scotland itself at this point was good enough. Mention has been made of Raith Rovers, but another team doing well were Airdrie (who had won the Scottish Cup the year before), who were challenging Rangers hard for the League Championship and the latter provided Willie Russell and Hughie Gallacher for the national team. In addition, Rangers, who would be this year's League Champions, had a fine side with a marvellous left wing pairing of 'tireless' Tommy Cairns and Alan Morton, 'the wee blue de'il', who had impressed everyone so much since his arrival from Queen's Park five years previously.

Rangers were odds on to become League Champions for the third successive year, but they had received a very nasty blow to their pride a couple of weeks before the international when Celtic suddenly turned on the style and beat them in the Scottish Cup semi-final to the tune of 5-0. Celtic had, if truth be told, been nothing other than an ordinary side that season, but with men like Patsy Gallacher and young Jimmy McGrory in their ranks, all things were possible. They would go on to win the Scottish Cup the following week in an epic and famous final against Dundee.

Rangers had a strange kind of problem with the Scottish Cup which they had not won now for 22 years since 1903. Much was the talk of hoodoos, jinxes and even curses from the dead of the Ibrox disaster of 1902. This piece of rubbish, incidentally, though widely believed and indeed peddled by religious and spiritualist quacks (who abounded in that age) conveniently ignored the fact that they had won the trophy in 1903, a year after the disaster, and that they had no apparent problem in winning the Scottish League or the Glasgow Cup! Nevertheless, Rangers' lack of success in the Scottish Cup troubled and upset their players and supporters.

Scotland in 1925 was at once prosperous and yet seething with industrial discontent. Trade had improved since the immediate post-war years, and unemployment was down, with the shipbuilding industry on the Clyde doing better than for some time. But this masked the true position, for key industries, notably the mines, were shaping up for a conflict that would explode the following year. Poverty was almost endemic in large parts of the country, and the wonder was the lack of political unrest, given the appalling lack of health and education facilities for the working class. Apart from the very rare exception, working class boys and girls were precluded from any university or higher education. Grants and bursaries did exist, but usually family circumstances compelled the youngster to get a job at the earliest opportunity, usually immediately after (or sometimes even before) the statutory school leaving age of 14.

Health care was shocking, as was borne out by the statistics of life expectancy and the prevalence of diseases which did not disappear until the birth of the National Health Service some 20 years later. Slum housing, particularly in Glasgow, would have disgraced a modern day third world dictatorship, and it was hard to believe that this was the 'second city' of a huge Empire which had just won a war.

Politically, Scotland had been disappointed in the short-lived nature of the first Labour Government of the previous year. The cult of Ramsay MacDonald had been intense in Scotland (he had been born in Lossiemouth), but the Messiah's rule had lasted only a matter of months, as he had headed a minority government. Even so, Glaswegian John Wheatley's Housing Act had given out a clear signal that local authorities must now take some sort of responsibility for housing. And there were now enough Labour politicians in Glasgow of the calibre of Manny Shinwell and Jimmy Maxton to indicate that the other cheek was not going to be turned for ever.

However the picture was not all bad. There were still entertainments. Apart from football itself, the undeniable replacement of religion as the 'opium of the masses', there was the cinema, the theatre and dancing. The cinema in particular symbolised the new age. Conservative opinion would tut-tut at the way it encouraged the flappers and undermined the traditional values of society, but girls (and a few older women as well) would spend Saturday night swooning over Rudolf Valentino as he made silent love to Gloria Swanson or Nita Naldi. Even more distressing for the middle classes was the thought that agitation was now rising for all women to get the vote. Women over 30 who owned property already did have this right, but this new movement demanded suffrage for every woman, including the working class ones.

The crowd at Hampden was a little disappointing at 92,000, but this was still vast and Hampden struggled to cope with a huge seething and swaying mass at several points on the terracing. Measures however had been taken to deal with this problem, for a steward on a huge mobile tower (not unlike a siege tower which the Roman Army would use to break down stubborn resistance from Gauls or Carthaginians) armed with a meagaphone, directed the crowd successfully to less-populated parts of the terracing. There were in addition Marconiphones, making their first appearance at Hampden. These were gigantic loud-speakers which barked out 'a stream of instructions to keep passage-ways clear'. As a result of all this, there were only three reported injuries, although one of them was an unfortunate gentleman from Stranraer who broke a leg.

The crowd had arrived from all over Scotland and contained quite a few 'trippers' from England who had brought their wives with them to do some shopping in Glasgow. Train was the normal method of transport, although 250 tramcars were also on duty to convey spectators from the city centre, and *The Scotsman* reported that supporters travelling from Dunfermline in 'a new motor bus' had a traumatic experience in the village of Condorrat when a wheel came off. However no-one was injured, and everyone got to the game in another bus. Tartan tammies were prevalent in the crowd, and the arrival of Davie Morris and the Scottish side was greeted with a huge cheer.

After their comfortable wins over Wales and Ireland, Scotland had been expected to win, and the first half hour showed them at their best with the mighty half-back line of Meiklejohn, Morris and McMullan spraying passes to a hard-working forward line and particularly to the two wingers, Alex Jackson and Alan Morton, who roasted their opponents. At one point, Jackson rounded Wadsworth and sent over a lovely cross which any of Cairns, Russell or Gallacher might have reached. On another occasion, a fine run by Tommy Cairns was stopped only by a determined tackle from Magee.

At the other end, Willie Harper the Scottish goalkeeper was a virtual spectator as Willie McStay and Philip McCloy gobbled up anything that came their way in a game that was distinctly one-sided. But Scotland did have to wait until just before half-time was approaching before they took the lead. This came when a ball from Alan Morton rebounded off a defender to HUGHIE GALLACHER who, after feinting to go to the right, suddenly turned and scored with a fierce drive high into the corner of the net from the edge of the penalty area.

It was the sort of goal that Gallacher had been scoring all year for Airdrie, and if he hadn't been a target for rich English clubs before, he certainly became so now, for the officials of the England team were mightily impressed. Hampden was a sea of acclamation, and seconds after the restart, Scotland really should have scored again, but goalkeeper Pym made a fine save from Alec Jackson. Then just on half-time, England nearly equalised, but Tottenham Hotspur's Jimmy Seed's poor shot was hit straight at the goalkeeper. Everyone would have been glad to hear the half-time whistle a minute or two later, but England had really done well to restrict the score to 1-0 at half-time.

As is often the case, however, the interval cuppa seemed to revive England, and for a short spell in the early part of the second half they attained supremacy and really should have equalised and possibly gone ahead. This was when Manchester City's Frank Roberts twice eluded the otherwise vice-like grip that Dave Morris held over him and tested Harper with two shots. The first was hard but straight at Harper, but the second needed an acrobatic leap from the goalkeeper to turn the ball over the bar. Hampden once again roared its appreciation.

Scotland now settled once again, as wing-halves Meiklejohn and McMullan took a grip of the tussle. England were seldom a threat for the remainder of the game. Scotland's forward line, well lead and marshalled by the mercurial Gallacher, clearly revelling in front of the huge adoring crowd (about ten or twelve times more than what he had been used to at Airdrie), spread the ball about to each other, particularly to the brilliant Alan Morton whose runs and crosses earned frequent rounds of applause from the 'crowd on the terracing and the spectators in the stand,' as one newspaper report (with a touch of snobbery) put it.

It was outside-right Alec Jackson of Aberdeen, the youngest man on the field, who was responsible for the decisive goal which finally killed off the Englishmen. He picked up a pass from Tommy Cairns, beat one or two of the tiring English defence, then rounded Wadsworth and shot for goal. Pym did well to reach the shot but he could only parry it as far as the ever-ready HUGHIE GALLACHER, who had the easiest of jobs to nudge the ball into the net before being overwhelmed by a tidal wave of his own men offering congratulations.

Less than five minutes remained, and the rest of the game was played out in a noisy atmosphere of ecstatic joy with tartan tammies being hurled in the air (as was the custom of the time) and possibly never returning. No-one seemed to care. All that really mattered was that Scotland had beaten England, and were therefore champions of the world.

A more sober note appeared on Monday when *The Scotsman* damned with faint praise, saying that this was a poor England team with 'mediocrity written all over them', and that Scotland, although competent enough, had a few deficiencies. McCloy, for example, had shown some lapses of judgement, Russell and Cairns were too slow and Gallacher did not shoot often enough. But this 'wet blanket' judgement of the scribe did little to dampen the enthusiasm of the nation which received a tremendous boost from this performance. In 1925, any kind of boost was much welcomed.

v ENGLAND 5-1
Wembley; Att: 80,868
31 March 1928

T WAS WITH distinct pessimism that the Scottish nation approached their visit to Wembley on 31 March 1928. The omens were far from good. A year previously, Scotland had lost to England at Hampden – the first time on Scottish soil since 1904, and for the first time ever at Hampden since its construction in 1903. This result had been greeted with mourning and lamentation of Biblical proportions, for Scotland did not lose very often in the 1920s.

In early 1928, there had been two further setbacks to the national team. One was a defeat at home, at Firhill, to Ireland when a team of ten Home-Scots and Jock Hutton, once of Aberdeen but now of Blackburn Rovers, conceded an early goal to the incredulous Irishmen and failed to get back into the game. It was only the second time that Ireland had ever won in Scotland. That was bad enough, but then a fortnight later the English League had come to Ibrox and defeated their Scottish equivalents 6-2.

The Selectors were then accused of panicking when the team to travel to Wembley was announced and only three Home-Scots – Jack Harkness of Queen's Park, Jimmy Dunn of Hibs and Alan Morton of Rangers were picked. Celtic fans were annoyed at the dropping of Willie McStay and were particularly incensed at the exclusion of Jimmy McGrory, who had scored the Scottish League's two goals in the Ibrox debacle and who had been the only 'shining light in the gloom' as the *Glasgow Herald* had put it. But McGrory had had a bad game against Ireland – and in any case Hughie Gallacher, once of Airdrie but now with Newcastle United was now available after suspension.

Rangers' fans were not a great deal happier. The half-back line against Ireland had read Muirhead, Meiklejohn and Craig. They had been totally eclipsed in that game and dropped en masse for the Wembley trip. Even the sole Ranger Alan Morton had been considered lucky to retain his place, for many felt that Alec Troup of Everton, having a great season for the Toffees alongside Dixie Dean, was a better player.

The problem was that so many of the Scotland team were unknown to the Scottish public. Jimmy Nelson of Cardiff City, for example, or his full-back partner Tommy Law of Chelsea were hardly household names, and to counter the menace of Dixie Dean, the Selectors had even gone to Bury to find a fellow called Tom 'Tiny' Bradshaw. Jokes were made about going to Bury to 'dig up' someone from his deserved obscurity – when Davie Meiklejohn, already a legend at Ibrox was available! A cartoon appeared of the three Scottish Home-Scots sitting in the train going to London and looking for a supporter to make up a hand of Bridge with them. But, as the wags said, there were plenty of 'dummies' in the team.

And yet at least three members of the forward line had served a glorious apprenticeship in Scottish football before moving on. Alex Jackson had been a great right-winger with Aberdeen before he moved to Huddersfield Town, where he had been part of the first team to win the Football League three times in a row, and the two close friends, Hughie Gallacher and Alex James, had cut their teeth with Airdrie and Raith Rovers respectively. Gallacher in particular, earning his twelfth cap, had scored a hat-trick for Scotland against Ireland in 1926, the year after he had comprehensively earned the love of the nation for his two goals that defeated England at Hampden.

They were going to this magnificent stadium called Wembley, already the envy of the world, built in the early part of the decade almost as a huge victory emblem to let the world see who had won the Great War. There were also the more mundane reasons of making money and in the short term alleviating some of the dreadful unemployment in London. It had opened in 1923 and Scotland had played the first international there in 1924 – a creditable 1-1 draw, but then unaccountably the 1926 international had been played at Old Trafford in Manchester, and 1928 therefore was only the second time that Scotland had played at Wembley. On this occasion King Amanullah of Afghanistan and his Queen would be there as guests of the British Royal Family who would be represented by the Duke of York, the second son of King George V. He was a shy young man with a stammer who had married a Scottish wife, Lady Elizabeth Bowes-Lyon of Glamis Castle, in 1923. They had a two-year-old daughter called Elizabeth, and the Duke was a genuine football fan who would enjoy his trip to Wembley.

Wembley! The very name conjured up notions of wealth, opulence, royalty and imperialism in stark contrast to the very real poverty that was afflicting most of Scotland and indeed England at that time. The General Strike had come and gone less than two years previously, but the aftermath was bitter and vindictive with the coal owners having all the power they wanted to victimise those who had joined the strike and to impose any sort of terms on the miners for the sake of their evil profits. The rest of the Labour movement could only look on in despair, while bodies like the Church of Scotland washed their hands of this very real problem and concentrated instead on the diversions of illicit sex and drink and the supposed menace to society brought by the Irish to Scotland.

Nevertheless, in spite of the blatant and obvious poverty that they faced, some families scraped together enough to treat themselves to a weekend in London. There were very few who left Central Station, Glasgow or Waverley Station, Edinburgh, but those who did would remember the occasion for the rest of their lives. For those who preferred other pursuits, the Oxford versus Cambridge Boat Race was on the Thames that same day, although it would have been difficult if not impossible to attend both functions. The fare from most Scottish towns to Euston Station on the overnight train was 25 shillings and six pence (about £1.28) – something that a working class family could possibly aspire to if they were prepared to make a few sacrifices – but of course there was a great deal more expense involved in that, and one would be exceptionally naïve not to mention the fact that, for a large part of the Scottish travelling support, it was all about drink.

London's streets were far from 'paved with gold'. Indeed, the Scottish visitors would have remarked on the amount of drunks and beggars at railway stations and underground stations in possibly even greater numbers than one would have expected in Scotland. In addition to this miserable picture was the weather, with rain falling steadily all day. The result was that, in stark contrast to two years earlier when thousands of Scots in Manchester had sung songs about Loch Lomond and Bonnie Prince Charlie while inviting the Manchester mill-girls to speculate on what, if anything, they might be wearing under their kilts, the few Scots in London were hardly noticed and spent the Saturday morning in department stores and restaurants, with only a smattering of tartan being seen at Trafalgar Square and Piccadilly Circus.

Wembley was not quite full, with 80,868 in attendance, as referee Willie Bell started play in the miserable conditions. Bell, from Hamilton, was a much respected official who had refereed the Scottish Cup Final of 1920 and was due to officiate at the Final again in a fortnight's time. His linesmen were one from each country, a Mr Morrison from Scotland and Englishman Mr Stanley Rous, who would in later years become President of FIFA .

Such was the tension at the start that Scotland's goalkeeper Jack Harkness felt faint and had to lean against a post until he recovered his composure. The intensity of play took everyone by surprise. Normally in big games like internationals and Cup Finals, there is a settling-in period of cat and mouse football, but not here, for England hit the post in the first minute but the ball was cleared before a forward could pounce. Scottish nerves were hardly settled by this occurrence, but then almost immediately play swung to the other end. Fine work by Scotland set Alan Morton, 'the wee blue de'il', up for a charge down the left wing. He beat his man and fired hard across the goalmouth to the head of ALEX JACKSON on the right side who put Scotland 1-0 up.

It is often said that the best football is played in the wet. This is particularly true of Scottish teams, but on this occasion both teams served up some breathtaking stuff with Jack Harkness in the Scotland goal probably the busier keeper. But then, in the crucial minute just before half-time, came the moment that changed it all, and ALEX JAMES would for the rest of his life say that this was his best ever goal. He picked up a misplaced pass on the centre line, played a quick one-two with Jimmy Gibson, charged forward, exchanged another quick one-two with Alex Jackson before hitting a low drive from the edge of the penalty box, struck with such venom and pace that the hitherto excellent Arthur Hufton got nowhere near it. 2-0 to Scotland. Half-time came soon after, and Scotland left the field superbly confident about the rest of the game, although a more objective analysis might have suggested that they were lucky to go in two goals ahead. England were closer to them than that.

It was, however, a totally different story in the second half. Perhaps buoyed up by the second goal just before half-time or perhaps seeing that England were now deflated by the same event and the realisation that Scotland's nippy, small forwards were far more suited to the wet than were their more cumbersome English counterparts, Scotland simply took command. Wing-halves Gibson and McMullan were absolutely on top of their game. In the 65th minute a carbon copy of the first goal saw Scotland three ahead. Once again Alan Morton crossed for ALEX JACKSON to head home. A minute later the game was over as a contest when Hughie Gallacher was fouled on the edge of the box, and while some Scottish players yelled for a free-kick, the ball rolled gently to ALEX JAMES who scored.

The game was now finished as a contest, and England would have reason to be grateful to the Scottish referee Willie Bell who might well have given four or five penalties for Scotland, but he was bending over backwards to be seen to be fair, in the opinion of many observers. But yet another goal came Scotland's way as a result of a cross from Alan Morton to ALEX JACKSON, although this time it was a mere tap in for Jackson, who scored with his foot rather than a difficult header. The Scottish fans, beside themselves with joy, were even prepared to be magnanimous and cheered when BOB KELLY scored a consolation goal for England from a free-kick more or less on the final whistle.

So 5-1 it was, a great victory, much celebrated in the city that night (the rain had eased off!) and much talked about in the Press of both countries for days afterwards. Someone (no-one quite knows who) coined the alliterative phrase the 'Wembley Wizards', and this name has stuck. It was a great example of Scottish football at its best (and the presence of eight Anglos in the team convinced any doubting Englishman just how much their domestic game owed to Scottish stars), but this victory had to stay fresh in the Scots' memory for a while, because Scotland's next three visits to Wembley in 1930, 1932 and 1934 ended in heavy one-sided defeats.

v IRELAND 7-3

Windsor Park, Belfast; Att: 35,000
23 February 1929

Scotland:	Ireland:
Harkness (Hearts)	Scott (Liverpool)
Gray (Rangers)	McCluggage (Burnley)
Blair (Clyde)	Flack (Burnley)
Muirhead (Rangers)	Miller (Middlesbrough)
Meiklejohn (Rangers)	Moorhead (Linfield)
McMullan (Manchester City)	Steele (Fulham)
Jackson (Huddersfield Town)	Chambers (Bury)
Chalmers (Queen's Park)	Rowley (Southampton)
Gallacher (Newcastle United)	Bambrick (Linfield)
James (Preston North End)	Cumming (Huddersfield Town)
Morton (Rangers)	Mahood (Belfast Celtic)
Referee: Mr Fogg, England	

A S THE SCOTTISH party sailed from the Broomielaw on the Friday before the game, the hope was expressed that Ireland had now 'settled down'. The civil wars and struggles for independence now seemed to be over, and although Ireland was divided bitterly against itself, there seemed to be no reason to fear for the security of the Scottish team. In 1921, 1923, 1925 and even 1927, there had been cause for concern, but it now seemed that football was once again more important than politics.

Northern Ireland had won its struggle (at the cost of much blood) to remain British, although at least one third of its population wished it otherwise. That was dangerous and the problem would not be resolved for the rest of the century. Belfast in 1929 was perpetually awash with Union flags and British colours, and public buildings would contain *de rigueur* a portrait or two of King George V and Queen Mary. Being British was very important to the Ulstermen, for the privilege had almost been taken away from them.

It is noticeable at the time that the football team was referred to, in the British Press at least, as 'Ireland', although the country or the province called itself Northern Ireland, as distinct from the Irish Free State in the south. In fact, very little football was played in the Irish Free State and even in the old days it had been played more frequently in the north. This was presumably because it was perceived as a British game and therefore encouraged in Ulster, whereas 'football' to a southern Irishman was more likely to mean Gaelic Football, or perhaps Rugby. It so happened that the Scotland rugby team were also playing in Ireland that day, in Dublin. The Scottish rugby team would be as happy as the 'Association' team in the outcome of their game.

In 'Association football' (already called 'soccer' in some quarters to distinguish it from other codes) Ireland were generally considered to be the weakest of the four countries. They had had one great season in 1914 when they won the Home International Championship, but apart from that, their successes had been isolated. They had beaten the Scots in 1903, 1910 and 1928. The last mentioned game at Firhill twelve months ago had inflicted severe damage on the Scottish psyche, had lead to a total recasting of the Scottish side including a 'cap in hand' approach to some Anglos and the result had of course been the Wembley Wizards.

This team contained four Anglos. The Home-Scots consisted of four from Rangers, one from Clyde, one from Hearts and one from Queen's Park. The fact that there were none from Celtic did not necessarily reflect political considerations in Northern Ireland (although Mahood of Belfast Celtic playing for Northern Ireland was less than welcome with some of the Orange crowd and was commonly referred to as 'the Fenian') but more because Celtic were in a trough of their own making at this time in their history (they would, for example, lose to Hibs that day) leaving Rangers to run the roost in Scotland.

But Rangers did indeed have a fine team with men like Meiklejohn and Gray in their defence, and of course the great Alan Morton on the left wing. The 'wee blue de'il' was now approaching the veteran stage but there was as yet no sign of him slowing down nor any lessening in his sometimes mesmeric ability to beat defenders and send over inch-perfect crosses for his forwards to score from.

Much talk centred on the two wee men in the forward line, the two friends Alec James and Hughie Gallacher. Both from the same area of industrial Lanarkshire, both similar types of players, both incredibly able footballers – and both, sadly, imbued with the Scottish ability to destroy oneself on occasion. Both gave the impression of being streetwise and well versed in how to survive life's storms, but both had the ability to upset the wrong people, (especially managers and referees) and Gallacher in particular made some horrendously bad decisions in his life.

Gallacher had already made his mark with Airdrie and Newcastle United, winning the Scottish Cup and the English League respectively with them, and this year he had already scored a hat-trick for Scotland, when Scots forwards had demolished a strong Wales defence at Ibrox in October. Gallacher was such a versatile centre-forward – very tough and never afraid to get even with the bruising centre-halves that 1920s football produced and with the ability to shoot, dribble, pass and head. He was much loved by the Scottish fans, if a wheen less so with administrators. There were also those who argued that the best player in the Scottish team was Alec Jackson, lately of Aberdeen but now with the mighty Huddersfield Town. Alec played on the right wing and had scored a hat-trick in the Wembley Wizards game of the previous year, but it was not goal scoring that he was really famous for. He was a goal maker, and normally a totally unselfish player. Wingers often work in pairs, and with Jackson on one wing and Morton on the other, Scotland, on their day, could be fearsome opponents for anyone.

35,000 attended this game, including a small Scottish support attracted by 'excursion' offers from various travel companies, but for the supporters back home, there would be no radio broadcast, and they would be dependent on the early evening papers for the result. As was the way, groups of supporters would gather outside newspaper offices, hoping for someone to come out and tell them if anyone had scored, or place a placard in a window. They would then rush to buy the evening paper whenever it was printed.

Rain had fallen steadily in the morning and indeed in the days before the game, but it had now eased off, and the surface, although wet, was conducive to good football. And it was good football that Scotland produced, on occasion being described as 'breathtaking' and 'out of the ordinary' by the Irish press. Within the first quarter of an hour, GALLACHER had scored a hat-trick, two of them made by the creative Alec Jackson who had torn past his opponent Hugh Flack of Burnley as if he didn't exist and crossed for Gallacher to net. The other had come from a fine inter-changing move with James. It began to look as if the game was to be embarrassing for the Irishmen.

But Ireland rallied, and somewhat fortuitously, DICK ROWLEY of Southampton pulled one back and for a while, the game was open and evenly contested up to half-time. Before the break, both sides had scored – ALEC JACKSON for Scotland cutting in from the wing when the defence expected a cross, and DICK ROWLEY again for Ireland. The second goal for Ireland just on the half-time whistle led to a crowd disturbance and an invasion of the park, not caused by hooliganism but rather exuberance and a certain amount of overcrowding.

With the scoreline 4-2 in the favour of Scotland, the consensus of opinion was that this was a great match, especially for an international where fewer goals tended to be scored than in club matches. Gallacher was every bit as good as they said he was and that Ireland in such an open game had at least a chance of a high-scoring draw or even a win.

It seemed that Ireland only had a chance because the attack-minded Scots, in particular the outstanding midfield of Muirhead, Meiklejohn and McMullan, were pushing forward and leaving gaps at the back. In addition, goalkeeper Harkness had suffered an injury and did not look as fit as he might have been. In the Scotland dressing room the half-time talk was led by Jimmy McMullan, who was determined to keep playing the normal Scottish attacking game and to 'give Hughie more goals'.

Hughie was not likely to miss such an opportunity. Whatever might be said of his attitude off the park, there was seldom any problem with him on the field. He worked hard, was unselfish and for the 90 minutes was committed to no other cause than winning the game. Six minutes into the second half GALLACHER scored again, this time simply through the centre-forward's greatest skill of being in the right place at the right time. This made it 5-2, and they had not yet played an hour when Ireland scored again, this time through JOE BAMBRICK, a goal that gave particular joy to the Windsor Park crowd for he was a Linfield player. It came from a corner kick, and after the goal was scored there was a slight interruption to play while Harkness received further medical attention.

Once more the Irish crowd scented possibilities, but Scotland simply took command. Their sixth goal was the one which had a certain amount of controversy about it, because GALLACHER and James seemed to kick the ball at the same time. Some newspapers gave the goal to James, others to Gallacher. It mattered little for Scotland, but Hughie was insistent that it was his, claiming that as he and James were of similar build (and of course in 1929 there were no numbers on the jerseys), it was easy for press men to make a mistake. Interestingly enough, nowadays, websites and record books tend to agree with Hughie and to give him five goals for the match, something that is a record for a Scotland game. In 1929 it was the joint record (shared with Steve Bloomer and Howard Vaughton of England) for any international, until the same Joe Bambrick who had just scored for Ireland, notched six against Wales the following year.

ALEC JACKSON, the best player on the field in spite of Hughie's five goals, scored Scotland's seventh near the end. So ten goals were scored in this international, the highest amount since Scotland put eleven past Ireland in 1901 at Celtic Park. The goals had all been well wrought and well taken by Gallacher and Jackson, but the rest of the team had also contributed hugely to a massive Scottish success. Yet *The Scotsman* newspaper, which often tended to undervalue some good Scottish performances, had some serious reservations about this game, saying, 'they [Scotland] won with such ease that the match could not be regarded as an international in the true sense of the term'.

This seems to be grossly unfair, conveniently forgetting that a year previously Ireland had beaten Scotland in Glasgow, and paying little credit to the excellent play of the Scottish team who left the field to the cheers of a sporting Irish crowd. It was also an insult to Ireland, most of whose players were full-time professionals with English clubs like Bury, Burnley and Middlesbrough. It also ignores how well Scotland played against Wales a few months previously, and Scotland's excellence would be proved in six weeks time when they beat England as well.

Remarkably this was not the first time that Hughie Gallacher had starred in a 7-3 victory in Belfast. In November 1925 he had banged in five goals with his usual cheeky insouciance for the Scottish League, annoying some members of the crowd so much that he had been warned to watch his back as he ventured into Belfast after the match to visit relatives. Cocksure Hughie was sure he would be fine, but, according to his own telling of this story, was startled when gunfire sprayed bullets over a nearby wall as he casually walked near Queen's Bridge. Typically Gallacher had the last word. "I will have to extend my stay in Belfast," he joked. "It seems I still haven't managed to teach the Irish to shoot straight."

It would be a fair bet that Gallacher celebrated his most recent success rather well that night, albeit without having to dodge the bullets, along with a few wilder spirits like his old pal Alec James, while the rest of his team mates looked on tolerantly. This was a team of true professionals. They realised that they were lucky to earn their living from playing football, and that to make a success of their career they would have to buckle to and restrict themselves to only moderate pleasures. They also perhaps realised that with true geniuses like Hughie Gallacher, such rules were inappropriate...

v FRANCE 2-0
Paris; Att: 25,000
18 May 1930

Scotland:	France:
Thomson (Celtic)	Thepot
Nelson (Cardiff City)	Anatol
Crapnell (Airdrie)	Capelle
Wilson (Celtic)	Lauren
Walker (St.Mirren)	Banide
Hill (Aberdeen)	Chantrel
Jackson (Huddersfield Town)	Kauffmann
Cheyne (Aberdeen)	Pavillard
Gallacher (Newcastle United)	Pinel
Stevenson (Motherwell)	Delfour
Connor (Sunderland)	Korb
Referee: Mr Van Praag, Belgium	

S COTLAND BROKE NEW ground in 1930 when they went to France to play a full international game. In the previous year of 1929 there had been a tour of Norway, Germany and Holland but it had been a far from full strength Scotland team which had undertaken it, and for a while there was a dispute about whether they were 'real' internationals or not. But now France, a better developed footballing country, who had played an annual fixture with England more or less throughout the 1920s, wished to play Scotland. Scotland agreed and sent a team which could be said to be a reasonably full international side to play at the Stade Olympique du Colombes in Paris in May 1930.

The idea that football began and ended in the British Isles died hard. For a long time, if Scotland beat England, they could reasonably be described as the champions of the world, but the game was now more and more taking on an international aspect. The Great War had certainly developed the game in France and Belgium, as all the British regiments had their football teams, and many Scottish and English ex-patriates were doing a great deal to introduce the game to countries in South America in particular.

Since the Great War, there had been several tours of Scottish teams to Europe and to North America (and in 1923 Third Lanark had toured South America) but they had been half-hearted, patronising sort of affairs in which football had not been taken too seriously in games like 'A Scotland XI v Toronto' or 'New York All Stars v The Scots'.

It had almost been a missionary exercise, but it was noticeable that tours tended to be to rich countries, where there was money to be made, or where there was a large Scottish ex-patriate population. Canada was particularly popular.

This summer in particular, however, there would be one great development called the World Cup to be held in Uruguay under the auspices of FIFA, which had been formed in 1904. The British countries had been the leading lights of FIFA in the early days, but in recent years had fallen out with them about 'broken time' payments to men who were amateurs but needed to be compensated for loss of earnings from their normal jobs. Scotland and England therefore were not invited to the feast in Uruguay, and it is a token of British insular arrogance (they had after all won the Great War and the affairs of 'Johnny Foreigner' were none too important) that neither Scotland nor England even seemed to discuss the idea of healing the breach with FIFA and joining the World Cup. This attitude would continue for many years.

To be fair, a trip to Uruguay, however complicated in the 21st century, was a hundred times worse in 1930. The voyage would take three weeks, and would be outrageously expensive without any great guarantee of any money at the other end in those unstable, inflation-ridden, under-developed and dangerous (kidnapping was a serious problem) countries of South America. It is however less easy to explain why this attitude continued in 1934 and 1938 when the World Cup was held in Europe.

But France would be part of the 1930 World Cup. Indeed it had been the brainchild of two Frenchmen, Jules Rimet and Henri Delaunay, and although they were disappointed that the tournament was not to be held in France, they felt duty bound to attend. They also felt that they needed a practice game against top-class opposition and this is why they invited Scotland for a game. Scotland had indeed been recognised as unofficial 'world champions' since before the Great War, for they tended to get the better of England more often than not.

But Scotland were on a low in 1930, largely due to an almighty 2-5 thrashing at Wembley which avenged the Wembley Wizards' victory of 1928. Much of the controversy centred on Hughie Gallacher whom Newcastle refused to release for that fixture, even though Arsenal, Chelsea and Huddersfield Town released their men to play for Scotland. The selectors then ignored the obvious candidate to replace Gallacher at centre-forward in Jimmy McGrory of Celtic, and a Flodden ensued. Some said that Hughie himself, having quarrelled with certain members of the Scottish establishment, had preferred to stay with Newcastle (to play a vital relegation game) rather than Scotland. Be that as it may, Hughie was back for the French trip.

No Rangers players were available but given that five of them had featured in the 2-5 defeat, that was perhaps no bad thing. On the other hand, they had won both the Scottish League and the Scottish Cup that season, so they were unquestionably the best team. Four men were given their debut – goalkeeper John Thomson of Celtic, centre-half George Walker of St. Mirren, Frank Hill of Aberdeen at left-half and James Connor of Sunderland, who was asked to take on the mantle of Alan Morton on the left wing.

In 1930 it was a great thing to be taken on a trip to Paris, even then the centre of romance, the arts and culture. The team would travel by train to Dover, then the ferry boat the 'Maid of Kent', then train again to Paris, very aware no doubt that this was the same trip undertaken by thousands of Scotsmen in less happy circumstances during the Great War, something that still dominated the thoughts and minds of everyone, even after the interval of more than a decade. After the game, they would stay on in Paris for a week or so to do some sightseeing. The SFA had clearly not yet appreciated how Scottish footballers could behave when abroad!

1930 was a difficult year as the minority Labour government of Ramsay MacDonald struggled to cope with economic problems brought about by the Wall Street Crash in America the previous autumn, causing bankruptcies and unemployment on a huge scale all over a world which had, until that point, been showing signs of a slow recovery from the Great War.

The game was to be played on a Sunday. This caused a few ructions in Presbyterian Scotland as the Church of Scotland still believed that it could pontificate about such things. A few years previously, Eric Liddell had refused to run on a Sunday in the 1924 Olympic Games (in the very same stadium, it turned out), and had been much praised for his stance. But the Scottish footballers took the view that France saw no problems about games being played on Sunday, and cheerfully went along with the idea. 'When in Paris, do what the Parisians do' might have been the attitude. But letters appeared in protest in several newspapers, and the players were all sent to Hell by the lunatic fringe in the Highlands. The game went ahead regardless.

The arrival of the Scots provoked great interest in Paris, as British football was still on a pedestal in European eyes, and everyone seemed to know about the Scottish players, in particular 'le Gallacher' whose goalscoring exploits (and indiscretions) were clearly much talked about. They knew for example about his five goals for Scotland against Ireland in 1929. Hughie basked in the adulation, and the rest of his team mates enjoyed the reflected glory. Being Scottish in Paris was a distinct social asset in any case, because although the traditional Gallic distrust of the English was still prevalent, the Scots, well remembered as the 'ladies from Hell' who wore kilts in the Great War and whose bagpipes played their part in saving Paris in 1914, were very welcome. The Auld Alliance of Scotland and France against England was very much still alive.

The game itself was one sided with a couple of goals from HUGHIE GALLACHER, one in each half, and only the French goalkeeper Alexis Thepot keeping the score down to reasonable proportions. Alex Jackson was superb on the right wing, and the two wing halves Peter Wilson and Frank Hill kept up a constant supply of ammunition to the forwards. Possibly under orders from Scotland officials with an eye to good public relations, the Scottish players did not tackle hard, for the common belief was that the continentals were far too delicate for that! The Scottish players would have been surprised at several things in the 25,000 strong French crowd. In the first place, most if not all were sitting down, something not at all common in 1930 where only the toffs could afford seats in the stand. Another thing was that the crowd cheered the good moves of the Scottish and French alike and cries of 'vive le Gallacher' were heard. The game finished to a standing ovation and cries of 'L'Ecosse! L'Ecosse'.

The Scottish party then stayed on in Paris for a few days with obligatory visits to the Eiffel Tower and the Louvre as well as a few trips to the battlefields, particularly those of the Marne which showed just how close to Paris the Germans had actually reached. Some players would have had relatives or friends who had fought and perhaps died there, and this part of the trip was given due respect.

Other parts were treated less seriously, in particular the SFA's none too wise attempt to impose a curfew on the players. There is value in this action before a game, but when the game is over, it borders on the ridiculous. A story emerged that Gallacher had been caught out after hours and the next night found his bedroom door locked with him inside after a given time. But saying that, no centre-half could hold him, and therefore no hotel bedroom could either. Along with Frank Hill and one or two others, he climbed out the window and down the drainpipe for a night on the town.

This would hardly have been the first occasion upon which Gallacher had been in trouble, but this time when he got back to Scotland, he had two major shocks. Firstly, he discovered that he had been transferred in his absence and without his knowledge or consent from Newcastle United to Chelsea! He was deeply unhappy about this for he loved Tyneside and Tyneside loved him. But his indiscretions were rather too obvious for the Newcastle establishment. In particular Andy Cunningham, the recently appointed manager, ex-Rangers and a keen devotee of the notoriously strict regime of Bill Struth at Ibrox, did not like Hughie. Moreover, there was money and Chelsea were prepared to fork out over £10,000 for the prolific little Scotsman, close to the world record fee.

Secondly, Gallacher discovered that, aged 27, he had been dropped by his country's Selectors. The striker would not be recalled for four years, by which time he was over the hill physically, and perhaps also mentally. Gallacher ended his international career with a record of 23 goals in just 20 games, making him the third highest goalscorer in Scottish history, only being surpassed by Denis Law and Kenny Dalglish.

A thought must have occurred to the Scotsmen as they returned across the English Channel after their very successful trip. Why were they not going to the World Cup? If Scottish football was feted and well thought of elsewhere as it obviously was in France, why could they not take on the world? The French players had told them that they would sail in early June to Uruguay on the same ship as Rumania, Yugoslavia and Belgium in time for their first game on 13 July. It sounded a phenomenal experience and it was a shame that Scotland could not be there.

The World Cup was eventually won by the host nation Uruguay, but it was little mentioned in the Scottish press who were all far more interested in the fate of the Ashes, for Australia, with a talented young man called Bradman, were in England once again. But the trip to France was considered such a success that the Scots went back there in 1932. It would be a long time however – another war would have to intervene – before the French were invited to play in Scotland. It was simply believed that they would not attract a large enough crowd, and their standard would be so low that Scotland would have to field a 'B' side to make a decent game of it!

v ENGLAND 2-0
Hampden Park; Att: 129,810
28 March 1931

Scotland:	England:
Thomson (Celtic)	Hibbs (Birmingham City)
Blair (Clyde)	Goodall (Huddersfield Town)
Nibloe (Kilmarnock)	Blenkinsop (Sheffield Wednesday)
McNab (Dundee)	Strange (Sheffield Wednesday)
Meiklejohn (Rangers)	Roberts (Arsenal)
Miller (St.Mirren)	Campbell (Huddersfield Town)
Archibald (Rangers)	Crooks (Derby County)
Stevenson (Motherwell)	Hodgson (Liverpool)
McGrory (Celtic)	Dean (Everton)
McPhail (Rangers)	Burgess (Sheffield Wednesday)
Morton (Rangers)	Crawford (Chelsea)

Referee: T. Attwood, Wales

'INDUSTRIAL DEPRESSION does not affect the popularity of this game in Scotland,' said *The Scotsman* as it marvelled at the record crowd of 129,810 who saw this game, coming from all parts of Scotland and England, conveyed by train, car, tram and even on foot. This was indeed a time of huge industrial depression with unemployment spiralling apparently out of control, firms closing down, and even the rich and privileged members of society feeling the effects of what was going on. How then did so many people manage to get to Hampden? The answers are simple – one was the sheer love of the game, surpassing anything else in the country in the hearts of so many people. And the other was that football acted as a sort of escapism from the grim reality of the outside world. This phenomenon has frequently been seen in times of war, and in this case of economic catastrophe. People do need to bury their heads in the sand, or in this case, in a game of football.

The domestic game had perhaps more accurately reflected the depression in that crowds were disappointing, but there always seemed to be money enough for people to attend the big games. The best team in Scotland at the moment were possibly John 'Sailor' Hunter's Motherwell, but the League would be won by Rangers who fended off a strong challenge from a Celtic team having one of their best seasons for some time. Indeed it would be Celtic themselves who would win the Scottish Cup two weeks later, beating Motherwell in a dramatic final and replay. Both these games would also have big crowds.

There was another reason perhaps for surprise at the huge crowd at Hampden to see the England game. This was in the poor form of the Scottish team. The English clubs and their association were making it difficult, if not impossible, for Scotland to choose Anglo-

Scots like Alex James and Hughie Gallacher. This had been a constant theme over the past 40 years or so, but effectively it meant that Scotland could only choose Home-Scots (ie. those who played for Scottish League teams). The results that year had not been encouraging.

In October, there had been an insipid 1-1 draw against Wales at Ibrox, followed by a feckless 0-0 in Belfast against Ireland, but worst of all had been the 3-7 drubbing of the Scottish League by the English League at White Hart Lane in November. There were therefore very few grounds for confidence, but the Scottish support is forever optimistic, and the selectors did seem to have got a few things right. For example, they had chosen in the centre-forward position Jimmy McGrory of Celtic, a man who had been scandalously ignored up to now, to such an extent that some Celtic supporters had openly stated that they wanted Scotland to lose. The previous year at Wembley, McGrory had been passed over and when the announcer at Parkhead reminded the crowd that the half-time score was England 4 Scotland 0, the news was greeted with a loud, unpatriotic but totally understandable cheer.

But with McGrory now on board and goalkeeper John Thomson in goal, the Celtic supporters were now reconciled to the cause. Beside McGrory were two fine inside forwards in George Stevenson of Motherwell and Bob McPhail of Rangers. Despite the two wingers Sandy Archibald and Alan Morton now perhaps being a shade past their best, they were still producing the goods for Rangers. Other men like McNab of Dundee, Blair of Clyde and debutant Miller of St. Mirren had yet to prove themselves, and a great deal depended on how captain Davie Meiklejohn would perform and lead his men.

To add even more tension, the game had a very important spectator. This was the charismatic and now somewhat controversial figure of James Ramsay MacDonald, Prime Minister of Great Britain. He was Scottish and in his leadership of the Labour Party he had been almost a cult figure for several decades with people believing that he was the man who would rid the country of unemployment, capitalists, bosses and the gross inequalities in wealth. His opposition to the Great War had in some ways hindered his ambition, but there were many who would look at the huge disabled enclosure at Hampden that day with men commentating for the blind veterans, and the hundreds of limbless ex-servicemen and wonder whether Ramsay had not perhaps got that one right. But the fact remained that he was now the Prime Minister for the second time, albeit on both occasions depending on the support of the Liberals, and he was manifestly not solving the problems of poverty and unemployment, as he had been supposed to do.

The situation in fact had deteriorated, as shortly after he came to power in 1929, Wall Street in New York had crashed, causing all sorts of worldwide economic problems which no politician was able to solve. MacDonald no longer radiated the confidence that he once had. His wife had died many years before. He had never re-married and it was rumoured that he spent rather too much time 'talking to the dead'. What was in a lot less doubt was that MacDonald certainly spent too much time in the company of disreputable aristocrats, particularly ladies with whom he had an intense, although presumably Platonic relationship.

His appearance on the field at Hampden to meet the players led to a mixed reception. There were those who did not forgive him his 'conscientious objection' to the Great War as if this was some form of cowardice, but on the other hand, he was a Labour leader and football crowds in Scotland tended to vote for that party. He might yet turn the economic situation round, it was felt, so the grey-haired, slightly stooping figure was given more of a cheer than a boo as he appeared. In truth, the fans were far more interested in Bob McPhail and Jimmy McGrory, but it must have given a great thrill to men like John Thomson (with his mining background in Fife) to meet the great Socialist Messiah, however flawed he had now become.

A great deal of attention was now focussed on the great William Ralph Dean of Everton. His swarthy complexion and curly hair led him to be called 'Dixie', a name that he himself hated for it smacked of slavery – an emotive issue in the city of Liverpool. But he was a legend on the field, and his clash with Davie Meiklejohn would be a key issue of the game in the same way as the jousts of Jimmy McGrory with Arsenal's Herbert Roberts at the other end would be similarly decisive.

The game was to be broadcast throughout Great Britain, along with the Community Singing which preceded as the Glasgow Police Military Band, conducted by T.P. Ratcliff encouraged the crowd to sing 'Keep Right On to the End of the Road' and 'Ye Banks and Braes of Bonnie Doon' amongst other popular favourites before Mr George F. Allison, the sports journalist and director of Arsenal, who would later go on to take over as manager of the Gunners after the untimely death of Herbert Chapman, would provide the running commentary of the action all the way to the final whistle.

Meiklejohn won the toss and chose to play with the stiff wind, hoping thereby to blunt the early attacks of the Englishmen. In this he was correct and half-time was reached with the score at stalemate. The defenders had all done well with McNab and Miller impressing everyone with their creative play, and full-backs Danny Blair and Joe Nibloe blunting the edge of the England wingers.

England began the second half playing with the wind. They attacked fiercely and Dean almost scored in the first minute before the ball was scrambled away on the line. But at this point the Scottish forwards came into their own with McGrory now leading his line and distributing well to both wings. Scotland were now generally playing with more composure with the wind against them and their persistence paid off with a goal coming for Scotland in the 60th minute. They won a corner kick on the left. It was taken by Alan Morton and came to the feet of Sandy Archibald who shot for goal. The English goalkeeper, Harry Hibbs, could only partially stop the ball, and GEORGE STEVENSON of Motherwell was on hand to score. The roar for this goal startled everyone within a square mile of Hampden Park, including the many thousands who were still outside, unable to afford the entrance fee and longing for the last ten minutes when they would be allowed in free as the gates were opened for the crowd to go home. But scarcely had the noise died down, when Scotland scored again.

This time it was JIMMY McGRORY who was on the spot to nudge the ball into the net after Hibbs had failed to hold a Morton cross. Once more, bedlam erupted inside

Hampden, outside Hampden and in the living rooms of Scotland which (in increasing numbers) possessed a wireless.

This time there was the feeling of confidence that England were not now going to get back into the game. Meiklejohn was superb, McPhail and Stevenson controlled the midfield, Archibald and Morton could always take the ball past their markers as they charged up their wing, and McGrory was a constant menace, especially when his marker, Herbert Roberts, in sheer desperation went upfield to try to get the goal that would bring England back into the game.

John Thomson in goal had a quiet afternoon, for England's forwards never really threatened him. Their ideas were the one-dimensional – pumping the ball upfield in the wind in the attempt to find the head of Dixie Dean, but Meiklejohn was well on top of that ploy. Gordon Hodgson on two occasions had an opportunity from a distance, but misjudged the wind on both occasions and missed to the loud cries of derision coming from the now happy Scotland crowd, whose enthusiasm and pleasure was shared by the Prime Minister and his daughter Ishbel who were on several occasions seen to be on their feet cheering on Scotland.

Full-time came, and Hampden rejoiced. It was a victory as complete as it had been unexpected, and the Scottish crowd, who had talked in whispers about the 2-5 thrashing at Wembley the previous year, were now singing the praises of the team of men from the Scottish League, from Celtic, Rangers, Clyde, Kilmarnock, Dundee, St. Mirren and Motherwell who had put England to shame.

Life looked good, but it was as well that no-one would know what was around the corner. When in August Ramsay MacDonald 'turned Tory' and formed a National coalition government, thereby ratting on the Labour supporters who had adored him, his memory would never be forgiven, but that was nothing compared to the tragic death of Scotland's goalkeeper John Thomson, of Celtic who died in the most tragic of accidents on the field of play at Ibrox on 5 September 1931. But that had not yet happened. 28 March 1931 was a day of the greatest rejoicing, not least for those who did not have much to return home to. No job was there for them and only poverty and the dole queue awaited them. But at least there was a smile on their faces this weekend.

v **ENGLAND** 2-1
Hampden Park; Att: 134,170
1 April 1933

T WAS A fine spring day as the crowd of 134,170 packed themselves into Hampden Park. The game had been looked forward to, one felt, with even more enthusiasm than normally, for 1933 was a dreadful year for Scotland with no sign of the depression receding and with heavy unemployment prevalent. There was also the feeling of betrayal for their leaders had now deserted them. Ramsay MacDonald, the charismatic Scottish Labour politician, had jumped ship and formed a National Government in which he was the leader, but merely the figurehead, for everyone knew where the real power lay – with the Tories of Stanley Baldwin and Neville Chamberlain.

In addition there were the first stirrings of further trouble with Germany. A strange little man with a moustache called Adolf Hitler had appeared with an absurd salute and saying the most ridiculous things. It was hard to believe that he could possibly be as bad as the Kaiser but the Germans had allowed him to take over on 30 January of that year without any real opposition. He would have to be watched.

One bright spot however had appeared, and strangely enough for a Scottish crowd, it was for a team called England – the cricket team! It was in cricket where the Ashes had been won in Australia – and the captain was of Scottish descent with the very appropriate Scottish name of Douglas Jardine. With the spearhead of a young professional from Nottinghamshire called Harold Larwood and backed up by men like 'Bumper' Bill Bowes from Yorkshire and another Notts player Bill Voce, the Ashes had been won with all Scotland as well as England tuning in to the BBC 8 o'clock news in the morning to follow the Test matches. The Australians were moaning about aggressive bowling aimed at the body, but then again, they would, wouldn't they?

The crowd at Hampden on 1 April 1933 was a world record, and 134,170 is all the more astonishing when one sees it against the backdrop of unemployment, short time working and general poverty. Moreover that figure of 134,170 is probably an underestimate, taking no account of children lifted over the turnstiles or the amount of intrepid but impoverished young men (several hundreds of them according to some eye witnesses) who scaled the wall. Hampden had in fact beaten its own record, for it was the only stadium in the word capable of holding such a crowd. The magnificent and opulent Wembley had now been restricted to 100,000 following its disastrously unsuccessful attempt to hold the 1923 English Cup Final on its opening day ten years earlier.

Scotland's team contained ten Home-Scots and only one Anglo in Dally Duncan of Derby County. Within the ten Home-Scots, what was even more remarkable was that there were nine men from Glasgow teams, with only Andy Anderson of Hearts the exception. But the inclusion of James 'Doc' Marshall of Rangers was a result of unsavoury goings-on involving the immensely talented Wembley Wizard Alec James of Arsenal. James was an invaluable player, but there was always, as with many Anglos, a struggle between club and country for his services. 1933 saw Arsenal going for the English League Championship – they would eventually win it – and when James, after being selected for Scotland, pulled out through injury, eyebrows were raised. They were raised even further when he turned out for Arsenal that day, against Aston Villa. This effectively ended his Scotland career, and he was never totally forgiven in Scotland for this betrayal.

But there was no reason for anyone to feel betrayed about Jimmy McGrory. No-one could ever understand why the Scottish Selectors regularly ignored McGrory and never gave him a chance at Wembley, in particular. In the early days of his career it would have been difficult to displace Hughie Gallacher, but then again, Gallacher suffered from the same sort of temperamental and attitude problems that Alec James had about being available for Scotland. With McGrory, there was no such problem.

McGrory's prolific goalscoring could only be helped by the inclusion of his friend Bob McPhail of Rangers. Like McGrory, McPhail never played at Wembley. Yet Ibrox historians will maintain that this tall, elegant, straight-backed inside-forward from Barrhead was one of the best players that they have ever had. He was called 'Greetin' Boab' because of his constant moaning about things going wrong on the pitch, but off the field he was a thorough gentlemen.

The McGrory-McPhail friendship and combination was significant for other reasons as well. The Celtic-Rangers divide with all its sectarian rubbish is still sadly a strong factor even in the early years of the 21st century. In the 1930s, a time of economic uncertainty and instability, it was probably even worse as each faction could always blame the other for misfortunes, in the same way as, at the same time, Hitler was beginning to blame the Jews for the loss of the Great War and the Depression.

McGrory and McPhail were both practising members of their respective faiths, but both openly scoffed at the divisions that they caused. They were role models for their supporters, and both realised how lucky they were to be able to play football for a living. And when these two friends could play together for the same team, it became a very important union indeed.

There was a further Old Firm connection in the wing-halves where Scotland were blessed with two elegant and accomplished players in Peter Wilson and George Brown. Peter Wilson could frequently elicit gasps of admiration from the Parkhead crowd for his superb passing. 'Peter didn't pass the ball. He stroked it and caressed it,' it was said, and George Brown, fair haired and slightly more defensive minded had the uncanny ability to break up opponents' attacks 'even before they happened'.

The team was also unusual in that there were two men from Queen's Park in James Crawford and captain Bob Gillespie. The days when Queen's Park supplied virtually all the players in the Scotland team had long gone, but these two were deemed good enough to play for their country, for they had had a good season for Queen's Park, then doing well in the First Division. They did, in the eyes of the cynics, have an attraction for the parsimonious SFA in that, being amateurs, they did not have to be paid! Nevertheless they were given a round of applause by the Scottish crowd who contrasted their attitude that day with Alec James who seemed to have sold himself to the highest bidder!

Scotland had a surprise visit in the dressing room before the game from the great artiste Sir Harry Lauder of 'Roamin' in the Gloamin'' and 'Keep Right On to the End of the Road' fame. They then found themselves playing with the benefit of the sun and the wind towards the King's Park end of the ground. They began with some panache, and in one of their first attacks they opened the scoring. Bob McPhail released Dally Duncan down the left wing. He made space and crossed, where the ball beat everyone except JIMMY McGRORY who had the easiest of jobs to tap the ball in.

This occurred in only the fourth minute of the game and was missed by those who were still trying to gain entry. Once you had paid your money and got in, that was only the start of your problems, for you then had to fight your way onto the massive terracing and find a place from where you could watch the game in some sort of comfort. There was usually enough space at the bottom, but sadly all the latecomers tended to stay at the top. It needed strength of character to push one's way to the bottom!

The crowd was now, however, noisy and animated with every touch of the ball by a Scottish player being cheered. But England had some fine players, and having calmed the Scottish midfield by blocking tactics, began to exert some pressure on the Scottish defence, particularly testing Jakey Jackson in the Scottish goal whom they believed to be not as good as Jack Harkness or the late John Thomson. But despite Jackson appearing to be in fine form, he was caught totally by surprise on the half hour mark when GEORGE HUNT shot through a ruck of players and scored a goal which had the definite benefit of a little deflection.

Yet it was no more than the Englishmen deserved and the players left the field at half-time to the accompaniment of cheers for what had thus far been a fine game. The Scottish fans felt that a draw might well be a reasonable result here, for England would now have the benefit of the wind and the sun. Scotland had only ever lost once to England at Hampden Park and that had been in 1927 when a late error had allowed Dixie Dean to score. Scotland would have to guard against that. England did indeed dominate the first period of the second half, but gradually with full-backs Anderson and McGonagle gaining the mastery of the English wingers, the main English attacks came though the middle. A few chances were missed, one in particular by Joe Hulme who had meandered down the middle and then shot straight at the goalkeeper, before Scotland rallied with Peter Wilson clapping his hands and beginning to spray passes to both wingers. Peter the rustic from Beith, often called 'Celtic's country bumpkin', was superb that day, and was by some distance the best man on the park.

Scotland were well on top when there occurred the incident that would give birth to phenomenon which would become known as the 'Hampden Roar'. It was not true to say that Scotland fans at Hampden had been quiet in the years before 1933, but it was certainly the first time that the noise was christened with the famous term, for it was heard many miles away in other parts of the city. It was JIMMY McGRORY's finest moment in a Scotland shirt, but as Jimmy remained a modest man, it was very difficult to get him to talk about it, until Gerry McNee in 1975 persuaded him to say the following in his book *A Lifetime in Paradise*.

'... only eight minutes to go! The surging, inspiring crowd began a cacophony of bedlam as Doc Marshall of Rangers ... won the ball on our 18 yard line. He drew his man beautifully and sent his man across to Bob McPhail who beat two men and cut into the centre. I sensed the move in a twinkling and raced to the inside-left position just in time to pick up McPhail's inch perfect pass. The England full-back Tom Cooper advanced to tackle, but I shoved the ball past him and summoned the legs to chase after it as the bedlam of the crowd shaped itself into a mighty roar of anticipation. Keeper Harry Hibbs came out in a bid to narrow the angle but I gave the shot everything I had and the ball fairly exploded behind him. So too did the crowd. I'd never known anything quite like it. Often on the park I was very conscious of the crowd but this time it was quite impossible to ignore it ... One paper claimed that men came hurtling down the passageways as if shot by a catapult when I scored.'

The ecstasy, of course, is difficult to imagine in today's all-seater stadia, but McGrory's account gives some idea of the what it must have been like in that dangerously over-crowded Hampden of 1933.

England were now a beaten team, but accepted their defeat chivalrously with Harry Hibbs in particular seeking out McGrory after the game to tell him what a great goal he had scored. The nation now walked on air for a few weeks with those who had been at the game boring all their friends with detailed accounts of everything. "You'd think it was him that scored the goal, no' Jimmy McGrory!" said one wife after she had heard the story repeatedly.

And as for Jimmy McGrory himself, he was back at Hampden a fortnight later for the Scottish Cup final against Motherwell. Celtic won 1-0, and the goal was scored by McGrory himself. So if Jimmy had been the midwife to the Hampden Roar, he was now the godfather at its christening as well!

v **ENGLAND** 2-0
Hampden Park; Att: 129,693
6 April 1935

Scotland:	England:
Jackson (Chelsea)	Hibbs (Birmingham City)
Anderson (Hearts)	Male (Arsenal)
Cummings (Partick Thistle)	Hapgood (Arsenal)
Massie (Hearts)	Britton (Everton)
Simpson (Rangers)	Barker (Derby County)
Brown (Rangers)	Alsford (Tottenham Hotspur)
Napier (Celtic)	Geldard (Everton)
Walker (Hearts)	Bastin (Arsenal)
Gallacher (Derby County)	Gurney (Sunderland)
McPhail (Rangers)	Westwood (Bolton Wanderers)
Duncan (Derby County)	Brook (Manchester City)
Referee: Mr Thompson, Northern, Ireland	

ATURDAY 6 APRIL 1935 was a beautiful spring day. Optimism was in the air on several fronts. In the first place, it was the start of the good weather, one hoped, but also, economically, the corner seemed to have been turned; more and more people were back in work. The 'Doctor's Mandate' sought by the Baldwin/MacDonald National Government in 1931 seemed now to be working, and more and more firms were taking on men who had been idle for so long. A closer look at this phenomenon, however, might well have revealed a sinister reason, for it was noticeable that spare parts for armaments were in demand, as were things like tin helmets and sand bags. There was more than a slight uneasiness about the world situation.

Opinion was still split about Adolf Hitler, the man who had galvanised Germany in recent years. His methods had been questionable, but Germans were also now back working again, building massive roads, for example. Yet there was something untrustworthy about him, for he did seem to be limbering up for a struggle against someone. He did not like the Treaty of Versailles, nor Jews, nor Russia, but although we would have to watch him, there did not seem any likelihood of him becoming another Kaiser – yet.

Mussolini, the dictator of Italy, on the other hand was a vainglorious blowbag, making noises about wanting an Italian Empire in – er, Abyssinia, where most of the land mass was desert. We could laugh at him – even the Italian ice cream men ridiculed his preposterous pretensions. 'Mussolini no buono' was often heard when the ice cream cones were being served. Yet he and Hitler seemed to be friends, and that could be very dangerous.

The Duke of York was coming to Hampden today. His father, George V, was now an old and sick man, and the day was fast approaching when the Duke's brother, the Prince of

Wales would take over. What a contrast there was between the two Princes, sons of the king. One was handsome and heavily involved in yachts, fast cars, even faster women, yet did not hesitate to speak his mind about dreadful things like poverty and unemployment to the embarrassment of the Government. The Duke of York on the other hand was quiet, reserved, shy and apparently had a massive stammer. But he was a football fan and had seen Scotland on previous occasions, notably the day of the Wembley Wizards' victory in 1928. He was even a Scotland supporter, it was rumoured, for his wife was Scottish from Glamis Castle. And his father-in-law, the Earl of Strathmore, was an unashamed lover of Forfar Athletic and frequent attender at their home games.

Scotland had had a mixed autumn in 1934. They had embarrassingly lost to Northern Ireland, then the Scottish League team had lost to the English League, but the national side had redeemed themselves with a creditable win over Wales at Pittodrie. With respect to these opponents, however, what really mattered was the game against England. As always the selection had caused debate. The little-known George Cummings of Partick Thistle had been given his first cap at left-back, displacing Celtic's Peter McGonagle, and the Celtic fans had more cause for distress when Jimmy McGrory, hero of 1931 and 1933, was overlooked in favour of the ageing Hughie Gallacher, who had, frankly, seen better days and had won just one cap since being banished from representing his country after his misdemeanours in Paris five years previously.

Bob McPhail, 'Greetin' Boab' or 'Barrheid Boab', was clearly one of the best players in Great Britain at the moment, but this meant him displacing Charlie Napier at inside-left. This would involve replacing a Celt with a Ranger, and in what looked like an attempt at 'appeasement' (to use a word that would soon become commonplace) of the alienated Celtic support, Napier ('Happy Feet') was put on the right wing, a position with which he was not familiar. This move was much criticised in the press but the much reviled Selectors would have the last laugh.

Three Hearts men had been chosen – Anderson, Massie and the new discovery Tommy Walker. No relation to the great Bobby Walker of a generation previous, this young slick-haired youngster had the makings of being a great inside-right. He had impressed at Pittodrie against Wales, but would he have the temperament for the big occasion? And what about Alec Massie at right-half? There would be experience beside him in the shape of the Rangers duo of Simpson and Brown, Simpson, in particular, was keen to do well, for he had a four-and-a-half-year-old son, Ronald, to impress.

As it happened, Hearts and Rangers were at that very moment embroiled in another struggle. They had played at Hampden the previous Saturday in the Scottish Cup semi-final and in a thrilling game of football, Hearts had delighted their vast travelling support with a 1-1 draw. They were now due to play each other in the replay the following Wednesday for the right to take on Hamilton Accies in the Final, and hopes were high that Hearts' trophy famine, which had prevailed since 1906, would soon be coming to an end.

Scotland's goalkeeper that day was Jakey Jackson, once of Partick Thistle but now of Chelsea, and England's goalkeeper was particularly abused by the Hearts section of the Scottish crowd, for he was called Harry Hibbs. It was his third visit to Hampden and he was generally agreed to be a great goalkeeper, known like many keepers of that time (Jack Harkness, Jerry Dawson and the late John Thomson) for his chivalrous behaviour and seen frequently before the game and after, talking not to his team-mates but to the other goalkeeper, as if they were the third team on the field.

Soon after midday it was obvious that the good weather and improving economic situation were going to produce a huge crowd. Two years earlier 134,170 had swarmed to Hampden, and the overcrowding had been described as dangerous. On this occasion, with a full 40 minutes to go before the start of the game, the decision to close the turnstiles was taken by the panicky SFA and Queen's Park, acting on advice from the police whose men with walkie-talkie telephones reported huge build-ups of people at various areas round the ground. This decision in itself caused chaos, and there were several incidents of exit gates being rushed, men climbing over walls and even when the Duke of York's car arrived, about a hundred rushed in along with it as the gate was opened. The official crowd was given as 129,693, although at least a thousand more got in illegally, and tens of thousands arrived to find that they were too late, and were compelled to settle for listening to the roars of the crowd.

Some hostelries round about Hampden hit upon a good idea – a harbinger of things to come in the distant future – by rigging up their wireless (or radio as it was sometimes now called) in their bar, so that customers could at least listen to the game if they had been denied access to the ground. This idea was only a limited success for it is of course very difficult to persuade drunken men to be quiet all the time, but at least the commentary reached some of the excluded.

Inside the ground it soon became obvious that some of the players were overawed by the crowd. The noise was perpetual and almost deafening, and some players gawped at the sight of huge crowds swaying at the top of the terracings. A number of fainting cases occurred – hardly surprising given the heat and the crush – but very few injuries were sustained. At one point, apparently, the Duke of York, a kind and compassionate man, expressed concern about the welfare of the huge crowd on the terracing.

Ironically in view of all the fuss to get into the game, the standard of play was poor. To a certain extent, this sort of thing is likely to happen in internationals where with the best players of each country on view, they are likely to cancel each other out. This was certainly the case with Hughie Gallacher, rendered impotent by his Derby County team-mate John Barker, who knew exactly how Hughie played. Hughie, of course, was now getting old and did not train as hard as he should have. It was also true, however, that the Scottish half-back line of Massie, Simpson and Brown had a stranglehold on midfield. The problem was further up the field. Only Tommy Walker impressed in the Scottish forward line.

The heaving masses on the terracings had little to cheer them until two minutes from half-time when Scotland forced a corner on the right. Charlie Napier ran across to take it. Although naturally a left-sided player, Napier kicked the ball with his right foot, low and hard, and the ball looked as if it were heading straight for the arms of Harry Hibbs until DALLY DUNCAN bent down to head the ball into the net. Hibbs was aghast that his defence had not given him more cover and spent the remainder of that half gesticulating to Hapgood and Male that they had given the goal away. There was the predictable Hampden explosion of joy on the terracing and half-time was spent with everyone slapping each other on the back and liberally dispensing drinks from bottles, it still in 1935 being legal to drink alcohol at football games.

But the Scotland players knew that more would be needed if they were to win this game. Douglas 'Dally' Duncan, the canny Aberdonian, would repeat his success early in the second half and once more it was from a Charlie Napier corner, although this time it was a well placed cross, and DUNCAN rose majestically above the defence to head home. Scotland were now two up, and England never really looked like getting back into the game.

The longer the second half progressed, the more men like Massie, Brown, McPhail and debutant Cummings took over. Long before the end, England were a well beaten side and would be much criticised by their own journalists who cursed their luck in having a Press ticket. They therefore had to be allowed in, whereas they felt they would have been happier standing outside and not having to watch such rubbish. At least that's what the pieces they wired down to Fleet Street said.

The Duke of York was seen to clap the Scottish moves, standing up at the end to give a standing ovation to the Scotland team. It was hard to imagine that by 1937, the next time that England played at Hampden, this self-effacing, profoundly shy man would be preparing for his Coronation as King of Great Britain. Not only that, but he would be called upon to lead the country through her direst days.

The teams had now played each other 59 times, and Scotland had won 27 to England's 18, with 14 draws. Scotland maintained their proud record of having lost at Hampden only once since it was built in 1903 – that being the disastrous year of 1927. The trend that was emerging though was for Scotland to win at Hampden and England at Wembley. Next year the Scots would have another opportunity to put an end to all that.

In the summer, Scotland took their players on an unofficial tour of North America. They sailed on the luxury liner the Aquitania which had swimming pools, cinemas and everything that rich people in the 1930s would want. They arrived in the new world to be greeted enthusiastically by members of the Scottish diaspora, and won all 13 games against poor opposition in a light-hearted tour. Tommy Walker's boyish looks and handsome features made him a special attraction and Tommy rose to the occasion by playing some brilliant football, earning comparisons with Babe Ruth, the legendary American baseball player.

A thought occurred to some supporters: Scotland were the best team in the world – why did they not enter the World Cup (which had now been won by Uruguay in 1930 and Italy in 1934) and prove it? The next tournament would be in France in 1938. Why shouldn't the Scots be in with a chance?

v GERMANY 2-0
Ibrox; Att: 50,000
14 October 1936

Scotland:	Germany:
Dawson (Rangers)	Jakob (Ragensberg)
Anderson (Hearts)	Munzenberg (Dusseldorf)
Cummings (Aston Villa)	Munkert (Nuremberg)
Massie (Aston Villa)	Janes (Dusseldorf)
Simpson (Rangers)	Goldbrunner (Munich)
Brown (Rangers)	Kitzinger (Schweinfurt)
Delaney (Celtic)	Elbern (Beuel)
Walker (Hearts)	Gellesch (Schalke)
Armstrong (Aberdeen)	Siffling (Mannheim)
McPhail (Rangers)	Szepan (Schalke)
Duncan (Derby County)	Urban (Schalke)
Referee: H. Nattrass, New Seaham	

THIS GAME WAS all about propaganda, pomp and show. That it failed in its objective was entirely due to a fine performance by a good Scottish team who showed the world that, whatever was happening in political and military terms throughout Europe, as far as football was concerned, Scotland were a force to be reckoned with. 1936 was the year in which Hitler tried to show off to the world. He had just staged the Berlin Olympics in which he had suffered a major embarrassment when the blue riband sprinting events had been won by a black American called Jesse Owens, who thereby delivered a telling blow to the nonsense of any 'master race' theory. Hitler could not bring himself to present the gold medal, and tried to pretend that it did not happen.

But plenty of unpleasant things were also happening in Spain, where the Republican government was under attack from the fascists of General Franco and their supporters of Mussolini, Hitler and (shamefully) the Roman Catholic Church. The British Government (equally shamefully) persisted in Anthony Eden's policy of 'Non-Intervention', something which sounded fine but in fact meant that the Republican Government would be deprived of support from Great Britain, France and the USA ,who might have been expected to help and would have to rely instead on the prickly, inconsistent and brooding dictatorship of Stalin's Russia. In autumn 1936, the fascists were girding themselves for an all-out attack on Madrid, where food rationing had been introduced and anti-air raid measures were being practised.

In these circumstances, many people in Scotland found it incredible that a team from Germany was coming to Ibrox to play football. Certainly some people at Leith Docks thought so, for they had scrawled over warehouse walls slogans like 'Mit Hitler Nieder'

(Down With Hitler) or the cruder Anglo-Saxon 'F*** Hitler' for the benefit of the 400 Germans who arrived on the ship Hamburg-Amerika Reliance to see the game. But these were rich, middle-class Germans who smiled benignly at the Scottish crowd, most of whom were attracted by curiosity to see what a 'Hun' looked like rather than by any political hostility to Germany. International relations were helped as well when some Germans offered their lunch parcels to some thin-looking Leith waifs.

Hitler had already scored a propaganda coup by sending the official team party via his Luftwaffe. It was believed that this was the first time ever that a football team had flown to a game, and Hitler was not slow to show to the world what a fine airforce he had. The Germans were clearly under orders to be pleasant and friendly, and the Scots, as represented by George Graham the SFA Secretary and Willie Struth the manager of Rangers, taking shelter under the all-encompassing but vacuous cliché that 'politics should not interfere with sport', were perfect hosts.

Visits of foreign teams to play in Scotland were still very rare. Indeed only Austria in 1933 had played a full international match in Scotland before. Scotland had been on several tours of Europe – they had drawn with Germany in Berlin in 1929 – but a visit of Germany was a great attraction. Feelings towards Germany were divided. There were those who still remembered the trenches and the Kaiser (and if one forgot, one only had to look at the huge amount of men now in their forties and fifties who had lost limbs or who had bee blinded), but on the other hand there were those who admired the way that Hitler had pulled them round again, restoring pride to a broken nation. A little wisdom from our leaders, they felt, and there need never be another war in Europe.

In any case Britain had problems of her own. True, unemployment seemed to be on the wane, but there were still pockets of the country where the problem was huge. Men had just walked from Jarrow in Newcastle to protest, but no-one, other than a few members of the Labour Party were prepared to meet them. And rumours persisted about the new King Edward VIII. The foreign press told stories about his involvement with an unscrupulous American lady called Wallis Simpson, and hard though the British establishment tried to prevent these stories reaching the British public, it was becoming more and more difficult.

It was a dull but dry and somewhat windy day as 50,000 made their way to Ibrox that afternoon. Some may have been shocked to see a swastika flying, but it was the official flag of the guests, and in any case the flag did not yet convey the nuances of evil that it would in a few years time. Similarly the German team came out and performed the Nazi salute to the crowd (as did the entire German press contingent), and did likewise at the end of the game. They were applauded politely by the crowd, many of whom in later years would become thoroughly ashamed of themselves for so doing. But at least the Scottish players did not perform that salute, unlike the England team in Germany in 1938 who were ordered by the craven British Foreign Office to do so.

Such were the traffic jams outside the ground that the game had been delayed for 15 minutes as the German team bus struggled to get through the Scottish crowd, most of whom stopped and gawped at them but showed no hostility to the obviously athletic and prosperous Germans. Inside the ground it was a different matter, though, for the public address system had failed to inform the crowd of the reason for the delay, and Glaswegian crowds revealed their traditional dislike of being deprived of football with catcalls, boos and the throwing of missiles.

Disappointment had been expressed that there was to be no radio commentary of the game, but the BBC explained that commentaries were usually for Cup Finals and 'England games' but promised that the result would be 'available' at 6pm and that at 10.25pm that night, there would be a five minute report of the game. All the evening newspapers, however, in Glasgow, Edinburgh, Dundee and Aberdeen offered a special edition with a report on the game. They were all distinctly unhappy with the delay, for it did not help with their deadlines.

The teams came out to a huge cheer and the Govan Pipe Band who had been trying in vain to entertain the crowd during the delay now played both anthems – 'God Save The King' and 'Deutschland Uber Alles' – surely in the circumstances ironic choices. The King would last only another couple of months before being effectively 'sacked' and Germany would indeed try to prove to the world very soon that they were superior to everyone else!

Scotland's team was a strong one, and it was confidently expected that they would beat their visitors very easily. But they were contained by an impressive, strong German team who tackled robustly but fairly and played correctly and courteously. They were being avidly cheered on by the sizeable contingent who had arrived at Leith that morning, supplemented by a few supporters who had travelled all the way from Germany by train.

The game had almost started with a sensation, for Germany netted in three minutes, only to have it ruled out for offside. The decision, even to the Scottish Press, seemed a little harsh, and quite a few fans felt that it would have been a good thing for Germany to go ahead, for that would have forced Scotland to attack more.

Szepan and Elbern were singled out as fine players by the Scottish press and the hard tackling full-backs Munzenberg and Munkert were praised for their ability to keep Scotland's wingers Jimmy Delaney and Dally Duncan quiet. Scotland were marginally the better team at half-time but there had been a marked reluctance on the part of their forwards to shoot, a reluctance that was all the more surprising when goalkeeper Jacob had on several occasions shown a clumsiness in handling the ball. One shot from 'Greetin' Boab' McPhail earned the description of 'einen bombenschutzen' by a German journalist, but half-time arrived with no score. The Germans had acquitted themselves well (they were all part-timers and had never played before such a huge crowd in their lives) and had deserved the applause they got from the Scottish crowd for some fine moves.

In the second half, however, Scotland took control and it was JIMMY DELANEY who scored halfway through the second half. Delaney's instincts were to move inside when the ball did not come to him on the wing, and thus he found himself in exactly the right position in the penalty area to score when a shot from Tommy Walker was only partially saved by goalkeeper Jacob. With time running out, and Scotland now well on top, DELANEY scored his second, a much better goal. This time it came from a fine lob through from Walker who spotted Delaney in a good position on the edge of the box, and Jimmy found the net from a difficult angle. Unfortunately Delaney injured himself slightly in scoring that goal and was taken off, but thankfully soon recovered. Shortly afterwards, Scotland should have had a penalty when Munkert handled a shot from Aberdeen's Matt Armstrong, but Mr Nattrass of England said no. The game finished with Scotland well on top, but with Germany earning a few friends through their occasional good moves.

The game over, both teams and their officials proceeded to the St. Enoch Hotel for a meal and speeches by both sets of officials – James Fleming of the SFA, Fritz Randolf of the German FA and, for good measure, James Wilton of the Irish FA to give the neutral point of view. Presents were exchanged, everyone patted each other on the back, and the hope was expressed that nations could play each other in 'friendly rivalry without any malignity' on the football field. It was a well-intentioned piece of international relations, and rather poignant in view of what was just round the corner.

The result was well received in Scotland, a nation in which football was going from strength to strength as crowds were thrilled by Alex Massie, George Brown, Tommy Walker and Jimmy Delaney. It was almost as if they all knew what was coming and that life in the meantime meant enjoying oneself as much as one could.

History does not record how this result was received at Berchtesgaden. Did the Führer fly into a rage, blaming everyone but himself, alleging 'betrayal'? Or did it make him all the more determined that the rest of the world should be punished? It had indeed been a bad few weeks for Herr Hitler on the sporting field. First a black athlete called Owens, and now a Scotsman called Delaney had given him grief. Time, then, to renew assaults on Spain and to demand Austria and Czechoslovakia!

Meanwhile Scottish poets made up verse about how Hitler had been 'put off his tea' by the redoubtable Jimmy Delaney, and how Göring had been sick below the bed and Mussolini had been shunned for mentioning the result. It was a momentary relaxation in tension, and gave the Scottish nation the chance to laugh – not at the German nation, for their players had been fine ambassadors for their country and the game, but at their ridiculous Führer with his bizarre nightmarish dreams of word domination.

v ENGLAND 3-1

Hampden Park; Att: 149,547

17 April 1937

Scotland:	England:
Dawson (Rangers)	Woodley (Chelsea)
Anderson (Hearts)	Male (Arsenal)
Beattie (Preston North End)	Barkas (Manchester City)
Massie (Aston Villa)	Britton (Everton)
Simpson (Rangers)	Young (Huddersfield Town)
Brown (Rangers)	Bray (Manchester City)
Delaney (Celtic)	Matthews (Stoke City)
Walker (Hearts)	Carter (Sunderland)
O'Donnell (Preston North End)	Steele (Stoke City)
McPhail (Rangers)	Starling (Aston Villa)
Duncan (Derby County)	Johnson (Stoke City)
Referee: Mr W. McLean, Northern Ireland	

SO GREAT HAD been the crushing experienced by supporters at the 1933 and 1935 Scotland v England internationals at Hampden Park, that the SFA decided that this game would be all-ticket. If the intention had been to limit the crowd, it was a total failure, for the ticket supply was not controlled, forgeries were easily made, children were lifted over turnstiles, and as usual, quite a few athletic young men managed to scale the wall. The official figure varies but most settle on 149,547, a world record. But that is only the official figure. *The Scotsman* newspaper, for example, is prepared to believe that the crowd might have been as high as 180,000 – roughly the population of a city like Dundee.

The late 1930s were, like the early 1920s, a boom time in many respects. The depression was clearly over, and full employment was restored – but with conflict looming in Europe, everyone in their heart of hearts knew change was one again coming.

It was already underway in Spain. Shortly after this game a town called Guernica would be eliminated by the German Air Force working on behalf of General Franco, who had no qualms about blitzing Madrid either. The British Government who, in conjunction with France and even the USA, might have put a stop to this barbarism, decided on a plausible but bogus 'No Intervention' Policy, effectively doing nothing while Italy and Germany supplied Franco with the evil trade of weapons to destroy his own people.

The road to Hampden that day for those who had travelled to Mount Florida station was therefore full of earnest young men distributing leaflets and encouraging the crowd to join the International Brigades to save Spain. Already these bands of volunteers had heroically saved Madrid, but they were desperately short of men and supplies. With the pessimistic but prophetic slogan 'Spain today, tomorrow Scotland', they urged the need to fight Hitler

Hamilton Crescent 1974. A boy watches Scotland v England from the vantage point of a cab.

The Scotland team which beat England 1-0 in 1884 to make it a record five years in a row of victories.

The famous Wattie Arnott of Queen's Park and Scotland who, as a boy, claimed to have watched Scotland v England by the method depicted in the picture at the top of the page. He then went on to play 14 times for Scotland.

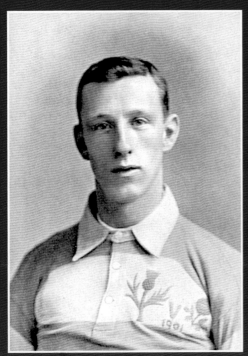

Alex Smith of Rangers and Scotland in the Rosebery colours.

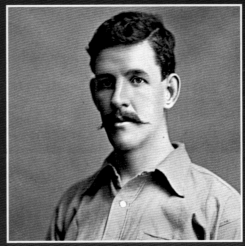

Jack Bell of Dumbarton, Everton, Celtic and Scotland.

The Scotland team (in their Rosebery colours) who beat England 2-1 before the world's first ever six figure crowd of 102,741 in 1906 at Hampden's inaugural staging of Scotland v England. Alex Raisbeck of Liverpool is the captain with the ball between his feet.

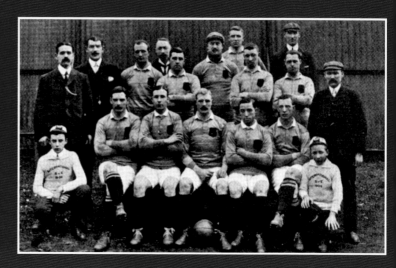

The great Jimmy Quinn of Celtic and Scotland who scored four goals against Ireland in 1908, and played a major part in the victory over England in 1910.

The 'wee blue de'il' - Alan Morton of Queen's Park, Rangers and Scotland.

A rare action photograph from the 1910 International between Scotland and England. Left winger Bobby Templeton has just collected the ball and is about to charge up the wing. The three Scottish defenders watching him are Andrew Aitken, Charlie Thomson and Jimmy Hay, and the partially hidden Scottish player is Sandy Higgins. Observe the dignified dress of referee Mr Mason.

A view of the crowd at the Scotland v England International of 1925.

The ball of the Wembley Wizards game of 1928.

An account in a contemporary football magazine of the famous game in 1933 when the Hampden Roar was born.

One of Scotland's first overseas ventures to France in May 1930. Hughie Gallacher is in the front in the centre of the picture.

Dally Duncan of Derby County and Scotland.

1937 was the first time that tickets were issued for International games. Notice the exorbitant 2/- (10 pence) charge. This did not prevent a record crowd appearing.

A picture of the huge crowd making their way to Hampden in 1937.

Tommy Walker of Hearts and Scotland.

Action from the 1938 game which Scotland won 1-0.

Jimmy Cowan of Morton and Scotland, the hero of Wembley 1949.

Jimmy Mason of Third Lanark (out of picture) scores for Scotland in 1949.

Programme cover for Scotland v Spain in May 1937.

Bobby Collins scores for Scotland against Switzerland in May 1957. Observe the ball wedged behind the stanchion and Scotland's bizarre orange shorts.

A young Denis Law.

Jim Baxter scores a penalty kick for Scotland at Wembley in 1963.

Campbell Forsyth, Alan Gilzean, Alex Hamilton, Jim Kennedy and Davie Wilson after beating England 1-0 at Hampden in 1964.

Tommy Gemmell, Eddie McCreadie (in an England shirt) and Jim Baxter accept the cheers of the crowd after the 3-2 victory at Wembley in 1967.

Ronnie Simpson and Jim McCalliog congratulate each other after the win at Wembley in 1967.

Willie Ormond is chaired off the field by Billy Bremner and Davie Hay after Scotland beat Czechoslovakia 2-1 in September 1973 to qualify for the 1974 World Cup Finals.

The moment that haunted Billy Bremner for the rest of his life. The ball rebounds of the post just too quickly for him to score and the ball goes past, and Scotland have to settle for a 0-0 draw against Brazil in the World Cup of 1974.

The goalposts are about to break after the 2-1 victory over England at Wembley in June 1977.

Kenny Dalglish scores the goal at Anfield against Wales in October 1977 which will take Scotland to Argentina in 1978.

Jock Stein, manager of Scotland 1978-1985.

Archie Gemmill turns away after scoring his famous goal against Holland in the 1978 World Cup Finals. It was Scotland's only moment of glory in an otherwise grim occasion.

Davie Cooper scores the penalty against Wales at Cardiff in 1985 which gives Scotland a play-off against Australia for qualification for the Mexico World Cup of 1986. Unfortunately this game was overshadowed by much darker events.

Andy Roxburgh, manager of Scotland 1986-1993.

Richard Gough of Dundee United, Tottenham Hotspur and Rangers who won 61 caps for Scotland between 1983 and 1993.

Craig Brown applauds the fans for the support in Euro 1996.

Ally McCoist scores the goal which gives Scotland a 1-0 win over Switzerland in Euro 1996.

Kevin Gallacher scores against Austria at Celtic Park in a World Cup Qualifier in 1997.

In the play-off of 1999, Colin Hendry gets his head to the ball before Paul Ince of England.

Gary Caldwell (pursued by Gary Teale) has just scored for Scotland against France at Hampden in October 2006.

The Scotland team which beat France 1-0 at Hampden in October 2006.

The Tartan Army, blue nipples and all!

Somewhere in the middle of all that is Jamie McFadden who has just scored for Scotland against France in Paris in September 2007.

before it was too late. The huge crowd was not unsympathetic but more interested in the football. There was a great deal to be excited about, in spite of the heavy rain which had fallen all morning. Even at Hampden where cover was limited, and for the hordes on the open terracing non-existent, this did not dampen the enthusiasm of the Scottish crowd, some of whom were not particularly well dressed for the occasion, wearing kilts and jackets rather than the more appropriate hats and coats. But they bred them hard in Scotland in the 1930s, and anyway the pubs on the way to the game offered means to warm oneself up! The hospitality was extended even to a few apprehensive Englishmen who were taken somewhat taken aback by the warmth of the Scottish welcome, something which dispelled the myth that Scotsmen were mean.

Most of the crowd had taken the advice of the authorities to be there early, but this did not help with the inevitable late surge who arrived just before kick-off. There was enough room, as always, near the front, but there was a reluctance to move forward, and the result was excessive crowding at the back and 46 people fainted – a number which would have been far greater if the weather had been warmer. The trick for a latecomer was simply to barge their way forward, and if you were on your own, you could join a group of tough-looking chaps who had no qualms about sensitivity, take hold of one of their flags and join them, as they marched down the terracing, belting out their songs like, 'Roamin in the Gloamin', however ludicrous the lyrics might be for a packed Hampden Park where there was a real danger of being crushed to death.

By this time the 'Hampden Roar' was a major factor. Even Englishmen like Raich Carter (his real name was the unlikely one of Horatio) of Sunderland, a seasoned professional if ever there was one, would admit to being intimidated and alarmed by it. England had taken the field to polite applause from a chivalrous Scottish crowd and were kicking in at one of the goals as Carter himself later wrote: 'It began with a murmur, rolling round the ground, and mounting up out of nothing into a swelling, terrific roar that came at us from all sides. I wondered what had happened. Then I saw the Scotland team running out.' Neither Carter and his team-mates nor anyone else present had seen or heard anything like it, and another England internationalist would later compare it to the noise of an air raid on London, with the stillness, then the ominous buzz, ever growing in intensity, then the thunderclap of noise...

Scotland had had a poor season. The Scottish League had lost to the English League the previous October, and although Scotland had beaten Germany in the autumn ('putting Hitler off his tea', it was claimed) they had then appalled their supporters by going down to Wales at Dens Park in December. Wales in fact were a fine team and would win the Home International Championship, but the Scots were less concerned about that than beating England, who had still only won once at Hampden Park. It would be five victories in a row at Hampden if Scotland won today.

From the start, it was clear that this was going to be a tough game with the England defenders coming in for a great deal of criticism for their heavy tackling on Scotland's more fragile ball players. Jimmy Delaney in particular was singled out for tough treatment by Sam Barkas, and Bob McPhail found it hard to get going as he was surrounded by

Englishmen every time he got the ball. Tommy Walker, well remembered by Englishmen for scoring the penalty last year, was also the victim of a few nasty tackles.

Normally in the wet, and on heavy ground, Scotland perform well, but it was England who gained a certain ascendancy the longer the first half wore on, and Stanley Matthews of Stoke City was making quite an impression on the right wing. England might have had a penalty for a foul on the Wizard of the Dribble, but equally Scotland had a goal chalked off for mysterious reasons. Then England struck. And it was a fine goal as well, earning a reluctant round of applause from the wet, bedraggled Scottish crowd. It was scored by FREDDIE STEELE, Matthews's Stoke colleague, who picked up a pass from Starling, found himself in space thanks to some negligent Scottish defending, ran ten yards and deposited the ball behind Jerry Dawson. Minutes later, just on the half-time whistle, he might have scored again, but this time his shot flew inches wide.

Half-time was thus spent in introverted thought as the huge crowd tried to cheer themselves up by listening to the Massed Pipe Bands, their kilts swirling in the rain. It was a very damp occasion now indeed, but then Scotland decided to use a piece of gamesmanship, by no means uncommon today, but unusual for the time. Aware of the huge Hampden Roar that they would get, Scotland delayed their arrival for the second half. The result was that England were out there waiting for them in the rain, with referee Mr McLean pacing up and down the touchline wondering what was going on, and the pipe band waiting primed to play 'Scotland the Brave', but there was no sign of the Scotland team. Just as everyone was beginning to think that something serious had happened, out they came. 'Scotland the Brave' totally disappeared, immersed in the wall of noise.

This was a technique similar to that employed at the same time by one Adolf Hitler, who would arrive a few minutes late – not too late, or else his crowd might have been discouraged – so that they were all in a frenzy waiting for him. One would hate to think that Scotland got this idea from that source, but the ploy was certainly effective for within two minutes Scotland, now attacking the King's Park end, were on level terms. The goal came after some fine work from Alec Massie of Aston Villa who passed the ball to his ex-Hearts team-mate Tommy Walker, who in turn beat a man and slipped the ball to FRANK O'DONNELL, who finished easily.

The crowd who had never exactly been quiet, now roared into life and the second half became a bedlam of noise, terrifying in its intensity and consistency. Scotland now knew that things favoured them, and that as long as nothing silly happened, they had a great chance to win. These were typical Scottish conditions, the crowd was obviously behind them, and one or two of the English defenders were tiring. George Brown at left-half was particularly prominent as Scotland went forward, but the crowd were disappointed by the performance of Douglas 'Dally' Duncan. He had been the hero of 1935 with his two goals, but today he was showing a disinclination to leave his wing to look for the ball and was indeed well deserving of his nickname 'Dally'.

But that could not be said of 'Greetin' Boab' McPhail, who ran about, after a poor first half, and having missed a chance early in the second half (when goalkeeper Vic Woodley produced a great save) now began pointing, gesticulating, demanding the ball, using it when he got it to good effect and generally inspiring his colleagues. Delaney found that one way to avoid the attentions of Sam Barkas was to move inside and pop up in all sorts of surprising places like the other wing – a typical Delaney ploy which he had used on countless occasions for Celtic. Gradually the English defence were pegged back.

They were also finding the trickery of Tommy Walker hard to handle, and fouls became even more frequent, which pushed Mr McLean's tolerance to the limit. It was from one of the resulting free-kicks that Scotland eventually scored in the 80th minute. The ball from Frank O'Donnell came across the edge of the penalty area and centre-half Alf Young, hitherto outstanding, was not able to clear the ball properly and it fell to the unmarked McPHAIL who needed 'no second biddin' to blast the ball home, and unleash a tidal wave of joy on the terracing behind.

If the Scotland fans thought *that* was good, there was more to come, for Scotland kept pressing and pressing, realising the truth of the old maxim that the best form of defence is attack, and forcing England to concede even more fouls. Only two minutes remained when McPHAIL got his second and Scotland's third goal. This time it was a brilliant manoeuvre from another free-kick where Delaney was the decoy, jumping too early as the ball came in but taking the goalkeeper and a defender with him and allowing the ball to fly over him to the head of McPhail. McPhail himself claimed that Delaney actually touched it on to him, but it mattered little. Scotland had won!

Those who listened to the radio commentary could not hear any words from the commentator but they knew what had happened, as indeed did most of Glasgow. "The hens went off the lay," said an aggrieved poultry farmer, but as he lived over 100 miles away from Glasgow, we may suspect an element of rhetorical exaggeration. Nevertheless, all Scotland soon learned that their country had once again beaten England, and as a result summer 1937 was a fine one, with the Coronation of King George VI and his Scottish wife Elizabeth, good weather, and an even more pronounced desire to stick one's head in the sand and to ignore the rapidly deteriorating world situation. Was it really as important as Scotland beating England?

v ENGLAND 1-0
Wembley; Att: 93,267
9 April 1938

Scotland:	England:
Cumming (Middlesbrough)	Woodley (Chelsea)
Anderson (Hearts)	Sproston (Leeds United)
Beattie (Preston North End)	Hapgood (Arsenal)
Shankly (Preston North End)	Willingham (Huddersfield Town)
Smith (Preston North End)	Cullis (Wolverhampton Wanderers)
Brown (Rangers)	Copping (Arsenal)
Milne (Middlesbrough)	Matthews (Stoke City)
Walker (Hearts)	Hall (Tottenham Hotspur)
O'Donnell (Blackpool)	Fenton (Middlesbrough)
Mutch (Preston North End)	Stephenson (Leeds United)
Reid (Brentford)	Bastin (Arsenal)
Referee: Mr Hamilton, Northern Ireland	

BY 1938 IT was difficult not to be affected by what was called the 'international situation', and this had nothing to do with the Scotland v England football international. German Chancellor Hitler felt that he was entitled to take over all Europe and seemed to have bewitched his people into following him. Already, he had taken over admittedly a not entirely unwilling Austria into what was tactfully described as an Anschluss (union), and he was now casting greedy eyes in the direction of Czechoslovakia.

A few perceptive people saw parallels between the Anschluss of 1938 and the Act of Union between Scotland and England in 1707. In theory they were agreed upon and negotiated. In fact it was the takeover of a smaller power by a larger one using threats, bribery, violence, blackmail and all the other tools of wicked dictators. In each case, the countries had a great deal in common, notably language and culture, and to an outsider there might have seemed to have been no harm in it. The reality of course (in both cases) was a great deal different.

In 1938 the fact that another terrible war (more terrible than even the Great War if one could believe the stories one heard coming from Spain where Hitler's 'dress rehearsal' was taking place) was inevitable and even imminent made everyone all the more determined to enjoy themselves. Football was flourishing as never before. Last year at Hampden had seen two unbelievably large crowds in successive weeks to see England defeated and then the Scottish Cup Final, and this year far more Scots than ever before clambered on to the Friday night trains to travel to Wembley. This might be the last chance they would have for some time to visit London supporting their national team and very soon Scots would be embarking on trains for far less pleasant places than Wembley, and to face a foe far more deadly and earnest than the English football team. Daylight had broken by the time that their trains reached the outskirts of London, and the travellers could see people going about their business, delivering milk, going to the newspaper shop, going to their work, driving buses – and always, always a few middle aged men in wheelchairs or with one leg or one arm – victims of the folly of 1914-18. They were not going to allow this to happen again, were they?

But it was happening again – in Spain. The beleagured Spanish republic, now largely abandoned by those who might have helped her, was still fighting for her life against the Satanic combination of Nazi Germany, Fascist Italy and Spain's own establishment and Church, while the rest of the world looked the other way and pretended it wasn't happening.

But football was the more immediate concern. Scotland had had a mixed season so far. A win over the English League at Ibrox had been followed by two terrible full internationals. Scotland had gone down to Wales and drawn with Northern Ireland. They had then rallied to beat a poor Czechoslovakian team who had come to Glasgow in December with several players more interested in asking for political asylum than playing football. One of them said years later that if he had had his wife and child with him, he would have done just that.

The talking point of the Scottish domestic season had been the performance of East Fife, that remarkable team from the Second Division who had reached the Scottish Cup final to play Kilmarnock. Killie, now managed by Jimmy McGrory, had beaten Celtic in an early round and Rangers in the semi-final, and would, one expected, beat East Fife in the final in two weeks time. After all, the Fifers had needed three games to get past St. Bernards in their semi.

The team chosen to play for Scotland at Wembley had caused controversy. Scotland's best player, Jimmy Delaney of Celtic, was injured and could not be considered, but Celtic fans, whose team won the Scottish League comfortably that year, could justifiably ask why no other member of that fine group of players was included. What was wrong with Johnny Crum, or Malky Macdonald or Frank Murphy? Rangers for their part felt ill-done by as well, with only captain George Brown from the Ibrox side in the team.

No fewer than four debutants had been chosen and it was a fair guess that David Cumming and John Milne of Middlesbrough, and Bill Shankly and George Mutch of Preston North End were hardly household names in Scotland. Preston, in fact, supplied four players with Andy Beattie and Tommy Smith making up the complement. More familiar would be centre-forward Frank O'Donnell of Blackpool, who had played for Celtic for a number of years but without ever really setting the heather on fire. And then, who was Robert Reid of Brentford? Even though the Bees were to finish that domestic season sixth in the First Division, it somehow just didn't seem right that a player from such a humble club was representing Scotland. Indeed, only three Home-Scots were in the team – captain Brown and two Hearts men, Andy Anderson the right-back and at inside-right the talented Tommy Walker, who had captivated the hearts of the nation by calmly taking a famous penalty in the wind at Wembley two years earlier, having to replace the ball several times in order to do so.

Andy Beattie at left-back would have the key job of marking Stanley Matthews of Stoke City, clearly one of the best players in the world with his dribbling and crossing skills. Cliff Bastin on the other wing was not Matthews's inferior by much, so the odds were really stacked in favour of England, who had already beaten both Northern Ireland and Wales.

But Scotland's four Preston players were a solid block, and North End were having a good season. They would finish third in England's top flight and in three weeks' time they would be back at Wembley along with Frank O'Donnell's brother Hugh to win the English Cup against Huddersfield Town. George Mutch would score the penalty winner in the last minute of extra-time, and Beattie would later become Scotland manager; and of course Shankly would become a legend at Liverpool in the same job.

Radio broadcasting was now commonplace and most Scottish people would follow the game by that medium. Television had even made an appearance by 1938 but only in the area immediately around London and only to a very few households. It would not reach Scotland until 1952, and therefore no consideration was ever given to televising the game, although history had been made in 1937 when the Sunderland v Preston North End English Cup final had been shown, in part, to the lucky few. 1938's event between Preston and Huddersfield Town would be screened in its entirety.

Ten years had now passed since Scotland had last won at Wembley. That had been the Wembley Wizards international of blessed memory, but since then, apart from the creditable 1-1 draw of 1936, performances had been poor and the drubbings severe. But TOMMY WALKER, the hero of 1936 also became the hero of 1938 with an excellent early goal. It was a header down from the reliable Frank O'Donnell which found Walker inside the penalty area. He cut inside, deceiving two defenders and giving the goalkeeper no chance.

But frankly that was about all the good football that one saw. England did have a few chances to equalise, notably Micky Fenton of Middlesbrough, who had a double chance late in the game. He shot, but it was parried by his Boro team-mate Dave Cumming. The ball then bounced back to Fenton, but instead of placing the ball calmly into the net, he foolishly shot the ball straight at the body of the goalkeeper, whose day it thus was.

David Cumming thus claimed his place in history. Circumstances brought it about that it was his one and only official cap for Scotland, (he would play in wartime international matches) and it was the first time ever that England had failed to score in a Wembley international – a record that would stay unequalled until a dull 0-0 draw with Uruguay at the start of the 1966 World Cup. Cumming, an unassuming Aberdonian had played for Arbroath until 1936 before joining Middlesbrough, and he is one of many players whose Scotland career was not given a chance to develop because of historical events that took place at the end of the decade.

The significance of this result and the consequent rejoicing is not really consistent with the standard of play. England in particular were attacked by their own Press for a lacklustre performance with only wingers Matthews and Bastin earning any sort of praise. Scotland had worked hard at blocking the supply to Matthews, knowing that if he got the ball anything could happen, and Beattie deserves a great deal of credit for his ability to get to the ball before Matthews did. On the odd occasion that Matthews got to the ball first, mayhem could follow.

The Scottish Press however were delighted. While conceding that this was one of the poorest games ever played between the two nations, a victory is nevertheless a victory, and Scotland retained her commanding lead in the series since 1872. As the trains pulled out of Euston and King's Cross Stations on Saturday night and Sunday morning, possibly most Scottish fans were too inebriated to bother, but those who did so must have wondered how long it would be before they would return. The next official meeting between the two sides in north-west London would be nine years away.

The summer of 1938 was a pleasant one, although the international tension cranked itself up a notch or two. England played in Berlin on 14 May 1938. They beat Germany 6-3 but that was hardly the main talking point, for the authorities had wanted the England players to perform a Nazi salute before the start. Such was the climate of 'appeasement' in the air that the Foreign Office in London gave the humiliated England players the orders to comply. It was one of the saddest moments of England's proud football history and did nothing to dispel Hitler's belief that that British Empire had legs of jelly.

After Celtic wrapped up the League and East Fife shocked the world by defeating Kilmarnock in the Scottish Cup final replay, Scotland beat Holland in a friendly. Then there was one big event remaining in Scotland that summer, which was the Empire Exhibition at Bellahouston Park, near Ibrox. An all-British tournament was held to celebrate the event, and in circumstances of the greatest rejoicing, Celtic won the trophy, beating Everton in the final, thereby dispelling the fallacy that the Scottish domestic game was not as good as the English one. That was on 10 June, the same day as the Test Match series between England and Australia began at Trent Bridge, with Don Bradman and the rest of the Aussies renewing their struggle against England for the Ashes in a contest almost as old and certainly as keenly anticipated as the annual battle between England and Scotland in football.

Yet the curious thing was that whenever the pressures on England became other than sporting, both their 'enemies' Scotland and Australia rallied to her cause. Give or take a few crackpots, neither the Jocks nor the Aussies ever said anything like 'This is England's war. We're staying out!', and both nations rallied to the defence of London when she was attacked so brutally by evil enemies. Yet in 1946 the Victory international in football between Scotland and England was fought as intensely as ever, and England spent the winter of 1946/47 being thrashed by friends and allies Australia at cricket. Indeed during the war itself, there had been all sorts of unofficial internationals, including for example impromptu ones between soldiers on sand in Africa and scarred battlefields in Italy. Even then 'beating the English' was important, but no-one ever wanted them beat in anything other than sport.

v ENGLAND 1-0
Hampden Park; Att: 139,468
13 April 1946

Scotland:	England:
Brown (Rangers)	Swift (Manchester City)
D. Shaw (Hibs)	Scott (Arsenal)
J. Shaw (Rangers)	Hardwick (Middlesbrough)
Campbell (Morton)	Wright (Wolves)
Brennan (Newcastle United)	Franklin (Stoke City)
Husband (Partick Thistle)	Mercer (Everton)
Waddell (Rangers)	Elliott (West Bromwich Albion)
Dougall (Birmingham City)	Shackleton (Bradford City)
Delaney (Manchester United)	Lawton (Chelsea)
Hamilton (Aberdeen)	Hagan (Sheffield United)
Liddell (Liverpool)	Compton (Arsenal)
Referee: Mr P. Craigmyle, Aberdeen	

T IS A SHAME that this game is regarded as an unofficial 'Victory' international rather than a full one for which caps are awarded. It seems odd that in 1946, almost a year after the end of hostilities in Europe, that 'proper' internationals could not resume, but that was what was decided at the start of 1945/46 season when the Japanese war was still on, and when it seemed unlikely that teams could have their best men available. In fact at Hampden that day, both sides were more or less at full strength.

It is a myth, although widely believed, that wartime football was not taken seriously. In fact, if anything, the reverse was the case and it was even more important than otherwise for fans needed something to take their minds off the very real horrors that were surrounding them. Cinema and theatre answered a similar need, and entertainment was never more necessary than in war time. Football, in spite of all the shortages of strips, boots and even balls, had actually flourished during the years 1939 to 1945, not least in the Armed Forces themselves where every regiment would have its team for lulls during fighting and to ward off the inevitable boredom of Army life.

But Scottish footballers had fared badly during the second world war, regularly and repeatedly losing to England to the tremendous distress of those Scottish supporters who could listen to the radio commentaries of these games on the BBC World Service in Cairo, India, Italy, South Africa and on board ship in the mid-Atlantic. In fact it would never be believed that peace was truly back until England had been beaten by Scotland.

And yet, peace *was* obviously back, as more and more soldiers came home with their demob suits and hats, some from the Japanese theatre so thin and emaciated as not to be recognised by their wives and mothers at the railway station. Air raids had stopped. No more did families dread the telegram from the GPO with the dire news that someone had been killed. Food rationing was still in force, but there was a gradual easing of restrictions. The evil Nazis had been wiped from the face of the earth, the sadistic Japanese had literally been bombed into submission, and even in Britain the old order of the Conservatives had been ever so gently pushed aside by the new and vigorous Labour Government of Clement Attlee, Aneurin Bevan and Manny Shinwell, elected with an overwhelming majority in July 1945. Never in British history had there been such a clear indication that change was being asked for ... and it was going to come!

To say that optimism was in the air in April 1946 was stating the obvious. There was even a funny sort of prosperity as soldiers had arrived back home flush with years of arrears of back pay and with very few goods to spend it on. So there was definitely money to go on train journeys to football matches and to take newly reunited wives and families with them. The women could do what they would in Glasgow, the men would go to the football to watch Scotland versus England.

Scotland and England! Once again they had proved to the world that they were an unbeatable combination, as they had done since the Seven Years War of 1756-1763. Rightly did they sing their songs about being the 'mother of the free'. Never in history had this been more obvious than in the liberation of Italy as the cries of 'Viva England! Viva Scotland! F*** Mussolini!' had assailed the ears of British soldiers from the impoverished victims of the Fascist jackals. To a stammering, nervous Scottish RAF man, "Wonderful people, you Scots," had been said by the Prime Minister himself, the epitome of England and Empire. The two countries had done it again!

Now, though, the glory days were past, and it was a different kind of glory that was now being sought, that of victory on the football field. From an early hour, Glasgow that spring day was crowded with people – some still in uniform, others with demob suits and raincoats (even though the weather was dry), others clad in more shabby attire, because clothing was still rationed. Scotsmen, Englishmen, a few curious Americans, Australians, Poles and other displaced persons from the chaos that was still central Europe were there – and even a few Italian and German ex-Prisoners of War who had not yet been repatriated and who in some cases didn't want to be. Comrades in arms had agreed to meet each other, for there was a large English presence of those who had come up for the day and would meet Scottish army friends to go to the game and then have a drink at night. It was a great chance to meet up again for those who had shared the greatest dangers together.

And Hampden Park was still there! The biggest football stadium in the world, now over 40 years old, had survived. The huge terracings, the old stand which had seen so many Cup finals and international matches, the newer smaller stand built in the mid-1930s – everything was still in place as the crowds made their way to the game. England's team bristled with stars – Shackleton, Lawton, Compton, Mercer, Swift – how often had those names been heard on the wireless on wartime sports programmes? And now they were here in Glasgow in the flesh!

The Scottish team had been much dissected and discussed by fans since the New Year. It was remarkable in that there were brothers in the full-back positions; Davie Shaw of Hibs and Jock of Rangers. The half-back line contained Partick Thistle's Jackie Husband, reckoned to be the best in the business but who was unfortunate in that his best years had coincided with those of the war, and up front the strength seemed to lie in the wingers. Willie Waddell had starred for Rangers during the war years and had been one of the few Scotland players to play well in all the disastrous internationals. On the other wing was Billy Liddell of Liverpool, a man who was less well known to Scottish crowds but who had earned a good reputation while playing for RAF teams and with his club who would finish as Champions in the first post-war League season of 1946/47.

Somewhat controversially Jimmy Delaney was in the centre-forward position. Delaney had already had a remarkable career which was soon to become even more so. He had been a tremendous right-winger for both Celtic and Scotland before the war, but then on the eve of conflict had shattered his arm and had been out of action for over two years. He had been transferred to Manchester United (to the great distress of his fans) in February, and was now not considered good enough to displace Willie Waddell on the right wing. But he was far too good to be left out altogether and thus was selected at centre-forward, a position which he clearly did not like as much as right wing, where he could use his pace to good effect. Many people felt that this was a mistake and that his inclusion was merely a sop to the 'Celtic' element of the Scottish support who still considered Jimmy to be one of their own, even though he was now wearing the red of Manchester United rather than the green and white of Celtic.

Community singing was the order of the day before the start of the game. All the old Harry Lauder favourites were there – 'Mary, My Scots Bluebell', 'Keep Right On to the End of the Road' and 'Just a wee Deoch an' Doris' as well as a few of a more recent vintage; for example Vera Lynn with her 'Bluebirds Over the White Cliffs of Dover' and 'Roll Out the Barrel'. The National Anthem was treated with the greatest respect by fans of both nations.

The game itself turned out to be a disappointment with defences well on top and opportunities to score few and far between. The highlights were the funny things that happened such as when Denis Compton, who in a few years time would become a hero of English cricket but who also played football for Arsenal, collided with a corner flag at the King's Park end of the ground, breaking it in the process. There was a delay before another flag could be found, and during this time a souvenir hunter ran on to the field, seized half of the broken flag and disappeared back into the crowd.

Peter Craigmyle of Aberdeen was the referee. He had been officiating now since just after the Great War (or the First World War as it was now called) and was much respected and imitated for his somewhat theatrical style of officiating. He loved to have the world look at him as he pointed majestically and slowly after making a decision. The crowd enjoyed his performance – a sure sign of it being a poor game when the referee is the centre of attention.

Delaney had seemed out of sorts, well policed by Stoke City's majestic centre-half Neil Franklin and Jimmy clearly yearned for a return to the wide open spaces of the right wing. Tommy Lawton similarly was getting little change out of Frank Brennan and both Shaw brothers were having good games. Neither goalkeeper Bobby Brown nor Frank Swift was particularly troubled, and the game was to all intents and purposes, fizzling out.

Scottish fans were quite satisfied with a 0-0 draw. This was a very fine England side, and a draw was respectable, whereas a few of the defeats during the War had been anything but. Shoulders were shrugged, handshakes were exchanged with English fans who, with their cockney and 'ee, ba gum, lad' northern accents would say things like 'Cheers, Jock'. It was a very friendly experience. In any case, football would really only start again next season...

Barely a minute remained when George Hamilton of Aberdeen was fouled half way inside the English half on the main stand side of the field. There seemed little danger and the exodus of those who wanted to avoid the queues for trains and trams continued. Raymond Glendinning in the BBC Radio commentary box said that "Scotland would have to score now if they were to break the deadlock".

It was Jackie Husband of Partick Thistle who took the kick. He seemed to have hit it too hard however, for the ball swung across the English goalmouth, and the defence visibly relaxed. But Husband had found the head of Willie Waddell on the far side of the pitch, and he turned the ball back to find the inrushing JIMMY DELANEY who scored a simple but effective goal. Craigmyle paused, looked at his linesman to make sure that everything was legal, then pointed theatrically up the field as bedlam reigned on the Hampden terracings.

Those who had left early now heard the almighty roar which greets a goal, and cursed themselves for their precipitate departure, while those who were listening at home on their old battered wirelesses which not so long ago had been urging everyone to 'Fight them on the beaches' went as crazy as those in the ground. In blocks of Scottish council houses where every household was listening to the game, the noise became a miniature Hampden Roar of its own, followed by another one soon after as Glendinning told the world that Craigmyle had whistled for full-time.

It would be some time before that goal could be seen by the adoring masses. There was as yet no television in Scotland, but there were the newsreels which appeared at the cinema to show events about a week after they happened. Men would take their girlfriends to the 'flicks' again and again just to see the newsreel footage of that goal – a simple one, but one which meant so much to a football-starved nation.

v ENGLAND 3-1
Wembley; Att: 98,188
9 April 1949

Scotland:	England:
Cowan (Morton)	Swift (Manchester City)
Young (Rangers)	Aston (Manchester United)
Cox (Rangers)	Howe (Derby County)
Evans (Celtic)	Wright (Wolverhampton Wanderers)
Woodburn (Rangers)	Franklin (Stoke City)
Aitken (East Fife)	Cockburn (Manchester United)
Waddell (Rangers)	Matthews (Blackpool)
Mason (Third Lanark)	Mortensen (Blackpool)
Houliston (Queen of the South)	Milburn (Newcastle United)
Steel (Derby County)	Pearson (Manchester United)
Reilly (Hibs)	Finney (Preston North End)
Referee: Mr Griffiths, Wales	

I T IS COMMONLY assumed by social historians that the late 1940s were times of hardship, with the word 'austerity' frequently used to describe the poverty and shortages caused by the aftermath of the Second World War. This is not entirely true, for although many things remained on the ration – sweets, fruit, clothing – general prosperity had begun to rise, and more and more people were beginning to enjoy a better life than they had experienced in the 1930s.

The media – mainly newspapers – encouraged this belief that times were harsh. In reality for the working class life was beginning to get better. Not least because the new Labour Government pledged to create a Welfare State and were quite happy to use hyperboles like 'New Jerusalem' at their conferences. The working classes were beginning to get a taste of the good life. Indeed most of the complaints about 'austerity' came from the better off middle classes, living for the first time through times of economic hardship under a government not primarily dedicated to their welfare.

Certainly, London had never seen so many Scottish supporters descend on it as it did in 1949, and this time it was remarked upon that there were a great many women and children among them, travelling down on the overnight sleepers to be joined by a huge amount of ex-patriate Scots now living in London. Sadly two of them never made it, for John Wilson and George McDuff fell out of a train at Old Cumnock after some silly drunken horseplay, and there was a distressing amount of idiotic pulling of communication cords to stop the trains.

But the Scots had clearly been saving up for the event en masse and were determined to enjoy London, a city now beginning to recover from the dreadful pasting that it had taken from the Luftwaffe in 1940 and 1941 and from the V2 pilotless aircraft that had threatened to win the war in the later years even when Germany was apparently on her knees. Yet, there were still many areas of London that had their bomb sites, where even apparently healthy buildings had had to be destroyed for fear of them having been destabilised by collateral damage.

Saturday morning saw the obligatory trips to Trafalgar Square, Piccadilly Circus and Downing Street, hoping perhaps for a glimpse of the taciturn little man called Clement Attlee who was now spearheading the social revolution, or even Buckingham Palace where lived (along with his extrovert Scots wife) the quiet, unhealthy but dignified man who had led the British Empire through its most turbulent days. His daughter Princess Elizabeth and her husband the Duke of Edinburgh would attend the game, leaving presumably their five month old baby Charles in the hands of experienced nannies. 'Look, there's Willie Woodburn,' a supporter might have said looking up at the famous clock face that had so often symbolised the free world, for 'Big Ben' was the nickname given to Rangers and Scotland's centre-half.

Scotland had had a good season. It was often said that when Rangers do well, so do Scotland. This was certainly true of 1949. Rangers were destined to win all the domestic honours, and Scotland had already beaten Wales and Northern Ireland. Wales had presented few problems, but the Irishmen had been leading 2-0 after five minutes before Scotland rallied and won 3-2, Billy Houliston of Queen of the South scoring the winner at the death.

That Rangers had done well this season was due to their 'Iron Curtain' defence. The 'Iron Curtain' of course was a phrase coined by Winston Churchill to describe the inscrutable and impenetrable tyranny that was the Soviet Union and their post-war infiltration of much of eastern Europe. Rangers' defence was similarly impregnable and it was no surprise that Geordie Young, Sammy Cox and Willie Woodburn were chosen for Scotland's trip to Wembley, particularly after the disappointing defeat of the Scottish League by the English League in March when too many goals had been leaked.

It is not often that a man from Queen of the South becomes a national hero but Billy Houliston had done just that against Northern Ireland with his late winner, and now here he was playing his second international carrying the nation's hopes. The first Doonhamer ever to be capped for Scotland, he was being played at centre-forward at the expense of Lawrie Reilly who was on the left wing, in theory at least, for it was felt that the two could interchange positions to confuse the English. The right winger was Willie Waddell of Rangers, commonly known as the 'deedle', who had been absolutely inspirational against Wales, scoring two of Scotland's goals.

The inside forwards, generally regarded in that age as the playmakers of the team, were Jimmy Mason, a cheerful extrovert from Third Lanark, and the man often rated as the best footballer in the British game, Billy Steel. Such was the strength of Scottish domestic football in 1949 that Steel was the only Anglo-Scot of the eleven. He was a great distributer of the ball with a fine shot, but was often regarded as a difficult character off the field. He would soon sign for Dundee and become a Tayside legend.

Celtic, East Fife and Morton all supplied one player each in Bobby Evans, George Aitken and Jimmy Cowan. Cowan had come into the Scotland team in the wake of last year's disaster at Hampden against England. He had impressed everyone in the Scottish Cup semi-final and final of 1948 when he had played well against both Celtic and Rangers, and he had made several appearances for Scotland this season, although he had been out for a spell with a broken arm. He was lithe, agile and courageous and one of the best goal-keepers that Scotland had produced for some considerable time.

England had two of the greatest wingers of all time in Stanley Matthews and Tom Finney, also two of the finest gentlemen ever to grace the game. It was obvious that if Scotland were to win, this pair would have to be tamed. Much therefore would be demanded of Young and Cox, as if the wingers could get to the byline and cross the ball there was the head of Jackie Milburn of Newcastle United to finish the job. 'Wor Jackie' was already a folk hero on his native Tyneside, and it would only need a goal or two to make him a hero of all England.

Scotland were due to tour North America in the summer, sailing on the Queen Mary. There would be no official internationals, but it would clearly be an incentive for men to play well and get a chance to see the New World. It would be nice to do so as champions of Britain and as they had already beaten Wales and Northern Ireland, all they had to do was win at Wembley. Since 1924, Scotland had played there eight times, winning in 1928 and 1938, drawing in 1924, 1936 and 1947, but losing heavily on three successive visits in 1930, 1932 and 1934.

Television existed in 1949 but had not yet reached Scotland, although it was projected to do so by 1952. But there would be radio coverage from the 'stadium of the twin towers' for those who were not at Wembley from Raymond Glendinning, a genial sportscar driver and general sporting expert, who always said in a cheery piece of fence-sitting that, "although I favour England, this does not mean I do not like Scotland!" Glendinning would be commentating on the BBC Light Programme to all of Great Britain whereas the Scottish Home Service would cover a Shinty match! The Scottish Home Service would however have a highlights programme called Sportsreel from 6.27pm until 7pm, followed by Scottish Country Dance music and then the famous Scottish radio soap opera about a family called the McFlannels.

This game is often referred to as 'Cowan's Match', and the Morton man thoroughly deserved all the plaudits that he got, but it would be inaccurate to assume that Cowan single-handedly kept England at bay for the whole 90 minutes. This is not so, for Scotland were far and away the better team, but at two vital stages of the game, the form of Cowan proved pivotal to Scotland's success. The first of these stages was in the first half hour when the superb play of Matthews and Finney created a number of chances for their forwards, as England threatened to take Scotland apart. Twice Cowan saved from Mortensen and once from Milburn, and another occasion saw Cowan beaten on the rebound from a save ... only for Sammy Cox to appear from nowhere to clear his lines.

It is often said in football that you must score when you are on top, otherwise the pendulum will swing the other way. This was exactly what happened here, for gradually under the inspiration of Cowan, Young and Cox got control over England's two wingers, and the Scottish wing-halves, George Aitken and the red headed Bobby Evans took a decisive grip on the midfield area.

JIMMY MASON was on hand to take full advantage of a cross from Lawrie Reilly, side-footing the ball into the net off a post. It was a fine goal, and England now looked a little dispirited as Scotland finished the first half strongly. It was more of the same after the interval, the second goal coming from BILLY STEEL, who walked the ball into the net after a brilliant one-two with Billy Houliston. That was in the 52nd minute and by the hour mark, Scotland were three up when a great cross from Willie Waddell found LAWRIE REILLY whose diving downward header created an explosion of sound from the now delirious travelling Scots who could shortly afterwards be seen doing impromptu eightsome reels on the standing terracing area of Wembley.

But there was a sting in the tail as England pulled a goal back when MILBURN deflected a Mortensen shot goalwards with only 17 minutes remaining, and England, having gained their second wind, took over from the now exhausted Scottish midfield. More goals might have come and England almost scored in a late scrimmage when Milburn seemed to get in the way of a goalbound shot, then Pearson hit the bar. In addition Cowan made at least four good saves. It was clearly Scotland's day.

The final whistle blew to signal Scotland's first Home International Championship triumph since 1936 and their first 'triple crown' of beating all three home countries since 1929. The fans invaded the field, making a bee line for Jimmy Cowan and attempting none too successfully to chair him off the field, almost dropping him twice. It was as well that Jimmy held the ball better than the Scottish fans held him, it was said! More heroes' receptions were seen at Glasgow Central Station when the team arrived home on Sunday night, the police having to deal with serious overcrowding caused by the fans of a triumphant nation who had now recorded their first official victory over England for more than a decade.

v **SPAIN** 4-2
Hampden Park; Att: 88,890
8 May 1957

Scotland:	Spain:
Younger (Liverpool)	Ramallets (Barcelona)
Caldow (Rangers)	Olivella (Barcelona)
Hewie (Charlton Athletic)	Campanal (Sevilla)
McColl (Rangers)	Garay (Bilbao)
Young (Rangers)	Verges (Barcelona)
Docherty (Preston North End)	Zarraga (Real Madrid)
Smith (Hibs)	Gonzales (Real Madrid)
Collins (Celtic)	Kubala (Barcelona)
Mudie (Blackpool)	Di Stefano (Real Madrid)
Baird (Rangers)	Suarez (Barcelona)
Ring (Clyde)	Gento (Real Madrid)
Referee: Herr Dusch, West Germany	

SCOTTISH PEOPLE IN 1957 did not really know very much about Spain. The tourist boom of the 1960s during which everyone seemed to be holidaying in Spain was still some way off. In the 1950s we knew that Spain had sunshine, wine, bull-fighting, donkeys, broad hats called sombreros and cigars. There was a chap called Don Quixote, who rescued damsels in distress, and another fellow called Don Juan who seduced and ruined them. There was a dance called the flamenco, everyone rattled castanets and they played a game called pelota. But they also played football. This would be the first time that they had ever played against Scotland, but recently the exploits of a team called Real Madrid had come to everyone's attention through the BBC. Real had won the first ever European Cup final against Reims in 1956, and had just defeated Manchester United to reach the final in 1957. They played good attractive attacking football, and they supplied several men to the Spanish national side, so Spain would be good.

There was another side to Spain, of course, one that the British establishment tried to gloss over. 20 years previously when the world record crowd had arrived to see the England game there had been posters all the way from the Mount Florida railway station to Hampden Park encouraging people to join the International Brigades to fight against fascism in Spain and its leader General Franco. Now that man was still dictator. He'd had the sense to use Hitler and Mussolini to help him gain power but to refuse to help them when they were fighting the bigger boys in World War II. As a result, he had survived but still many were surprised that the Allies had not wiped out fascism in Spain the same way as they had done in other parts of Europe.

Spain was now at peace but it recalled the dictum of the Pictish chief Calgacus in 84 A.D. who had said, 'where they create a desert, they call it peace'. Spain was a repressed nation, with gross problems of poverty and underdevelopment, making a few noises now and again about communism in order to get some patronising support from the USA and with a population which needed football to cheer it up. In football, a further legacy of the Civil War was the bitterness between Real Madrid and Barcelona. There was a little of the Celtic v Rangers about this one, but the feelings went further and deeper than that. One team had won the Civil War and had the dictator as one of its unashamed supporters, the other was the vanquished with a permanent chip on its shoulder.

Scotland, meantime, was prospering with the Welfare State set up by Labour in the 1940s and wisely retained by the Tories in the 1950s producing real benefits in health and welfare as many of the horrible diseases of the past were progressively being eradicated. The Prime Minister was a sensible man called Harold Macmillan who had taken over from Anthony Eden at the turn of the year. Eden had led the world to the brink of another war in his Suez fiasco. Macmillan, on the other hand, rejoiced in the nickname 'Supermac' and famously said that "we have never had it so good". In fact, he even had one effect on Scottish football: the very talented inside-right of Airdrie and Rangers was called Ian McMillan. Ian had so much control over a football that he was nicknamed 'The Wee Prime Minister'.

This match was the first real World Cup qualifier that Scotland had ever played. For the 1950 and 1954 World Cups, the Home International Championship had been used for the British clubs, but for 1958 in Sweden, all the Ss had come together – Spain, Switzerland and Scotland, and it now seemed that the SFA had 'wised up' to the idea that the World Cup tournament might just be here to stay and that money and prestige could be gained from this tournament.

Incredible as it might seem, Scotland still had no team manager. The team was chosen by 'Selectors', men appointed by the SFA for that purpose. There had been a team manager in 1954 – Andy Beattie – but he had let them down by walking out on Scotland in the middle of the World Cup finals, and after that no-one had seen any great need to appoint another manager. In recent years, however, the selection system was coming under increasing pressure, for it was failing to produce the goods. It was now, for example, six years since Scotland had beaten England, the longest gap in the twentieth century.

Scotland had disappointed their fans by losing to England at Wembley a month previously. It had only been a narrow 1-2 defeat, but Scotland had scored first and failed to capitalise. The Scottish goalscorer was Tommy Ring of Clyde, one of the very few Second Division players ever to be chosen for Scotland, because Clyde were technically still in the Second Division at that time, even though they had already secured promotion. Domestically, Rangers had won the Scottish League First Division, Celtic had won the League Cup, but for a change a less fancied team, Falkirk, had won the Scottish Cup. Attendances were high, and Scottish football was booming.

The game kicked off at 6.45pm on Wednesday 8 May, the time being chosen as the latest that could guarantee a finish in daylight. Given the murky conditions, that looked decidedly problematical. The weather had taken a slight turn for the better, but it had been absolutely dire for the past 24 hours or so, rendering the pitch heavy. This would naturally suit the Scots more than it would the Spaniards, even though Scotland had a few lightweights in Bobby Collins, Jackie Mudie and Gordon Smith in their forward line. George Young, the much respected Scotland captain had announced his retirement after the World Cup qualifiers of May 1957 were completed, but he was playing this night along with other Ibrox men like Eric Caldow, Ian McColl and Sammy Baird. Alex Parker of Falkirk was a late call off and his place was taken by John Hewie, a South African of Scottish descent who played for Charlton Athletic. Hewie came in at left-back, allowing the versatile Caldow to play at right-back for Parker.

Arguments centred on the wisdom or otherwise of including Jackie Mudie in the team. Jackie, a Dundonian, had played for Blackpool alongside Matthews and Mortensen and had won a medal in the English Cup final of 1952, but his four previous appearances for Scotland had seen no great successes. It was felt, particularly in the wet conditions that a larger, more bustling type of centre-forward might be appropriate. The game against Spain however would be Jackie's finest hour.

The rain was easing, but it was still a miserable night and it said a great deal for Scotland's support that 88,890 turned up, wading through puddles to get to turnstiles and being prepared to stand on uncovered terracing as they listened to the Military Band of the 1st Battalion Royal Scots Fusiliers. One had to be tough to be a real Scotland fan in the 1950s. One had to be able to accept defeat manfully and stoically and also to have the fortitude to brave appalling conditions. Fortunately, those who did just that would be lucky enough to see a great game and a really first-class Scottish performance. There is a school of thought which believes that Scotland plays its best football in the wet. They would have evidence for that belief here.

Scotland drew first blood about halfway through the first half when MUDIE took two bites at the cherry from a corner kick. He hit the bar with his first effort but followed up and headed home the rebound. This was no more than Scotland deserved and the large crowd showed their appreciation. But then Spain equalised with a real fluke goal when KUBALA found himself in front of the Scottish goal but miskicked, in so doing deceiving Tommy Younger into diving the wrong way and allowing the ball to trickle apologetically over the line for a crazy equalizer. Scotland were not to be outdone. Before half-time, Tommy Ring, who had caused the Spaniards all sorts of trouble on the left wing, was brought down in desperation by Olivella. Herr Dusch did not hesitate – a penalty it was, and ice cool JOHN HEWIE did the needful to send Scotland in at half-time with a 2-1 lead.

The second half was played at an even faster tempo than the first, and it was clear that Scotland were gradually wearing down the Spaniards, even though the visitors were back on level terms within minutes of the restart when SUAREZ netted a rebound after Younger could only parry a Gento shot.

But the last half an hour saw some inspirational Scottish play. Their determined attitude against a team who were none too particular in how they stopped them won the hearts of the Hampden crowd and it was like old times again with a Scotland team playing fast aggressive football. 20 minutes remained when Scotland went ahead for the third time in the game when a pass from wee Bobby Collins bisected the static Spanish defence to find MUDIE, who set Hampden alight with a crisp shot. And if that was good, there was even better to come ten minutes from time when a long ball from the excellent Ian McColl found Collins who beat his man, then, after a quick one-two with Gordon Smith, sent another ball into the penalty box for JACKIE MUDIE to complete his hat-trick. There was now no way back for Spain who had been well and truly beaten by a superlative Scottish side who thoroughly deserved the plaudits of their fans.

Euphoria reigned in the Scottish press the next day with banner headlines like 'Super Scots Skittle Spaniards', and for a few days everyone was convinced that Scotland would win the World Cup next year. It was certainly a fine performance, arguably the best against foreign opposition since Germany had been beaten in 1936, and it showed that, at Hampden at least, Scotland need not fear anyone.

A feature of Scotland's play had been the wingers – Gordon Smith and Tommy Ring. Using the excellent service supplied by inside-forwards Bobby Collins and Sammy Baird, the two wide men had rounded the Spanish defence time and time again, and with such players on board, confidence was justified.

But sterner tests awaited. Scotland were now off to Europe to play Switzerland and Spain away from home, and sandwiched between them was a friendly against the World Cup winners West Germany. Not exactly a doddle, but Scotland were striding towards their first World Cup finals with confidence.

v **SWITZERLAND** 2-1
Basle; Att: 48,000
19 May 1957

Scotland:	Switzerland:
Younger (Liverpool)	Parlier
Caldow (Rangers)	Kernen
Hewie (Charlton Athletic)	Koch
McColl (Rangers)	Grobety
Young (Rangers)	Frosio
Docherty (Preston North End)	Schneiter
Smith (Hibs)	Antenen
Collins (Celtic)	Meier
Mudie (Blackpool)	Vonlanthen
Baird (Rangers)	Ballaman
Ring (Clyde)	Riva
Referee: Herr Seipelt, Austria	

WHILE NATURALLY apprehensive about flying (a first experience for many of the squad), Scotland were nevertheless in rare good humour as they flew out of Prestwick Airport for their tour of Europe to play Switzerland, West Germany and Spain. The euphoria was understandable, for they had just completed one of their best ever results by beating Spain at Hampden.

The World Cup was a new and exotic tournament in 1957. Scotland's only previous experience of that event had been a terrible one when they lost 0-1 to Austria and 0-7 to Uruguay in the finals in Switzerland in 1954. Now by bitter irony they were flying to Switzerland to play the hosts in the very ground in Basle where Uruguay had dealt out that spectacular thrashing. Tommy Docherty was the only playing survivor of that day nearly three years ago, but the whole nation had been traumatised.

But this was a different Scottish team, and one which seemed to be taking, at last, the concept of a World Cup seriously. In 1950 they had (incredibly) refused to go unless they were British Champions. Having been pipped by England they had declined FIFA's invitation. 1954 had been half-hearted to say the least. The 1958 finals would be held in Sweden and there was a determination that Scotland would be there. The win over Spain had excited the fans, making them forget about the unlucky defeat at Wembley by England, and encouraging the nation to feel good about themselves once again.

Switzerland, the land of clocks and snow and Alps and rich people who made their fortunes out of war by staying neutral and selling commodities to combatant nations, had played Scotland three times before. Scotland had won in Geneva in 1931 and at Hampden in 1950, but had gone down in Berne in Scotland's dreadful year of 1948. They were not considered to be top notchers in World football, but they would be efficient, organised and hard working. Scotland feared that the heat would count against them.

In that respect at least they were wrong. Central Europe frequently attracts extremes of weather, and although the temperature was not cold, it was wet, very wet in Basle. This, of course, to a nation that plays so much of its football on wet pitches between November and February was a bonus, and Scotland would feel at home, it was felt.

They would also know that, in a rare move for the 1950s, the match would be televised live to several nations and Scotland would get the second half. This decision was not achieved without more than a little reluctance by the SFA, for they were traditionally against the televising of matches. There was an added dimension on this occasion because the game was to be played on a Sunday. To a Calvinistic country like Scotland, this did not sit very well with the Establishment with all their Church connections. Scotland was way out of line with other countries in this respect, and indeed had played games on Sundays before in foreign countries – but never had they been televised. Letters were written by the Godly to protest. Television, after all, itself was the work of the Devil, and this sort of thing just proved it. This opinion was screeched and thundered by men from the Highlands and Islands (and a few from Glasgow and Edinburgh who should have known better), but the SFA agreed to the second half being televised live on the grounds that there were no other football matches on in Scotland at that time, and therefore the 'deterrent' factor of stopping people attending live matches did not apply. The cynics also suspected that the size of the fee offered by the BBC to show the game was a potent factor as well. Religion is all very well ... as long as it does not get in the way of money making.

In Scotland in 1957, television ownership was expanding but was far from universal. The middle classes in the leafy suburbs of Edinburgh and Glasgow would tend to own one, but for many of the working classes it was still an expensive item, in spite of all the attempts to woo them by rental and hire purchase deals. Nevertheless, everyone knew someone who had one, and neighbours, grannies and aunties were suddenly courted to open their house for the vital 45 minutes from Basle. But the televising of the game had one bizarre side effect. The game would be in black and white (for colour television was a good 10 or 15 years in the future) and the teams would look very similar, as Switzerland wore red shirts and white shorts while Scotland wore blue shirts and white shorts – indistinguishable to the TV viewer. Nobody seems to have thought of this before Scotland left, for they could have brought a set of white shirts or even worn the Rosebery colours as they had done as late as 1949. There was thus a problem, eventually resolved when the Swiss loaned them orange shorts! This caused a little hilarity in the Scottish camp. In the first place it was a hideous combination of navy blue, bright orange and red socks – just as well that it was only on black and white television! – and the Rangers players like Sammy Baird and Ian McColl joked that they were perfectly at home in a combination of blue and orange, but what about men like Bobby Collins, Tommy Ring and Tommy Docherty, who were not of the same persuasion?

On a more serious note, for another Rangers player, captain George Young, this would turn out to be his last game for Scotland. He had announced his retirement as from the end of the tour, and it so happened that he was not picked for the other two games. It was therefore his 53rd and last cap. It was a fine game to go out on, for he was, as so often in the past, outstanding in the middle of the defence.

Scotland were taken aback by the size and volume of the crowd which revealed a fanaticism that one did not normally associate with Switzerland. In addition, Scotland seemed to be wearing the wrong sort of studs on their boots, for they lost their footing several times and made many defensive errors. Goalkeeper Tommy Younger looked distinctly ill at ease, and in the first half hour of the game, Scotland were extremely fortunate not to be more than one down. The goal was scored by VONLANTHEN after a well worked move with Meier in which the Scottish defence looked non-existent.

But this Scotland team did not lack character and, inspired by Docherty and Young, gradually took command of the game, bringing the two wingers Gordon Smith and Tommy Ring into action. Smith was generally regarded as one of the best right wingers that the Scottish domestic game had seen, but his performances for Scotland had been sporadic and fitful, doing little to justify his domestic reputation with Hibs. Conversely Ring, with the reputation of a wild boy, could be absolutely devastating on his day. As the wingers came more and more into play, it was from a corner kick that Scotland equalised and once again it was JACKIE MUDIE, the hero of Hampden 11 days earlier when they had beaten Spain, who scored, heading home a corner which the Swiss had disputed so much that it disturbed their defensive concentration.

Thus it was that Scotland went in 1-1 at half-time so that the television viewers joined the game on level terms. Spain and Switzerland had drawn their game, so a draw away from home for Scotland would be an acceptable performance, whereas a win would be a large step towards qualification, as Switzerland had yet to come to Hampden in the autumn. The second half saw Scotland gradually taking control of the game with Baird and Collins, the inside-forwards, benefiting from obvious Swiss exhaustion. In addition, both of these men could dribble – a skill that could be counteracted by a massive tackle, but the Swiss were reluctant to do that. Indeed it became obvious that on the heavy ground and with a slow pace, Scotland would be the stronger team at the finish. It just remained to be seen whether they could score and earn themselves a win. The flickering black and white screens back home, still subject to interference from next door neighbours' motor bikes or vacuum cleaners (two other phenomena of the increasingly prosperous 1950s), were now being watched with increasing interest, passion and optimism as Scotland began to exert a little pressure on the Swiss.

The 70th minute brought a goal. Scotland won another corner on the right, and it was taken by Gordon Smith. The ball came across and BOBBY COLLINS, for some reason totally unmarked, was able, in spite of his lack of inches, to rise high and head the ball downwards past goalkeeper Parlier, who was deceived by the bounce. The ball lodged itself between the stanchion and the net, an image that the TV cameras caught to produce bedlam in living rooms back home.

20 minutes remained and the Swiss crowd who had been becalmed after Scotland's first goal and thunderstruck after their second, now got behind their team again and roused

them to greater efforts, knowing that their chances of qualification would be virtually gone if Scotland won. Scotland did not always help their own cause by being short with pass backs more than once, and relying on Tommy Younger to save them. Younger however had got over his earlier hesitation and uncertainty and made several good saves in the latter stages, one of them from point blank range after the rest of the Scottish defence seemed to have fallen asleep.

Scotland for their part might have added to their tally, but the Swiss goalkeeper Parlier was also in fine form. The full-time whistle brought great rejoicing to the team, the few supporters in the ground (some Scottish soldiers serving in Germany had saved up some leave to come and watch the game) and the many supporters back home who now enjoyed their Sunday tea with the knowledge that one more win over Spain in Madrid next week or Switzerland in Hampden in November would be enough to send Scotland to Sweden.

Press reaction was varied. *The Scotsman* said that 'some Scottish players probably realised that they would never again play so badly and be on a winning side'– a rather harsh judgement which did not take into account that it was a valuable win over a fine side away from home, whereas the *Daily Record* was more positive: 'the Scots were the more solid lot ... and went on to deserve their victory', whereas much tribute is paid to the 'mighty midgets' Bobby Collins and Jackie Mudie who were also described as 'lionhearts'.

Perhaps the real triumph in this game was the victory of reality. The idea that 'continentals' were flashy footballers who faked or exaggerated injuries and had little in the way of guts and stamina died hard in Scotland, even when failures against continental and South American teams would indicate that it was the Scottish game which had problems. This game, shown to the Scottish nation, clearly indicated that this was not so, and that European teams, particularly on their own patch, were hard to beat. Fortunately this Scottish team had the determination and professionalism to do just that. As Lewis Grassic Gibbon in his *Scots Hairst* would say, 'Ye need smeddum for that!'

v **SWITZERLAND** 3-2
Hampden Park; Att: 58,811
6 November 1957

Scotland:	Switzerland:
Younger (Liverpool)	Parlier
Parker (Falkirk)	Kernan
Caldow (Rangers)	Morf
Fernie (Celtic)	Grobety
Evans (Celtic)	Koch
Docherty (Preston North End)	Schneiter
Scott (Rangers)	Chiesa
Collins (Celtic)	Ballaman
Mudie (Blackpool)	Meier
Robertson (Clyde)	Vonlanthen
Ring (Clyde)	Riva

Referee: Mr R. Leafe, England

T HE YEAR 1957 had been a mercurial one for Scotland, with defeats at Wembley and in Madrid, but victories in a glorious spell in May over Spain at Hampden, Switzerland away and West Germany (the World Cup holders) away – the last one only a friendly, sadly – and then most recently, a feckless 1-1 draw against Northern Ireland in which the Irish had been very unlucky.

The bottom line of 6 November 1957 was that if Scotland beat Switzerland at Hampden, they would qualify for the World Cup in Sweden. A draw would lead to complications and play-offs, but a win would see Scotland through because their two opponents Spain and Switzerland had obliged Scotland with a 2-2 draw, something that helped neither of them.

The players were well motivated certainly, as were the ever loyal fans who refused to desert them. The game had to be played on a Wednesday afternoon in November as Hampden would not have floodlights for another four years yet, and 58,811 were persuaded to take an afternoon off work or to tell a lie to an incredulous employer or headmaster about yet another auntie's funeral or a sore back in order to support their country. This was an era of full employment, prosperity even, but industrial growth and productivity would have to take a back seat for at least one afternoon.

Football in Scotland was still reeling from the League Cup final of 17 days previously in which Celtic had beaten Rangers 7-1. The extent of that beating had been as spectacular as it had been unpredicted, and it was no surprise that three Celtic players, Bobby Evans, Willie Fernie and Bobby Collins were selected to face Switzerland. The left wing was an all

Clyde affair of Archie Robertson and Tommy Ring – Clyde that remarkable side who were in the middle of a four year spell in which they won the Scottish Cup (1955), were relegated (1956), promoted (1957) and won the Scottish Cup again (1958). The unusual was part of Clyde, but everyone agreed that their left wing was devastating. The team of the season, however, was destined to be the fast-developing Hearts.

The Scotland team had to be changed from its original selection when Gordon Smith of Hibs was pronounced unfit and Alec Scott of Rangers was sent for. This was no real blow because, although Smith was a marvellous player, he was somewhat fragile and had seldom been seen at his best for Scotland, whereas Scott was stronger and more direct. The centre-forward was Jackie Mudie of Blackpool who had been the hero of his country in the triumph against Spain in May, and the captain was Tommy Docherty. There was no more committed or determined character.

It was a fine, crisp, November day when the game kicked off at 2.30pm, the crowd having waded through a fair amount of autumn leaves on the walk from Mount Florida railway station. Another feature of November is the low sun, excessively troublesome to those in the North Enclosure who would be glad to see a few clouds drift in as the sun began to sink. The game would be broadcast on the radio, and those who had the latest luxury of a transistor radio or a 'portable' (erroneously called Portobello by some, a mistake which caused a false belief that there was a factory in the outskirts of Edinburgh which made them!) were beseeched by their workmates to bring it along that afternoon for updates when the 'gaffer' (or foreman) was not looking. Schoolboys worked out that if school finished at 4pm a quick charge up the road might allow then to hear the last five minutes or so. Ah, but the radio in these days took a few minutes to 'warm up', so it would have to be switched on at lunchtime, broadcasting to an empty house and wasting electricity, so that the final stages could be listened to!

The band before the start inspired the fans with a few rousing Scottish favourites like 'Rowan Tree', 'The Barren Rocks of Aden' and of course 'Scotland the Brave'. Scotland started kicking towards the King's Park end of the ground, against a team playing in a brilliant orange strip which dazzled a few spectators who had never seen such a thing before.

But despite all the anticipation and careful planning, the game was dull. The Swiss team would hardly have been satisfied with a draw, but it was clear that their tactics were to frustrate the Scots and hope for a quick breakaway and a late goal perhaps. Scotland charged at them, but the snazzy orange strips were always in command, not disdaining the pass back to their goalkeeper (it was of course legal for the keeper to pick up the ball from a back pass in 1957) or the punt up the field, and Scotland's attacks grew more and more desperate as the first half wore on, with, in particular, Willie Fernie (the mastermind of Celtic's recent 7-1 beating of Rangers), unable to produce what his fans demanded. But then, virtually out of nothing, it happened. No patient build up, simply a long and accurate through pass from Tommy Docherty to ARCHIE ROBERTSON and the Clyde man had enough sense not to delay but to shoot once and make it a good one.

But then almost immediately Scottish self-destruction took over again, as Tommy Docherty mis-kicked a ball out of defence so badly that it went across the park right to the

Swiss left winger RIVA who needed no second invitation to equalise. It was a bad mistake, but that hardly excused the heartless types who took their frustration out on the hapless Docherty by booing him every time he touched the ball for the remainder of the first half.

The Swiss were now heartened and the half ended with Scotland indebted to goalkeeper Tommy Younger, once of Hibs but now of Liverpool, who had to make a few fine stops. Half-time was passed in pensive silence as those who had brought thermos flasks enjoyed their cup of tea and the less provident queued at the inadequate catering facilities. The dream of next summer in Sweden looked far away, for Scotland's performance was far below par.

The second half saw better football from both sides, and noticeably the crowd became more animated as Younger several times saved well. Then Scotland went ahead. The goal originated from Willie Fernie, one of the few out and out dribblers in the Scottish game, who weaved his way in and out of several tackles before passing to JACKIE MUDIE who hit a fine shot. This was a goal fit to qualify Scotland for the World Cup, and something approaching the Hampden Roar was heard to greet this piece of brilliance, but then realism set in. There was still over half an hour to go, and the Scottish defence had boobed before. Would they do so again?

Switzerland now threw everything into the attack, and Scotland were distinctly lucky when right-back Alex Parker of Falkirk cleared off the line after Younger could only parry a fierce shot. Then immediately after that, and before the buzz of animated conversation died down, a long ball from Bobby Collins found ALEC SCOTT on the right wing just inside the Swiss half. Frankly he looked yards offside, and everyone stopped, including for an instant Scott himself who apparently expected a flag and a whistle. Neither came, and he ran on and scored past an incredulous goalkeeper who was busier shouting at the referee than remembering the golden rule of 'Play to the whistle'.

The goal was given, and the situation wasn't helped in Swiss eyes by the fact that the referee and linesmen were Englishmen. The Swiss mentality failed to appreciate the difference between Scotland and England and had convinced themselves that an English referee would side with a fellow British team! (In fact, Scott was possibly onside when the long ball was played from Collins, but this fine point would cut little ice with the demented and much put-upon Swiss). Angrily, they surrounded the officials, protesting animatedly and even laying hands on them, while the Scottish players, quite correctly waited calmly for the restart, reckoning that they were still two goals ahead and that the Swiss with someone now to blame for their defeat, would lose heart. All that Scotland needed to do now was the keep calm. Let the Swiss waste their own time!

For a while that seemed to work, but 'keeping calm' has never been a great Scottish characteristic, and once again a mistake allowed the Swiss in with a chance. Ten minutes remained when the previously outstanding Younger totally missed a ball from a corner kick and VONLATHEN reduced Hampden to an eerie silence as he scored.

Thus the Scottish nation was condemned to ten minutes of purgatory. The school boy who had left his mother's radio on all afternoon so that it would be 'warmed up' rushed home to hear George Davidson and Peter Thomson in an agitated state. No attempt was made to be unbiased as "Well played, Caldow!" and "Good! Evans breaks it up again" was heard, along with "The referee is again looking at his watch...". The game was being broadcast on BBC World Service so Scottish people abroad, soldiers in Cyprus, merchant seamen on the high seas, and even those living in England could share the tension. It could also be followed in Spain by anyone with an elementary knowledge of English or even enough common sense to follow the tone of the commentators and the roar of the crowd.

The sun had now gone, and it was distinctly gloomy in the crepuscular conditions of Hampden. The lights went on in the Press Box and the Stand, a clear sign that there was not long to go, but the referee would still not blow for time, allowing an inordinate amount for the few injuries that there had been and for the lengthy delay as the Swiss had argued the toss about that goal.

Eventually "Sweden, here we come!" said the commentator as Mr Leafe relieved the pressure on bladders and bowels throughout the land by pointing to the pavilion for fulltime. It was therefore a happy Scottish crowd which made its way back to cars and the queues for the trains. Tea, the traditional Scottish meal which got the blame for obesity and early deaths half a century later, was much enjoyed that night. Scotland had been invited to the feast of the World Cup finals.

So too had all the other British countries, as it turned out, and Scottish newspapers the following day tempered their joy with comments that this had been far from a vintage Scottish performance and that comparisons with more famous pre-war Scottish teams like the Wembley Wizards were not really appropriate. Still, Scotland had got the better of Spain and Switzerland, and they would be there in Sweden next summer. Rumour had it that the games would be televised. Was this an appropriate time to badger mother about whether we could afford a television?

v NORTHERN IRELAND 6-1
Windsor Park, Belfast; Att: 41,000
7 October 1961

Scotland:	Northern Ireland:
Brown (Tottenham Hotspur)	Gregg (Manchester United)
Mackay (Celtic)	Magill (Arsenal)
Caldow (Rangers)	Elder (Burnley)
Crerand (Celtic)	Blanchflower (Tottenham Hotspur)
McNeill (Celtic)	Neill (Arsenal)
Baxter (Rangers)	Peacock (Coleraine)
Scott (Rangers)	Wilson (Glenavon)
White (Tottenham Hotspur)	McIlroy (Burnley)
St. John (Liverpool)	Lawther (Blackburn Rovers)
Brand (Rangers)	Hill (Norwich City)
Wilson (Rangers)	McLaughlin (Shrewsbury Town)
Referee: Mr Finney, England	

YOU COULD SAY 1961 was a topsy-turvy year for Scotland. It was a significant year as well, for World Cup qualifiers were being played. But 1961 will always be recalled with horror by Scottish fans because of the 3-9 Wembley drubbing. The Wembley game was, by any standards, bad, but what should be remembered as well was the Scottish fight back, because by the time the team sailed to Northern Ireland on Friday 6 October, they had in their World Cup qualifying section beaten the other Ireland, Eire, twice (home and away) and won and lost to Czechoslovakia.

Eire were not a bad side in 1961 with men like Noel Cantwell, Charlie Hurley, Johnny Giles and Joe Haverty on board, but it was safe to say that Czechoslovakia presented the greater threat to Scotland's participation in the following year's finals. This was conclusively proved when the naïve Scotland side went down 0-4 in Bratislava, but then Scotland's resilience was shown when they beat the Czechs 3-2 at Hampden on the afternoon of 26 September (Hampden now had floodlights but they would not become operational until later that autumn). As goal average or goal difference did not count for the 1962 World Cup, this meant a one-off play-off in neutral Brussels against the Czechs on 29 November.

In the meantime Scotland had two Home International games against Northern Ireland in early October and Wales in what would turn out to be the first ever international under the floodlights at Hampden. There was thus a dual purpose in these two games. In the first place winning the Home International Championship was an end in itself in the early 1960s, but also there was the far more important World Cup, for which these games would provide the Selectors with food for thought for the vital play-off.

The World Cup was to be played in summer 1962 in faraway Chile, so faraway and little known in fact that one Scottish player when talking about it on a radio interview pronounced it as if it rhymed with 'mile' rather than 'chilly'! World Cup qualification was now looked upon as something important for Scotland because the globe was now shrinking and it was no longer the case that beating England was the *only* thing that mattered. It did matter, however, that 3-9 defeat was a constant thorn in the flesh of the whole nation, and it was something that needed to be exorcised.

Things were beginning to change, albeit slowly and reluctantly, in the Scotland set-up. There was now a manager in place called Ian McColl. He had a good tactical brain on him, as events would prove, but strangely he had no say in the selection of the team, something that was done by Selectors by vote. This system had been very successful for the Australian cricket team for many years, and to be fair, it had not been a total disaster for Scotland. (Scotland in 1961 had still beaten England more often than vice versa) but it creaked and reeked of a bygone age. One would like to think that McColl was consulted at least unofficially about who he wanted in the team, but there would be no guarantee. However, there was now a clear sign that a 'supremo' was needed, but there was still a reluctance to allow this to happen.

Scotland's victory over the Czechs had owed a lot to Denis Law. No-one doubted the multi-talented Law's commitment or attitude, but the problem was that he played in Italy for Torino, who now turned awkward about releasing him to play international football. There was little that Scotland could do about this – there had in the past been many problems with players who played for English clubs – but, as it happened, Law was allowed to play in the World Cup play-off, but not in the two British games. This was a blow, but it did open the door for others, in this case Ralph Brand of Rangers. Ralph was a member of a very talented Rangers side who won the League in 1961 beating off a determined challenge from Kilmarnock whom they had also beaten in the League Cup final. But there had been a major shock in the Scottish Cup final when after a replay Celtic had gone down to provincial no-hopers Dunfermline with a very ordinary team but an extraordinary young manager who looked as if he could go places. His name was Jock Stein.

Over the summer, a great half-back line had emerged in Crerand, McNeill and Baxter. McNeill, one of the survivors of Wembley, had impressed for Celtic with his cool positional play, his marvellous heading ability and the fact that he was very obviously a leader. Crerand and Baxter may have played for different sides of the Old Firm divide, but they had a great deal in common. In the first place there was superb passing ability with control over direction even in the wind and the rain, and the uncanny knowledge of just how much weight to put on the ball so that it arrived exactly in front of a colleague's feet. They were also both prone to getting themselves into trouble (Crerand had been sent off in Czechoslovakia) and did not take kindly to authority unless they respected it. In that, they had much in common with the 'Angry Young Man' figure of drama and literature of the time, but the talent was awesome.

Law's absence meant that Rangers supplied three of the forwards – Brand and two excellent wingers in Alec Scott and Davie Wilson. The other two forwards were John

White of Spurs and Ian St. John, who had cut his teeth with Motherwell but was now playing for Liverpool. It was the Old Firm who supplied the full-backs in Dunky Mackay and Eric Caldow, and in the goal was arguably Scotland's best ever goalkeeper in Bill Brown of Spurs (formerly of Dundee), who had now been restored following some unhappy flirtations with Frank Haffey and Lawrie Leslie.

The behaviour of the fans at this fixture was puzzling. It must be said that everyone behaved, even the many alcohol-fuelled Scottish supporters who came across on the 'Royal Ulsterman' and other ferries. But their chants and cries would have puzzled a neutral observer. It would have to be said that most of the Scotland fans going to this fixture were also Rangers fans, for whom the fortunes of the Scottish team were secondary to the fortunes of Rangers. England supporters at Wembley that year had been amazed to hear a mocking chant of 'Haffey! Haffey! Haffey!' at the Celtic goalkeeper as the nine goals sailed past him, and other Scottish fans were embarrassed to hear offensive cries about the Pope.

What was even more puzzling was the behaviour of the Northern Ireland fans (mainly of the Orange persuasion) who booed the Celtic players in the Scottish team but also now and again turned on their own Bertie Peacock, now with Coleraine, but who had spent most of his career with Celtic. Peacock indeed was a bigot's nightmare, for he was an Ulster Protestant who had been one of Celtic's best ever players and captains. This was rather too much for the less well-educated to take in and accept. Incongruously wearing green scarves in conjunction with their Red Hand of Ulster flags and Union flags, they sang their sectarian songs, including the one from Ibrox which said, 'With Heart and Hand and Ralphie Brand, we'll guard old Derry's Walls!' – but the said Ralphie Brand was playing AGAINST them! One wonders what Ralphie made of it all.

Not only was BRAND playing for Scotland, he was not far from being their best player, scoring twice, while ALEC SCOTT scored a hat-trick from the wing, withDAVIE WILSON scoring the other. This meant that all six goals in the thrashing of the hapless Irishmen were scored by Rangers players, and a Glasgow evening paper ran the unfortunate headline of 'Ireland 1 Rangers 6'. Quite rightly this was seen as an insult to the other members of the team, and an embarrassment to the Rangers players themselves – including captain Eric Caldow, who had gone out of his way to stress the value of the three Celtic players and the three Anglo-Scots.

In truth, it was the unanimous opinion of the Press that Scotland's best player was Pat Crerand. The *Sunday Post*, in particular, was emphatic in stating the irony of a situation whereby the Irish crowd would be upset that so much of their destruction was caused by a 'callant by the illustrious name of Pat.'

It was in all truth a rather one-sided game, but what must be stressed is that Northern Ireland were no bad side. Within the last 12 months they had given West Germany a couple of good games, losing by the odd goal on both occasions, and later that autumn they would beat Greece and draw with England (at Wembley), and they had in their ranks men like Danny Blanchflower the captain of Tottenham Hotspur (who had that year become the first team to win a League and Cup double in England in the 20th century) and Jimmy McIlroy of Burnley.

But on this occasion, the young Scotland team simply swept them aside. Inspired by Crerand and Baxter, the team seemed unstoppable, and it was difficult to resist the conclusion that had these two been at Wembley in April, the debacle would never have happened. On this day the Scotland team clearly decided that enough was enough at six, and that little mileage was to be gained in humiliating their fellow professionals in front of their home crowd.

The Scottish Press was naturally ecstatic about this performance and predicted great things about what would happen to the Czechs in Brussels. The euphoria was strengthened when under Hampden's new floodlights (described by one newspaper as 'like fairy land') Scotland beat Wales 2-0 in early November, with an equally impressive performance, the goals this time being scored by Ian St. John. A week previously the Scottish League side had drawn 1-1 with the Italian League, and things looked promising for the vital game.

Scotland suffered from two things in Brussels. One was the lack of any passionate atmosphere – for the crowd was about 6,000 as the days of a large travelling support had not yet arrived – and the other was a changed team. Denis Law was available and played, but Scott and Wilson, the two wingers, were injured and had to be replaced by Hugh Robertson of Dundee on the left wing (a fair choice for Robertson and Dundee were having good seasons) but on the right wing, when Steve Chalmers of Celtic also reported an injury, the mantle fell upon Ralph Brand for no reason other than that he had been displaced at inside-left by Denis Law. Brand had at one point been a right winger, but Rangers had moved him to inside-left for good reason.

Yet Scotland almost made it. 2-1 up within the last ten minutes, a partially cleared shot was hammered home by a Czech to equalize. Then in the break before extra-time, Crerand and Baxter, normally the best of friends, fell out visibly about a water bottle, John White hit the junction of the post and the bar ... and it is almost superfluous to add that the Czechs then added two and Scotland limped out of the tournament.

And what a loss that was! Scotland beat England in April to lift the Home International Championship and then sat at home listening to the radio, reading newspapers and watching edited highlights (no live coverage on TV was possible from Chile in 1962) of a very poor World Cup in which Czechoslovakia reached the final. But what would a full Scotland team, like the one that beat Northern Ireland in 1961, have done?

v ENGLAND 2-0

Hampden Park; Att: 134,000
14 April 1962

Scotland:	England:
Brown (Tottenham Hotspur)	Springett (Sheffield Wednesday)
Hamilton (Dundee)	Armfield (Blackpool)
Caldow (Rangers)	Wilson (Huddersfield Town)
Crerand (Celtic)	Anderson (Sunderland)
McNeill (Celtic)	Swan (Sheffield Wednesday)
Baxter (Rangers)	Flowers (Wolves)
Scott (Rangers)	Douglas (Blackburn Rovers)
White (Tottenham Hotspur)	Greaves (Tottenham Hotspur)
St. John (Liverpool)	Smith (Tottenham Hotspur)
Law (Turin)	Haynes (Fulham)
Wilson (Rangers)	Charlton (Manchester United)

Referee: Mr L. Horn, Holland

ALL SCOTLAND v England games are important, but the 1962 fixture was looked upon as slightly more important than most. There were several reasons for this. One was that it was only a year since the 9-3 Wembley catastrophe which the nation was keen to wipe from its consciousness, for it had been much talked about on BBC Television, a relatively new medium of communication which had the ability to intensify emotions of ecstasy and grief. Another was that it was now 25 years since Scotland had beaten England at Hampden Park, something that horrified the older supporters in particular for they recalled that before 1937, England had only ever won once at Hampden. Since 1937 there had been two draws in 1956 and 1960 – unlucky ones, both of them – but the rest of the meetings had been unmitigated disasters with England clearly the better team in almost every case. Scotland's only triumph had been in the unofficial Victory international of 1946. For a proud nation like Scotland, this was hard to bear.

An additional source of frustration was that while England would be going to the World Cup in Chile that summer, Scotland would not. This rankled with Scots fans, because, the 9-3 defeat notwithstanding, many people felt that this Scotland team had tremendous potential. There was, for example, a tremendous half-back line in Crerand, McNeill and Baxter – all of them young and all immensely talented. Pat Crerand was by some distance the best passer of the ball in British football, and 'Slim' Jim Baxter seemed capable of doing virtually anything. Up front there were speedy wingers in the Rangers pair of Alex Scott and Davie Wilson, and there was also Denis Law, currently playing for the Italian glamour side Turin, but pining for a return to British football.

A certain boost had been given to Scottish self-belief in a fine 4-3 win for the Scottish League over the English League on 21 March. This game, which had been shown in part on STV from Villa Park, Birmingham, had been a good, if narrow win featuring a hat-trick from Davie Wilson and some fine wing-half play from Pat Crerand. And that, of course, was with only Home-Scots playing that day, it being a League international. The team for the full international would be supplemented by Anglos – some of them great ones.

There would be four Tottenham Hotspur players appearing, two for each side: Bill Brown the goalkeeper and the fantastic inside-forward John White for Scotland, with Jimmy Greaves (who, like Law, had had a taste of Italian football) and Bobby Smith for England. Young Bobby Charlton whose survival of the Munich air disaster of four years earlier had made him a world celebrity was one of the very few Englishmen (Tom Finney and Stanley Matthews being some of the others) whom the Hampden crowd loved. Less popular was Johnny Haynes who, six years previously, had scored the last-minute goal which had deprived Scotland of their deserved victory.

1962 was the year in which the 'affluent society' had arrived. Television ownership was now at more than 85 per cent of the population, more and more working class families could afford a motor car, and refrigerators and washing machines were now usually given as wedding presents as life became a great deal easier for housewives. Posperity was shared by the working classes to an extent never dreamed of before, a fact resented by some older members of society with their clear and vivid memories of the horrors of wars and economic crises of previous decades.

Slums were being demolished and housing schemes with indoor toilets became more prevalent, although not yet universal. Some working class families even aspired to owning their own house. On the football field, with the official abolition of the Maximum Wage (blind eyes had in practice been turned to it to for some time), players were beginning to earn fortunes. They were well trained, athletic and constantly in the spotlight, particularly of the television cameras. Today's Scotland v England game, like those of 1956, 1958 and 1960, would be televised live.

The downside of this new affluent society was that attendances at football matches were beginning to drop as people now had alternative entertainment. Football clubs had been slow to see this trend and only began to improve their grounds with covered enclosures and other amenities when it was too late. Hampden itself was a grim example of this. It was a ground with virtually no cover at all, unless you were one of the lucky and rich patrons who could afford a stand ticket. Its celebrity (it was still in 1962 one of the largest and most famous grounds in Europe) was belied by its general filth and neglect, and on a wet day, one really could do with wellingtons for standing on the exposed terracings!

This was not however a problem this lovely spring day of 14 April 1962 as 132,431 made their way by car, bus, British Railways, blue train (the Glasgow suburban service) or even on foot to Hampden Park. Some of the Scottish crowd, tartan bedecked as always, were a trifle over-dressed, as tammies and scarves were far more suited to colder weather. But it was now the fashion (and it had been for a few years) for football fans to wear scarves of their team's colours, and if you were supporting Scotland, this meant tartan was *de rigueur.*

Signs of the times were visible in the appearance of 'The Hampden Bowl' – a ten pin bowling alley between Mount Florida railway station and the ground. 'The Hampden Bowl' had previously been the term used for the physical location of the pitch, which was so much lower than the high terraces, and had often been used in connection with the breeze which tended to blow there. But this term had been hijacked for this new sport, recently arrived from the USA and featured on television, but would it ever overtake football as the Scottish national passion? One wouldn't have thought so, judging by the sheer amount of people heading for the game, the impassioned pleas from the tickletless and the loud raucous cries of 'Offeecial Program' or 'Scotland Souvenir Speeshul' from the vendors.

Inside the ground was the impatient build-up with traditional Scottish singers and this time a team of scantily clad females doing a synchronised dance routine with footballs, but this was only a prequel to the real thing, and the noise which had been growing in volume steadily reached its crescendo as Eric Caldow and Johnny Haynes led out their respective teams at 2.55pm.

There was a slight breeze, but not enough to spoil the game and Scotland started off playing towards the Mount Florida end. Early corners were forced as Scotland's wingers were brought into play, and goalkeeper Ron Springett of England, one of many excellent English custodians at that time, was forced into early action. But with less than 15 minutes on the clock, Scotland went ahead in a great move. A pass from Crerand found Law who drew the goalkeeper out of his goal and then crossed for the unmarked DAVIE WILSON to score, even though an England defender was just able to reach the ball, but could only deflect it into the roof of the net.

Hampden erupted and the noise lasted the rest of the first half with only a temporary lull when Caldow cleared off his line with Brown beaten by a Haynes drive. Scotland pressed and pressed and the feeling grew that if they kept this up in the second half, the 9-3 defeat of last year could be replaced by a bigger victory. Scotland were so very much in control.

But England's team manager, a gentleman with the unlikely and much parodied name of Walter Winterbottom (the manager of a Scottish junior team called Alex Somerville was given the name of Sandy Summerarse!) rallied his troops at half-time and England, with the benefit of the breeze, came out in the second half a more determined and organised outfit, although they never really gained control of the midfield where Crerand, Baxter, Law and White were simply magnificent, covering for each other, finding each other with inch perfect passes and giving the impression that they were lifelong friends.

The controversial moment of the game came halfway through the second half. For once it was England who felt cheated and the funny thing was that the newspapers and the media never really picked up on the truth. The incident occurred on the right, on the far side of the field from the main stand, with England now attacking the Mount Florida end of the ground. A cross from Greaves on the right found Johnny Haynes, who hit the ball from outside the penalty box. The ball smacked the bar and came down on what looked to many observers and newspaper photographs to be the over the goal line – more clearly so in fact than in the Geoff Hurst incident in the World Cup final of four years later at Wembley – but the ball bounced out and it was put behind the goal by a Scottish defender. The referee Mr Horn then shocked the media by awarding a goal kick to Scotland – surely the wrong decision.

It was only the spectators in the corner of the ground who knew the truth – and only the eagle-eyed among them! Before Greaves crossed, a linesman had his flag up because he thought the ball had crossed the line, and therefore the decision to award Scotland a goal kick was in fact the correct one! Referees were not allowed to discuss decisions then, there were no playbacks and everyone missed the key fact of the linesman's flag. It was possibly the wrong decision by the official in a marginal call, but Dutch referee Mr Horn accepted his linesman's verdict.

Scotland breathed again, but although they now took control of the game, they were still only one goal ahead, and they did not need to be reminded that Greaves, Haynes and Douglas were all capable of turning any game. Those who had waited since 1937 for a Hampden victory (how long ago, that was ! – the imminent Coronation of King George VI, the strident bullies of Germany, the posters inviting young men to go and fight in Spain, the record crowd, Jimmy Delaney, Tommy Walker, Bob McPhail...) now crossed their legs and bit the cushions on their sofas in darkened rooms where curtains excluded the sun from spoiling the picture on the black and white Defiant or Ekco TV, while their children revealed equal signs of tension.

But then relief came suddenly. Peter Swan handled in his penalty area to break up a move between Ian St. John and Denis Law. Penalty kick! Penalties had played a significant part for England in the 1960 game at the same Kings Park end of the ground, but this was a penalty for Scotland and we were well within the last five minutes. Up stepped captain Eric Caldow to do the needful. Eric was a total gentleman, loved by his Rangers fans and even respected by the Celtic ones for his gentlemanly demeanour on the field of play, and it was on his benign shoulders that the nation's future happiness depended. The Hampden Roar became the Hampden Hush as he stepped up – and sent the previously brilliant Ron Springett the wrong way.

The next half hour was a blur with people, in many cases total strangers, hugging, kissing, jumping on each other's backs and doing things which are only socially acceptable when Scotland have beaten England. The team did a lap of honour, and the Englishmen were gracious enough to accept that the better side won, with BBC commentator Kenneth Wolstenholme particularly generous in his praise of the Scotsmen. But this was no ordinary victory. It redeemed Scotland from many shames, and made the side of manager Ian McColl famous for many years. If only they had been going to Chile that summer...

v ENGLAND 1-0
Hampden Park; Att: 133,245
11 April 1964

Scotland:	England:
Forsyth (Kilmarnock)	Banks (Leicester City)
Hamilton (Dundee)	Armfield (Blackpool)
Kennedy (Celtic)	Wilson (Huddersfield Town)
Greig (Rangers)	Milne (Liverpool)
McNeill (Celtic)	Norman (Tottenham Hotspur)
Baxter (Rangers)	Moore (West Ham United)
Henderson (Rangers)	Paine (Southampton)
White (Tottenham Hotspur)	Hunt (Liverpool)
Gilzean (Dundee)	Byrne (West Ham United)
Law (Manchester United)	Eastham (Arsenal)
Wilson (Rangers)	Charlton (Manchester United)

Referee: Mr L. Horn, Holland

I T RAINED AS it does frequently in Glasgow, but nothing was likely to rain on the Scottish party as the tartan tammied hordes thronged their way from Hampden to Mount Florida railway station, and thence to the centre of Glasgow where the party really began. 'Scots Wha Hae A Hat-Trick' crowed the *Glasgow Evening Times,* pointing out that this was the first time that Scotland had beaten England three times in a row since the 1880s, when life had been quite different.

Scotland was booming in 1964. Prosperity and vibrancy were in the air, as the baby boomers of the 1940s began to take over. The Beatles were all the rage, but they were only the spearhead of the pop music which had taken over the nation and shaken the establishment to the core. Curiously enough, the aristocracy still ruled in the shape of Sir Alec Douglas-Home, appointed (not elected) Prime Minister six months ago after a sexual scandal involving the minister of war which had brought down Harold Mcmillan. But it was already clear in the shape of the up and coming Labour Party of Harold Wilson that such days were numbered. This was the era of the young. The now decadent and effete ruling class which had served Britain for so long was very soon to be given the elbow.

Even the football field seemed to be a more prosperous place as we now had super-fit, well-paid young men wearing shorter pants, football boots that looked more like shoes and playing with a ball that was not necessarily brown any more. Smart polo necks replaced the heavy old collars, and the shirts were light in weight. The football itself was not necessarily any better – in fact if anything the 1960s militated against the individual player – but it was certainly faster. This generation after all was the first where everyone had been well fed and well cared for by the National Health Service.

Fixtures against European teams were now played, and teams flew to games against Inter Milan, Sporting Lisbon and the mighty Real Madrid who had set all Scotland alight with their marvellous display at Hampden four years previously in the 1960 European Cup final. Floodlights, television coverage and acres of newspaper gossip about the game showed not so much that the times they were a-changing; they had in fact changed, and changed totally.

But there remained the primeval Scotland v England battle which was now not all that far short of its 100th birthday. Scotland was still haunted by the 3-9 drubbing at Wembley in 1961, but they had fought back to win 2-0 at Hampden in 1962 and edge it 2-1 at Wembley the following year. Another win therefore would give a much coveted three in a row, something that England had done as recently as 1957, 1958 and 1959, and which still hurt.

Both teams now had managers (a sign of the times, perhaps). Scotland had Ian McColl, although it was probably true to say that 'coach' might be a better description of Ian, for he had little direct say over the team which was still picked by Selectors. England's manager was Alf Ramsey who had been a doughty foe a decade previously and was rumoured 'not to like Scotsmen'. If this were true, it would have been unusual as most Englishmen would be happy to admit a soft spot for Scotland, admittedly very often in a patronising way, saying how they enjoyed their holidays at Lock (sic) Lomond, and then frequently causing offence by imitating (badly) Scottish accents or making weak jokes about what a haggis was or wondering why Scotsmen did not wear kilts more often etc. But Scotland was always their favourite country, they loved Edinburgh, the Hebrides and everything was 'cute' or 'quaint'.

Scottish feelings towards England were as complex as they had always been over the past millennium or so. There was the traditional dislike of the imperial power, but there had never been any strong desire to leave the comfortable, symbiotic relationship. The Scottish National Party had not yet emerged, and there were no, as yet, strong feelings of antipathy towards the Royal Family, other than in the minds of Celtic supporters with their love of the Ireland of their forefathers. In football, however, there would be 90 minutes of hatred.

In domestic football, 1964 was definitely Rangers' year. Celtic, from top to bottom, had such an ingrained inferiority complex that they felt they were not allowed to beat Rangers. Their good run in Europe was, as everyone pointed out, in a competition where Rangers were not their opponents. Rangers, on the other hand, while rampant in Scotland, had repeatedly failed in Europe, going down this season to an embarrassing tanking from Real Madrid, 0-1 at Ibrox, which was respectable, and 0-6 at the Bernabeu, which was not.

The Rangers team breathed Protestant supremacy, wealth and arrogance. They did indeed have some fine players, however, notably Jim Baxter who, for the moment at least was being held, to a certain extent, in check by the strict Rangers discipline. There were also Willie Henderson and Davie Wilson, two fine wingers who could pick up what Baxter offered from midfield and utilise it, and a tough character called John Greig, who had recently emerged. Celtic's two members of the Scotland team were Billy McNeill, the superbly inspirational captain and left-back Jim Kennedy who, some felt, was lucky to be in the team, but who had never really let Celtic or Scotland down. Dundee supplied two men – one was the charismatic and extroverted Alec Hamilton at right-back, and the other was the prodigiously talented striker Alan Gilzean. Dundee, in fact were the team that supplied the most threat to Rangers in those days. They had won the Championship in 1962 and done well in Europe in 1963. A key factor in this success was down to their ability to take a goal, mainly through Gilzean, a quiet, shy, retiring character from a village called Coupar Angus (for whom he played cricket in the summer) and who apparently once said that he did not really like football – it just so happened that he was good at it! He would go on to have a magnificent career for Tottenham Hotspur after he left Dundee following a rather bitter and nasty transfer saga.

The other Home-Scot in the side was goalkeeper Campbell Forsyth of Kilmarnock, and the two Anglos were John White of Spurs and Denis Law of Manchester United. Law was a remarkable player, but one about whom arguments raged among the Scottish support. No-one doubted his ability nor his love of Scotland. It was just that sometimes his attitude seemed wrong. Perhaps, like Dalglish 20 years later, he was such a good player that he was expected to be a world beater every time he put on a Scotland jersey. A mega-star like Law was not really allowed to have just a 'good' game; it had to be 'brilliant'. There was also John White, a consistently good forager and goalscorer for Spurs. He had already played 20 times for Scotland, and looked like a fixture in the team for many years. What no-one was to know was that he was fated to die on 21 July that year on Enfield Golf Course. It was a freak accident, for he was hit by a lightning bolt while sheltering under a tree during a thunderstorm. It is generally agreed that had he lived, he would have been considered one of the best players of all time. As it was, his record spoke for itself.

Scotsmen were glad of their tammies and tartan bonnets, for they kept their heads dry during the incessant rain which fell all day. Hampden offered minimum shelter, that being reserved for those rich enough to afford a stand seat at 10 shillings (50 pence). The majority of the crowd stood in the wet on the primitive, but still grandly impressive terracings which towered over the field of play but which tended also to be a channel for the downward surge of wind which had spoiled so many games at Hampden in the past.

The game was broadcast live on BBC TV and STV, but only to viewers in Scotland. In the 1960s a live football match on television was indeed a rare thing, although since 1956, the Scotland v England games at Hampden had been televised live, albeit often after a struggle with the SFA who kept saying that television was the thin edge of the wedge and that soon no-one would go to games in the flesh if they were all televised. This has since been proved to be rubbish, but was firmly believed by those in power at the time, and they were usually successful in preventing the transmission of the Scottish Cup final, for example. There was more than a touch of paternalistic Scottish Calvinism about all this, for Scotland's leaders were never good at allowing their people to enjoy themselves without feelings of martyrdom and guilt trips. Anyway, it being a rainy day, those who did not have tickets (133,245 did) sat down gratefully in their living room to watch the game.

That the times were changing was further proved by the half-time and pre-match entertainment. There was still a little of the Scottish stuff with pipe bands and singing, including the talented but distinctly over-exposed Andy Stewart with his 'Scottish Soldier', but there was also a pop group called Dean Ford and the Gaylords and an Invitation two mile race in which one Lachie Stewart featured. Lachie would some six years later win a gold medal for Scotland in the Edinburgh Commonwealth games. Some scantily clad young females (poor things in this weather) calling themselves the Glasgow Keep Fit Movement did a gymnastic routine and invited all sorts of suggestive and sometimes more blatant comments from the lecherous. A further decade or so down the line, and the women's movements would have put a stop to all that.

Scotland started off playing towards the King's Park end of the ground, but it took a long time for play to settle. The conditions were tricky, and there was also the undeniable fact that both teams were good enough to cancel each other out. If anything England had the better of the early play, but gradually the Scottish midfield of Law and Baxter began to exert some sort of command on the game. Half-time came however without either goalkeeper being seriously troubled. The Massed Pipes and Drums of the Argyll and Sutherland Highlanders attempted to cheer everyone up.

When the real entertainment started again, Scotland, now in command of the conditions, pressed and pressed with the Rangers wingers Henderson and Wilson coming more and more into the game. There were several penalty claims, never more so than in the 72nd minute when Alan Gilzean was clearly impeded when running in on goal. But Mr Horn was not impressed and pointed to award a corner kick on the left instead.

It was from this corner that the decisive goal came. Davie Wilson took it and ALAN GILZEAN rose above Bobby Moore and Maurice Norman to head home. Hampden erupted as total strangers grabbed each other, hugged, kissed and danced. It was no more than Scotland had deserved for their fine play, but there were another 18 minutes for England to come back. England did just that, and played better in the final stages than they had all game, forcing the Scottish defence to earn their pay. But McNeill, Hamilton and Kennedy were resolute and Forsyth was seldom troubled except when a Maurice Norman effort shaved the bar as time was running out.

But eventually Mr Horn blew for time, and Hampden, a microcosm of Scotland that day, exploded with joy. The game having been seen throughout the land, the joy was shared, and indeed it was great joy. The World Cup in two years time was to be held in England, it was said. You know, we could just about fancy Scotland to win it! Certainly, England had no hope...

v ITALY 1-0
Hampden Park; Att: 100,393
9 November 1965

Scotland:	Italy:
Brown (Tottenham Hotspur)	Negri (Bologna)
Greig (Rangers)	Burgnich (Inter Milan)
Provan (Rangers)	Facchetti (Inter Milan)
Murdoch (Celtic)	Guarneri (Inter Milan)
McKinnon (Rangers)	Salvadore (Juventus)
Baxter (Sunderland)	Rosato (Torino)
Henderson (Rangers)	Lodetti (AC Milan)
Bremner (Leeds United)	Mazzola (Inter Milan)
Gilzean (Tottenham Hotspur)	Rivera (AC Milan)
Martin (Sunderland)	Bulgarelli (Bologna)
Hughes (Celtic)	Barison (Roma)

Referee: Herr Kreitlein, West Germany

FOOTBALL WAS QUITE clearly on a high in Scotland in autumn 1965, and most of the excitement centred around a man called Jock Stein. Appointed manager of Celtic earlier that year, he was now showing signs of awakening that sleeping giant and offering a real challenge to the hegemony of Rangers which Scotland had not seen for many years. The national team too had jumped on the Stein bandwagon by appointing him temporary manager of Scotland following the departure of Ian McColl to Sunderland.

The World Cup qualifying campaign this year had an added edge to it in that the finals would be played in England. With a little imagination, Scotland's game could be scheduled for, say, Sunderland or Middlesbrough and it would be like playing at home. In any case, Scotland felt that they *should* be there, or at least their fans did.

Scotland's fans had always been a wheen more interested in qualifying for World Cup finals than administrators had given the impression of, presumably because the administrators feared that it might lose them money. But things were totally different now. The mega-buck culture of football possibly had not yet totally arrived, but playing in the World Cup, especially if the finals were to be held just over the border, now brought prestige and finance. For these reasons, the SFA had moved to get Jock Stein, the best manager around, to do the job, and even though they could not dislodge him permanently from Celtic, they would settle for him on a part-time basis.

That is one way of looking at it. Another was that it was a cheap way of getting a manager in the short term without having to pay him too much. It might have been better to go for someone on a long term basis, but Jock it was who entered upon the job with as much enthusiasm as he showed for Celtic. It was a shame that he would be less successful with the national side than with his club, whose supporters he would soon lead to untold and unbelievable riches.

Scotland were drawn with Finland, Poland and Italy in the qualification group. The streetwise Italians had outmanoeuvred the SFA into agreeing that the last game would be in Italy, so that the Italians would be in the happy position of playing a home game at the end of the campaign. But Scotland had started well. Finland had been disposed of twice, albeit none too convincingly in either case, and there had been a very creditable draw in Poland, but it was the game against Poland in Scotland that had made life difficult. It is hard to analyse exactly what went wrong that night. Scotland had already appalled their followers by going down to Northern Ireland in the Home International Championship at the beginning of October and then eleven days later seemed to have committed hari-kari by losing through two late goals to Poland after having looked so comfortable for long periods of the game. An indication of the interest in this match lay in the astonishing crowd of 107,580 (a record for a World Cup qualifier) who turned up. Seldom have so many people been so shattered in such a short time as five minutes.

It was the era of six figure crowds at Hampden. Both the Cup finals of 1965 attracted enormous attendances, and when 100,393 came to see the Italy game, this meant that four times in the calendar year of 1965 Hampden had housed such huge crowds. Had England been at Hampden that year, there would have been another. It was astounding that such a small country could produce such attendance figures, and even the English and the foreign press were mightily impressed. Whatever Scotland lacked, it was not support or commitment, it being no uncommon sight on these evening games to see men coming in with their piece bags, having come straight from work.

Such enthusiasm deserved some kind of reward. The position was that if Scotland could beat Italy home and away, they would qualify. A win and a draw would lead to a play-off. It would take a major effort, and any rational analysis would have to favour the talented Italians to win both games, but hope has always sprung eternal for the Scottish fan, and the prize of a World Cup place in England next summer was indeed a tempting one.

Arguments raged up and down the land about certain players. Denis Law and Jim Baxter, for example, were as good players as one would find anywhere in the world, but Law had seemed out of sorts against Northern Ireland and Poland. Against that, of course, he did have experience of Italian football and his exploits for Manchester United meant that the Italians respected and feared him. Jim Baxter, until breaking his leg last year, had been outstanding for Rangers for a few seasons – but that was in the time when there was no strong Celtic to oppose him, and his career had not been helped by his move to join Ian McColl at Sunderland. Similarly, John Hughes had his backers. Once again the phrase 'on his day' had to be used in qualification to any statement involving the words 'world class', but his unorthodox style might just break through the Italians, as indeed could Willie Henderson whose crosses could be so deadly if they found the head of Alan Gilzean, who had scored the goal against England 18 months earlier.

As it turned out, Stein wielded the axe, and out went Alex Hamilton of Dundee and Pat Crerand, both of them carrying the can for the Poland fiasco. John Greig, Rangers' talented but hard midfielder was played at right-back and partnering him was his Rangers colleague Davie Provan, as Eddie McCreadie of Chelsea was suspended. In place of Crerand at right-half, Stein brought in Bobby Murdoch whom he was grooming for stardom in that position for Celtic, while a last minute injury meant that Billy McNeill had to be ruled out and was replaced by Ronnie McKinnon.

There would be no Denis Law, fuelling the suspicion that Stein did not approve of his sometimes apparently flippant approach to playing for Scotland, but Jim Baxter not only played, he was made captain. In the forward line, Henderson and Hughes were given the nod and were supplemented by Gilzean, the as yet inexperienced but determined Billy Bremner, and Neil Martin, the last named being perhaps a surprise. However Stein had been his manager at Hibs a year previously and knew Martin's capabilities.

It was Italy's first ever visit to Hampden Park, although some of their players had played in Scotland previously for one or other of the Milan teams in the European Cup against Dundee in 1963 or Rangers in 1965. Signor Edmondo Fabbri, the Italian team manager, (generally regarded as a lightweight without the personality of Inter Milan's Helenio Herrera for example), chose a team which he hoped would earn a draw. The Italians were regarded as experts in that field, and absolutely none of the 100,393 crowd expected a game of fast-flowing attacking football.

The game would not be televised, except in highlight form late at night. Given the huge attendance and passionate interest in the game throughout the land, this is perhaps surprising, but the argument always was that the reason why six figure crowds flocked to Hampden Park with such regularity was because the game was NOT on the 'box'. This argument had only partial validity, and it certainly seems now to be wrong, for crowds still go to Hampden to see a good game even when the game is televised. The BBC and STV would have paid handsomely, and it may be that the SFA missed a trick here.

There was also the moral argument. If the SFA wanted to make Scotland the nation's team (as it undeniably was) their games should surely be made accessible to the entire nation, including those unable to travel for reasons of health, work commitments or sheer distance. It was, of course, none too easy to travel from places like Aberdeen or Inverness on a Tuesday night to Glasgow. It was amazing however to see the amount of people who did just that.

It was therefore Hampden or the radio for the nation that night. Scotland started kicking off towards the Mount Florida End, but as everyone predicted, they ran into the equivalent of a brick wall as the Italians pulled their men back and remained superbly organised, knowing when to foul and when not to foul and generally frustrating the Scottish attacks by cutting off supplies to the eager wingers of Henderson and Hughes, both of whom became dispirited. Baxter and Murdoch supplied the ammunition, but it was difficult to pull the trigger.

Italy on the other hand attacked rarely but effectively, and it was as well for Scotland that Bill Brown in the goal was in top form and that John Greig and Davie Provan were able to clear their lines when needed. Gianni Rivera, reputedly the best player in the world, was in top form, and with him on the field, Scotland could never feel secure even in the limited objective of achieving a draw. The longer the game went on in the second half, the more the Italians retreated into their own shell, but it was a secure one. Gilzean had a good chance and Martin a half-chance, but nothing came of them, and the Scotland crowd's backing began to lessen as one or two of the weaker elements decided on an early exit, the better to avoid the appalling traffic jams that a six figure crowd would involve around the sadly inadequate road system.

But then it happened. The radio commentators were becoming more and more pessimistic and telling the disheartened nation that only two minutes remained when Baxter, who had been quiet for some time, picked up a ball in midfield and slid it through to, of all people, JOHN GREIG, who had deserted his defensive duties in sheer desperation of a goal arriving somehow, anyhow. John ran into space and beat the goalkeeper, who, frankly, for all Scotland's pressure had been distinctly under-employed.

Greig very soon disappeared under a rugby scrum of his team-mates, and shrieks of joy were heard from living rooms and bedrooms all over the country as the radio relayed the glad tidings to the nation. That goal would be replayed *ad infinitum* on the television for many months, and it was a great one, proving that it would need something special to beat that Italian defence. It was enjoyed time after time.

It did indeed give the nation a temporary feelgood factor, but this had to be tempered by the realisation that Scotland had still to beat Italy in Naples – a far taller order than winning before 100,000 eager fanatics at Hampden. A draw would produce a play-off. This made the defeat by Poland all the more galling, for if that had not happened, Scotland would only have needed a draw in Naples and even a defeat might have earned them a play-off. Not for the first nor the last time, Scotland had shot themselves in the foot.

In the event, player unavailability and faulty tactics led to disaster in Naples, and Scotland were reduced to being mere spectators of the 1966 World Cup. That was a shame, for Scotland in conditions that suited them and with their huge support behind them might just have done well. As it happened, Italy came to England in the summer and managed to lose to North Korea. Signor Fabbri was lucky to avoid a lynch mob when he returned home. But was it perhaps a blessing in disguise that Scotland weren't there? It would have been dreadful if North Korea had headed the list that already contained Paraguay and would one day be supplemented by Peru, Iran and Costa Rica...

v ENGLAND 3-2
Wembley; Att: 99,063
15 April 1967

Scotland:	England:
Simpson (Celtic)	Banks (Leicester City)
Gemmell (Celtic)	Cohen (Fulham)
McCreadie (Chelsea)	Wilson (Everton)
Greig (Rangers)	Stiles (Manchester United)
McKinnon (Rangers)	J. Charlton (Leeds United)
Baxter (Sunderland)	Moore (West Ham United)
Wallace (Celtic)	Ball (Everton)
Bremner (Leeds United)	Greaves (Tottenham Hotspur)
McCalliog (Sheffield Wednesday)	R. Charlton (Manchester United)
Law (Manchester United)	Hurst (West (Ham United)
Lennox (Celtic)	Peters (West (Ham United)

Referee: Herr G. Schulenberg, West Germany

THINGS WERE STIRRING in Scottish football in 1967. Celtic, Rangers and Kilmarnock were all going strong in Europe, and after some years of a drop in attendances, there were clear signs that the crowds were beginning to come back. There were several reasons for this – the main one being the resurgence of Celtic with their massive support – but whatever the cause, football was back on the agenda. Not that it had ever really disappeared, for the love affair of a Scotsman with his national game is an eternal phenomenon, but people were becoming more and more animated, and they approached the England game at Wembley with more than the usual excitement.

The reason? Scotland had suffered badly when England had won the World Cup the previous summer. The crowing and the gloating – officially sanctioned gloating on the BBC – had been hard to thole, but there was also the nagging feeling that Scotland could have done it as well. Ridiculous myths grew up that it was all the fault of the English that Scotland hadn't qualified – because their clubs wouldn't release Scottish players for World Cup qualifiers – but the truth was that it was the old Scottish characteristic of self-destruction that had led to our downfall in the failure to qualify. Yet what could not be denied was that Scottish talent would certainly have graced the World Cup stage in 1966, and now here, belatedly, a year later was the opportunity to show what might have been.

This was the first match in charge for the gentlemanly manager Bobby Brown. At first sight, he did not look cut out for the job. He had been a goalkeeper with Queen's Park and Rangers, and had established a reputation for being one of the most sporting and honest players in what could sometimes be a dirty game. He had made a good job of managing St. Johnstone, but a sterner test lay ahead in the poisoned chalice of the Scotland job.

He was fortunate in having both members of the Old Firm in top gear, and naturally leaned heavily on them. In addition he had three 'wild geese' in Billy Bremner, Denis Law and Jim Baxter – three superbly talented players with few equals in world football. If these three could all perform to their potential, nothing in the world could stop them. But the moulding of these three disparate and individualistic characters into an effective midfield unit would be no easy task. It would be the first real test of Bobby Brown.

Other choices were surprising. Jim McCalliog of Sheffield Wednesday, a total unknown, was given his debut, but Brown then shocked the footballing world by inviting Ronnie Simpson, at the age of 36, to take the goalkeeping job. This decision was taken in collusion with Celtic's manager Jock Stein, who stated that at that moment Simpson was the best goalkeeper around, better than younger man like Herriot, Ferguson, Cruickshanks and Forsyth, who were all credible candidates. Brown and Simpson went back a long way to their Queen's Park days at the end of the second world war, and Simpson did have a wealth of experience behind him, including a couple of successful visits to Wembley to win English Cup medals with Newcastle United in 1952 and 1955. He had even played there with the Great Britain Olympic Games team of 1948. In more recent times Simpson had won two Scottish League Cup medals and a Scottish League medal with Celtic, but to be an international debutant at the age of 36 did seem odd. Perhaps Brown's heart was ruling his head, people feared, and Scotland might regret the decision.

England, for their part, had cause to feel apprehensive about the impending meeting with the Auld Enemy. As is often the case, constant adulation can have a deleterious effect and there were clear signs that some heads were swelling to impossible proportions. In addition, some of the wiser elements in the team were uncomfortably aware that at least some of the jibes coming at them from Scotland and overseas were not without their validity. They had been allowed to play all their home games at Wembley, some of their football had been rather negative and the Argentinians possibly did not get a fair deal from the referee in the infamous quarter-final. It might also have been different if Pele's opponents had not set out to crock him and if England had therefore met Brazil – and then, of course, that ball was clearly not entirely over the line in the final! All these things may well have weighed on their minds, and there was also the undeniable fact that while Scottish club sides were doing well in European competitions, their equivalent English teams were nowhere in sight.

There was also the character of the manager Alf Ramsey. He could be indiscreet. His use of the word 'animals' to describe the Argentinian team would never be forgiven. He was also quoted by those who knew him as saying on several occasions that he did not like Scotsmen. All this was true, but also true was the indisputable fact that ever since the World Cup triumph, England remained unbeaten. Scottish fans would have to express some reluctant admiration for at least some of the English team. Goalkeeper Gordon Banks, for instance, was world class, as indeed was Bobby Charlton and perhaps his less immediately likeable brother Jack. Bobby Moore radiated composure, and the only change from the World Cup winning team, Jimmy Greaves for Roger Hunt, was hardly to the team's detriment.

The tartan-clad hordes who assembled at places like Glasgow Central Station and Edinburgh Waverley on the Friday night were following the traditional template, but they were a different breed – better fed, better clad than ever before, even singing songs of the Beatles and the Rolling Stones. Everyone moaned about the Labour Government of Harold Wilson and how badly he was doing with the 'balance of payments' and the 'gnomes of Zurich' (even though few people knew exactly what these phrases meant), but the truth was that everyone was really doing very well in an era of full employment and sustained prosperity, no matter how much the right wing press tried to convince us otherwise. In addition to those who travelled by rail, there was now another (admittedly still rather small) detachment of the Scotland support who could afford to go by air. The Tartan Air Force had been born, and they could wait until the Saturday morning before they travelled.

The Scotland hotel outside London opened its doors to reporters and photographers. As well as the usual 'we are all out to do well' and 'quietly confident' clichés, one could detect a determination in the likes of Baxter and Law, and there was a particularly vicious plot to wind up Alan Ball by mimicking his high-pitched voice and call him the 'Clitheroe Kid', a character in a radio programme of the time played by 4 foot 3 inch comedian Jimmy Clitheroe. There were the usual Scottish high spirits, as well, but there would be no 'night on the town' until after the game. This game was so important that Scottish self-destruction had to be put on the back burner – at least until after the match.

As was usually the case, more than half of Wembley was occupied by Scottish fans, raucously singing their normal repertoire of songs mingling nice romantic Robbie Burns and Harry Lauder songs with unpleasant stuff about England and the Queen, but concentrating mainly on the repetitive chant of 'Scotland! Scotland!' A few bagpipes made an appearance as well, but sadly discordant, tuneless and cacophonic.

England had been much criticised for their 4-3-3 formation, but Scotland were now employing something similar, although it was more 4-4-2 with Wallace and Lennox being the two strikers, joined from time to time by Law and McCalliog. Team formations, of course, do not win or lose matches. It is how well the players adapt to such formations that determine these outcomes. Today at Wembley, it was Scotland who were the more aggressive, more positive side.

Just on the half hour mark, Scotland went ahead. Willie Wallace, playing with the same aggression that his namesake used to show many centuries ago against the English in those much romanticised but dreadfully bloodthirsty wars, tried a shot which was blocked. The ball came back to DENIS LAW who gratefully accepted the offer, raising his arm in his characteristic manner as the tartan exploded all round Wembley.

Half-time came and went with Scotland supporters in a fervour, and the radio commentators mightily impressed by the Scottish commitment, but waiting for the English backlash. The game was not on television, for this was still the era of the curmudgeonly BBC and SFA combination which feared that the nation might be somehow enervated or demoralised if it was allowed to enjoy itself, so those Scottish supporters not at Wembley were gathered round radios which were now often part of a radiogram which also played Beatles records. Or there were transistor radios, sometimes very small boxes carried around and held close to the ear, for neither the sound quality nor the volume was particularly good, and they gave off a sort of a crackle, which became a mini-explosion when the commentator became excited.

Much was often made in later years about Jim Baxter playing keepie-uppie as if Scotland were totally dominant and toying with the opposition. Baxter did do this once or twice, but in reality the second half, although Scotland remained on top, was far too tense for that. England were not, after all, World Champions for nothing, and, albeit hampered by injuries to key players, fought hard against the nation which was their oldest opponents.

No further goals came until the last ten minutes when there was a veritable flurry with each side scoring twice. First BOBBY LENNOX became the first Celtic player to score at Wembley, then JACK CHARLTON, one of England's walking wounded and playing at centre-forward as the World Champions sought to upset the hitherto comfortable Scottish defence, pulled one back. Wembley was now in a raptures as Scotland scored again through debutant JIM McCALLIOG. The Dark Blues seemed home and dry at 3-1 with time running out. But Scotland never do things the easy way, and a moment's slackness saw GEOFF HURST ghost in unmarked to pull it back to 3-2.

The crowd and the commentators now seemed to think that anything could happen, and it was an uncomfortable minute or two for those in the tartan. England had specialised in late goals in the previous summer's triumph, but after some heavy pressure was soaked up by the Scots Herr Schulenberg signalled full-time and the Scottish fans simply took over. There was none of the hooliganism which would destroy goalposts on subsequent occasions but there was a certain amount of dancing and turf pinching by the delighted fans, as the Scotland players reached the security of their dressing room in the knowledge that they had become the first nation to defeat the 1966 World Champions.

Euphoria reigned rightly in Scotland for a long time after that, and those who delighted in Celtic's triumphs had even greater cause to celebrate when they became the first British team to lift the European Cup in May. But Scotland's success at Wembley had to be tempered by two considerations. One was why they could not have won the World Cup itself? Claims that the defeat of England meant that Scotland were now the World Champions were specious nonsense. And the other 'wet blanket' point made by the pessimists was that sooner or later, Scotland, being Scotland, would 'blow it' and ruin all the previous good work. They did just that. Less than a month later, they went down 0-2 (including a horrendous own goal by Tommy Gemmell) to the USSR at Hampden, and by October they had contrived to lose to Northern Ireland in Belfast 0-1, and it would have been more if Ronnie Simpson had not saved a penalty kick!

v CZECHOSLOVAKIA 2-1
Hampden Park; Att: 100,000
26 September 1973

Scotland:	Czechoslovakia:
Hunter (Celtic)	Viktor
Jardine (Rangers)	Pivarnik
McGrain (Celtic)	Samek
Hay (Celtic)	Zlocha
Holton (Manchester United)	Bendl
Hutchison (Coventry City)	Bicovsky
Bremner (Leeds United)	Panenka**
Connelly (Celtic)	Kuna*
Morgan (Manchester United)	Adamec
Dalglish* (Celtic)	Nehoda
Law (Manchester City)	Stratil
Sub	*Subs*
Jordan* (Leeds United)	Dobias*
	Capkovic**

Referee: Mr H. Oberg, Norway

T HIS YEAR, 1973 was a year of crisis. Few parts of the world would be unaffected by the Arab-Israeli war that was to start in October. Oil prices would rise with dire consequences for world economies. Great Britain was soon to have its own Government versus miners dispute, and the United States of America was obsessed by the long slow process of proving to itself (the rest of the world had twigged a lot earlier) that its President, Richard M. Nixon was telling lies about his involvement in the Watergate burglary of his opponents' headquarters. Scottish football was bleating on about suffering from low attendances, largely due to too many televised highlights. So all in all, it was as well that we had this game to cheer us up before the fun of three-day weeks, strikes, electricity and fuel shortages really started in the winter.

The 1974 World Cup finals were to be held in West Germany. It was a tournament which Scotland had sadly not been present at for the last 16 years. This was emphatically not due to lack of talent – the 1960s will remain a golden age of Scottish football – but due to lack of ability to deliver, particularly away from home, when the chips were down. This time life seemed different. Denmark had already been beaten home and away, yet the Danes had done well against the talented Czechs. This meant that victory for Scotland over the Czechs either home or away would ensure qualification from the three team group.

But 1972 and 1973 had been difficult years for the Scottish national team. Tommy Docherty had appeared as the manager and, for a while, convinced everyone that he was to be the Messiah to lead us to the promised land and make us forget the appalling truth that hung over all Scotsmen and Scotswomen still in 1972 – that England had won the World Cup in 1966. Tommy had good results against Denmark, but then succumbed, to the distress of the nation that adored him, to the monetary temptation of England and Manchester United. Twas ever thus, it was said. Robbie Burns used to tell us about the 'hireling few' that sold Scotland in 1707. But Tommy's departure was hard to take.

His replacement was Willie Ormond, a quiet, unpretentious man who had been a great player for Hibs and a good manager for St. Johnstone. But those pessimists who feared that he was not up to the job had cause for their despair in Willie's early performances. His first game, for example, was in February 1973 against England in a special one-off match to celebrate the centenary of the SFA. On a frosty, foggy night, Scotland went down 0-5. It was a spectacular, quintessentially Scottish self-destructive flop, but then things got worse. Scotland managed to lose again to England in May at Wembley, but only after they had shocked their own fans at Hampden by losing to Northern Ireland. They then played two ill-advised friendlies in midsummer against Switzerland away from home and Brazil at home – and lost them both, leaving Willie with only one success in 1973 – against a poor Wales side at Wrexham.

The omens were therefore anything but favourable as Scotland geared themselves for the visit of the Czechs on 26 September. But the Scottish fan remains optimistic, sometimes excessively and irrationally so, and pointed out things like how good the team's record was at Hampden, that the crowd, limited to 100,000 on police advice, would lift the team, that we had men like Kenny Dalglish and Billy Bremner and even the now ageing Denis Law who would see us home. Then the nation was given a great boost with the news that the game was to be televised live on STV. It is perhaps difficult for us to appreciate, some 36 years later, exactly what this meant. Live television coverage is now almost automatic, but in the 1970s Scottish football was still controlled by those of a Calvinistic persuasion who believed that nice things were bad for you and that if the game was on TV, somehow or other, the nation would become demoralised and effete. Not only that, but they would stop going to junior games and Second Division games and ... the arguments went on, but sometimes, enough money was offered and the game was allowed.

It meant that in a very real sense, the 11 men of Scotland would have the nation behind them in a very real sense. It was apparently not unknown for Scotland managers to reel off a huge long list of places in Scotland – Edinburgh, Benbecula, Hawick, Kyle of Lochalsh, Brechin, Elgin etc, then say: 'In every one of these places tonight, people are depending in you!' In effect, the nation stopped that night with evening classes, drama groups and keep fit classes all bowing to reality and having a night off so that men, women and children could watch Scotland try to reach the World Cup finals for the first time for years. Not everyone as yet had a colour television, but the news that the game was to be televised led to an upsurge in demand for this new innovation.

Ormond's team selection included George Connelly. It would be his first cap. This was an immensely talented young man, but who had serious personality problems and would be described by his team manager Jock Stein in later years as 'unable to cope with the psychological side of the game'. He had walked out of the Scotland party before the game against Switzerland in the summer, and many people wondered whether he was suitable to play in a game of this magnitude. But Ormond had consulted his old rival Stein, and Jock had given the nod. It would turn out to be a wise decision.

Further controversy surrounded the selection of Denis Law. It had seemed to many observers that his chances of going to the World Cup finals had passed, and what a shame it was that the world had not seen Denis in his prime on this particular stage. Law himself would be the first to confess that the best days of his footballing life were behind him, but he was still such a brilliant player that, even in the twilight of his career, Ormond felt that he might just be the man to lead Scotland to West Germany.

One or two other men were far from household names. Jim Holton had played before but without any real distinction, Tam Hutchison was also a debutant, and not everyone was convinced about Willie Morgan. On the other hand Colin Stein and Derek Johnstone might have improved things had they been available, and where was Jimmy Johnstone? Prickly, nervous and insecure, but on his day the greatest player in the world and one who could terrorise and twist his way round the burly and insecure Czechs.

The pundits had predicted that Czechoslovakia would pack their defence, be quite happy with a draw (for then they could qualify by winning the return match in Bratislava) and would even try, knowing the Scottish death wish of poor defending, to score a goal on the break. In this respect they were proved right, for Scotland opened strongly and had several shots blocked or saved by a well organised Czech defence who were not above a little 'raw meat' from time to time. Several Scottish players, notably Dalglish, were targeted by the brutal defenders, although Scotland were more than capable of looking after themselves. Certainly Billy Bremner gave as good as or as bad as he got.

The crowd, sensing that Scotland were in the mood, roared them on but on the half hour mark were stunned by an appalling Scottish goalkeeping blunder. Around this time, Scottish keepers were a standing joke on English television programmes and the cause of the Scottish custodian was not helped by Celtic's Ally Hunter on this occasion. Zdeněk Nehoda, in an attempt to take the pressure off his defence, tried a shot which one could not even describe as 'speculative' in that it was just a punt towards the Scottish goal, lacking any strength or venom. Hunter got both hands to the ball, but somehow or other it squirmed into the net.

The cauldron of Hampden was suddenly transformed into a cemetery and living rooms throughout Scotland lapsed into the mourning that one associates with a death in the family. In this case it was punctuated with a few curses and execrations, as poor Ally Hunter became neither the first nor the last Scottish goalkeeper to be turned into the nation's whipping boy.

The deathly atmosphere prevailed for a few minutes while Scotland regrouped from this blow. And regroup they did. It was a spirited performance at the end of the first half, and the goal which arrived, though unexpected, was not undeserved. Hard work by Denis Law won a corner, the impressive Tam Hutchison took it, up jumped a posse of players and it was JIM HOLTON who outjumped both friend and foe to head home. Those who had never heard of Jim Holton before, knew who he was now! The half-time whistle came soon afterwards and Hampden was once more seething with excitement as the teams went off.

The TV studio saw future Scotland manager Ally MacLeod in full flow. In one brilliant phrase he described the Czech defenders as a "bunch of crunchers" – an onomatopoeic phrase which was many times repeated in the next few days. But Ally, optimistic as ever, remained convinced that Scotland could "do it". The million or so viewers wanted to believe, but feared that the 'crunchers' might win the day.

Early in the second half, Ormond made a decision which would prove to be the match-winning one. The young and as yet still fragile Dalglish was obviously tiring, the victim of many a coarse tackle and Ormond took him off to bring on Joe Jordan of Leeds United for his fourth international appearance. Ormond had introduced the young Clelland giant to the international scene and clearly hoped now to get some of the aerial power that Jordan was making his name for. With 15 minutes of the game to go, it paid off.

A fierce Bremner shot rattled the woodwork and the ball rolled out to the right. It was chased and picked up by Willie Morgan who resisted the temptation to try a shot himself or simply blast the ball into the goalmouth. He hooked the ball back and it found JORDAN'S head for what was an archetypal Scottish goal that might have been scored by Jimmy McGrory.

Hampden and the nation's pubs and living rooms now went crazy, but the delirium was tempered by the thought that quarter of an hour still remained. Indeed those 15 minutes were like 15 hours as the Czechs, abandoning their destructive defending, now threw everything into the attack. But Scotland were well marshalled by Bremner and full-backs Jardine and McGrain now came into their own. Behind them Ally Hunter, grimly determined to make up for his earlier blunder, radiated a degree of confidence.

But the tension spread even as far as STV's renowned commentator, the much-loved Arthur Montford. Several times he allowed his bias to show with remarks like "Careful, now!" or "Watch your legs, Billy" when a coarse Czech tried to get revenge on Billy Bremner, who was seen as being responsible for an injury to Kuna. But Arthur's climax came at the death, when Denis Law broke through on goal. Impartiality became a thing of the past when Arthur bawled into his microphone "Come on Denis! Come on Denis!" Sadly, even with Arthur's encouragement, the ageing Denis could not deliver, but it mattered little, for the final whistle came soon afterwards to the delight of an exhausted nation, who had on that occasion kicked every ball with the team. Scotland, for the first time in 16 years, would be at the World Cup finals!

v **ENGLAND** 2-0
Hampden Park; Att: 94,487
18 May 1974

Scotland:	England:
Harvey (Leeds United)	Shilton (Leicester City)
Jardine (Rangers)	Nish (Derby County)
McGrain (Celtic)	Pejic (Stoke City)
Blackley (Hibs)	Hughes (Liverpool)
Holton (Manchester United)	Hunter* (Leeds United)
Johnstone (Celtic)	Todd (Derby County)
Bremner (Leeds United)	Bell (Manchester City)
Hay (Celtic)	Weller (Leicester City)
Lorimer (Leeds United)	Peters (Tottenham Hotspur)
Dalglish (Celtic)	Channon (Southampton)
Jordan (Leeds United)	Worthington** (Leicester City)
	Subs
	Watson* (Sunderland)
	MacDonald** (Newcastle United)

Referee: Mr van der Kroft, Holland

HE MAN OF the moment was Jimmy Johnstone. Earlier that week, Johnstone, after a night on the town with the rest of the squad, had been involved in an incident on the Ayrshire coast when he jumped into a boat and was heading in the general direction of the New World when the coastguard rescued him. This incident became, of course, great copy for the the newspapers and much was made of it. Even his team-mates at breakfast the next morning all sang to him: 'What shall we do with the drunken sailor?' It stayed a part of Scottish football mythology for a long time. Jimmy sadly died in 2006, and in late 2008 when a statue was unveiled to him outside Celtic Park, one of the motifs on the back was a rowing boat!

So would these shenanigans mean he would be left out of the team for the game against England? Possibly a stricter manager like his own team boss Jock Stein would have done so, but the tolerant Willie Ormond reckoned that Jimmy was too good a player to be left out, and he played. It turned out to be a wise decision, although the know-all journalists of some newspapers suddenly turned very moral and were critical of the decision to play the man who had (in their view) disgraced Scotland. In the case of some of the 'hacks', it was a case of 'the pot calling the kettle black', but that has never stopped any of them where footballers are concerned.

Jimmy and controversy had been no strangers. On at least two occasions, his club Celtic had 'rested' him for apparent indiscretions, and he had been officially suspended by the SFA on several occasions – usually for some violent piece of retaliation after suffering cynical and brutal foul after foul. Yet there was nothing malicious about Jimmy. He had lots of friends, not least in the Rangers and the England camps, and on his day his play was superb. Outside of football he was neurotic, insecure, frightened and irrational about things such as air travel and homesickness, but on the field he never lacked courage, being quite prepared for example to run again at a coarse Czech or Argentinian defender (who made the Scottish 'clug' men look like angels) a minute after he had been downed. He was above else an entertainer. Instantly recognisable with his diminutive stature and red hair, and opposition fans could appreciate and fear his talent. England's defenders would have probably been hoping that Jimmy would be ruled out of the game. Jimmy was, however, angry with the Press, and by the end of the game, he would show them via the medium of television exactly what he thought of them.

1974 was also all about the World Cup and the undeniable fact that Scotland would be there in West Germany whereas England would not. To say that this hurt England is stating the obvious, but even more hurtful was the fact that Australia had qualified, something the Aussies would not stop talking about while Scots kept joking about how they would love to play Australia – unless bad light stopped play before the lunch interval!

Sir Alf Ramsey had now been sacked by the English FA for the failure to qualify, with the likeable Joe Mercer put in temporary charge. But the team was going nowhere. They had let Ramsey down badly and they contained many names that would not have figured in stronger England teams of the past. Even the England supporters who appeared in fair number that rainy Saturday morning in Glasgow lacked their normal cockiness with none of the 'I'm lookin for a moose, Jock' sort of nonsense that they thought was funny. They were quiet and even reserved, although there were a few that were out and out nasty – the beginnings of a problem that English football has struggled to find an answer to over the last 35 years.

Scotland, on the other hand, were buoyant and optimistic. Some Scottish National Party supporters tried to hijack the occasion for themselves and linked their seven seats (which they had won in the General Election at the end of February) with Scotland qualifying for the World Cup. This was nonsense, of course, but there was something definitely stirring in Scotland that spring.

The domestic season had been a triumph yet again for Jock Stein's Celtic, who won a League and Cup double. Hardly surprising then that Celtic provided four members of the team – Johnstone, McGrain, Hay and Dalglish, and as Leeds United had won the English League, they too provided four men in Bremner, Jordan, Lorimer and goalkeeper David Harvey. Jim Holton of Manchester United, John Blackley of Hibs and Sandy Jardine of Rangers made up the other places. It was a strong side, and Scotland were able to leave men like Martin Buchan, Tam Hutchison and even Denis Law on the bench.

The World Cup winners had all left the England team by now with the exception of Martin Peters, but they had had a better couple of games than Scotland in the Home International Championship that season. They had beaten both Wales and Northern Ireland, whereas Scotland had played a shocker against Northern Ireland, going down to a late goal in a game which should have been played in Belfast but was brought to Hampden for security reasons. A few changes had been made for the Wales game including the dropping of Denis Law and Willie Morgan. Scotland played much better against the Welshmen and won 2-0. That victory had been the catalyst for the immoderate celebrations which led to the Jimmy Johnstone incident, but just to prove that Scotland had no monopoly on the brilliant but unstable, a talented English player called Stan Bowles suddenly went AWOL from the team's hotel. It was no uncommon phenomenon in those days for young men unable to cope with the emotional side of the game with all the publicity and glamour, plus the undeniable fact that, for the first time in history, they were earning far too much money.

The game would be shown live on television (this was by no means automatic in the early 1970s) and to an increasing number of houses in 1974 this meant 'colour'. Colour television had first appeared in the late 1960s but had been confined to only the very rich for a spell until the hiring or the purchase of a colour television became as much of a status symbol as television itself had been 20 years earlier. Not all programmes were filmed in colour, though, and one recalls a little duck that appeared on the side of a television screen when a programme was being advertised or trailed, uttering the words 'in colour' if appropriate.

Scotland's record against England in recent years had been anything but impressive. Since the famous victory of 1967, there had been bad luck in 1968, 1970, 1972 and 1973, but a couple of real hammerings at Wembley in 1969 and 1971 and the total disaster of February 1973, when a match which should have been a celebration of 100 years of Scottish football turned into a 0-5 thrashing of the first order.

So apart from other considerations, the Hampden crowd, who had not now seen a Scottish victory over England for ten years, were anxious to see their team do well. The weather was dire, but rain and a heavy ground are conditions that traditionally suit Scotland – for it is what we are brought up with – and Scotland certainly started well. For some reason or another, England did not have the impressive Kevin Keegan of Liverpool playing for them, yet he had been the outstanding player in their team for some considerable time.

Scotland started off playing towards the Mount Florida end of the ground, and fed the hungry Jimmy Johnstone. They had an early success inside the first five minutes (while some of the crowd had not yet made their way through the primitive and painfully slow Hampden turnstiles, their mood not helped by having to stand in puddles of water) and it was JOE JORDAN of Leeds United who scored it, although he had the help of the outstretched leg of Mike Pejic to deflect the ball past goalkeeper Peter Shilton who might have had it covered.

This early success encouraged the Scots, who kept thundering forward as roar upon roar of encouragement rolled down the Hampden terracings. Norman Hunter of Leeds United, a notoriously robust (to put it mildly) defender who rejoiced in his nicknames like 'Bites Your Legs', and Emlyn Hughes, much ridiculed for his squeaky voice, who was no shrinking violet either, could not get near enough to the Scottish forwards to foul them as the interchanging and short passing of Dalglish, Hay and Lorimer was a sight to behold.

Just before the half hour mark, Scotland went further ahead. Johnstone, Bremner and Lorimer all combined to set the young Kenny Dalglish (already earning his 17th cap at the age of 22) through on goal. His shot hit a defender, this time the luckless Colin Todd who was already having a dreadful afternoon, and ricocheted into the net, and this time the deflection was considered to be big enough to warrant the description: OWN GOAL.

Thus two pretty dreadful goals had been scored, but judging on the play Scotland were in no way unworthy of their two-goal lead. In fact, the TV panel unanimously and magnanimously agreed that Scotland should have been more goals in front, for apart from a couple of speculative shots which went over the bar, England had hardly been in the game as an attacking force. One pundit put it very well when he said that, "We now see why one team is going to West Germany and the other one isn't."

Of course, Scotland when two goals ahead have been known to throw it all away upon occasion, but not this time. They kept up the pressure with Bremner fighting tigerishly in midfield and Davie Hay also showing why several clubs in England were keen on him. Behind them the back four did all that was asked of them, and David Harvey had a very quiet afternoon, possibly enjoying himself listening to all the Scottish songs from the crowd behind him.

In desperation, England took off Frank Worthington and put on Malcolm MacDonald of Newcastle United. Known as 'Supermac', MacDonald had been the man who was supposed to bring the glory days back to the Tyne in the English Cup final of two weeks previously. Sadly he had failed to perform, and the Geordies realised that he was no Jackie Milburn – indeed Magpies fans are still waiting for a trophy, any trophy. MacDonald's appearance this afternoon was greeted with indifference from the English fans and with derision from the Scots, and in truth he made no difference at all, as Scotland finished the game as much on top as they had been all through.

It was then that we saw Jimmy Johnstone's revenge. Jimmy had no feelings of bitterness towards the Englishmen – indeed he had swapped shirts with goalkeeper Peter Shilton whom he respected and admired – but he was then seen on camera flicking two fingers towards the Scottish Press in the Press Box. Perhaps he was just indicating to his wife, or his mother or club manager Jock Stein that Scotland had just won 2-0 – but I don't think so. Lip reading has never been a widely practised skill in Scotland, but it looked for all the world as if he were saying to the Scottish Press who had so abused him this week something along the lines of 'Up you, you b******s!'

v BRAZIL 0-0
Frankfurt; Att: 60,000
18 June 1974

Scotland:	Brazil:
Harvey (Leeds United)	Leao
Jardine (Rangers)	Nelinho
McGrain (Celtic)	Pereira
Buchan (Manchester United)	Peres
Holton (Manchester United)	Marinho
Lorimer (Leeds United)	Piazza
Bremner (Leeds United)	Rivelino
Hay (Celtic)	Paulo Cesar
Morgan (Manchester United)	Jairzinho
Dalglish (Celtic)	Mirandinha
Jordan (Leeds United)	Leivinha*
	Sub
	Carpegiani*

Referee: Mr van Gemert, Holland

SCOTLAND IN THE summer of 1974 was an exciting place to be as it basked in the unusual position of being the only British team at the World Cup, and even enjoyed the support of the English – some of which was genuine and much appreciated, some of which was patronising and frankly insulting like, for example, the ITV panel all appearing in tartan jackets, calling themselves names like 'Brian McClough' and talking about 'Jocks'. And then there was also the advertisement for beer in which the Englishman sneered at everything to do with Scotland, but then admitted they were the team to cheer on in the World Cup and besides, 'your beer is good'.

There was for the first time for well over 200 years a political dimension to all this as well. In February 1974, the Conservatives paid the price for picking unnecessary fights with unions, particularly miners, and were replaced by the Labour Government of Harold Wilson. But it was a minority government, and there were also seven Scottish Nationalist MPs. Industrial Scotland had voted overwhelmingly for Labour, as it did traditionally, but rural Scotland, which could not bring itself to vote Labour, voted for the nationalists instead in places like Banff and Angus. While phrases like 'emerging nationhood' were probably political or journalistic exaggeration, it was now true that the Scottish dimension to politics could no longer be ignored.

And there was that song, 'Flower of Scotland' written by Roy Williamson of The Corries in 1967 with its dreary lyrics about sending Edward II home 'to think again' which had an overt political message, and this song, first heard in full volume at Hampden on the night of the qualification in 1973, had taken off over the winter, perhaps encouraging the bogus belief that Scotland could ignore the outside world with all its energy crises, wars in the Middle-East and the corrupt and increasingly unstable US President Richard Nixon, and bury its head in the Scottish sand and live off North Sea oil.

But nationhood could wait until the World Cup was over. The domestic season had been a fairly dull one with Celtic winning their ninth League Championship in a row as Rangers imploded. Celtic then won the Scottish Cup in a dull, one-sided final against the over-awed Dundee United. The first of the tiresome attempts to change the League structure had been announced. Starting in 1975/76 there would be a 'Premier League' and the naïve believed that somehow or other, this would solve Scotland's domestic problems.

The truth was that, Celtic aside, most of Scotland's talent now played in England. There was nothing particularly new in this, but it was certainly very pronounced in the squad selected by Willie Ormond to go to West Germany. Willie had gradually won first the respect, then the love of the Scottish nation for his ungrammatical interviews and his unpretentious style. Words like 'Aye' and 'ye ken' littered his conversation, but it was clear that he had a good football brain on him. He was far too tolerant with some of the wilder boys in the squad, but was wise enough to to realise that getting heavy with them would have been 'cutting aff yer nose tae spite yer face' as the Scottish phrase had it. The wild boys were all talented and had their role to play. Getting Scotland to the World Cup and the winning of the Home International Championship after the horrendous start of losing to Northern Ireland was enough to be going on with.

There was a little embarrassment first. As was the wont in those days, a World Cup song had been written and sung by those players and supporters who were not too appalled at the lyrics. 'Yub a dub a doo' had been the war cry of Fred Flintstone in the days of black and white TV a decade ago, and this was now adapted to a buttock-clenchingly awful song that went:

Yub A Dub A Dub A Doo
We support the boys in blue
And it's Easy! Easy!
Ring A Ding A Ding A Ding
Jimmy Johnstone on the wing
And its Easy! Easy!

Those who did not like 'Flower of Scotland' nevertheless had to conclude reluctantly that 'sending King Edward home to think again' was the lesser of the two evils!

The first game in Germany had been against Zaire, which Scotland won comfortably enough 2-0. It was generally described as 'not bad', although more goals would have been in order against the outsiders of the group. The big test would be Brazil who had drawn unimpressively 0-0 with Yugoslavia in their opening fixture.

Brazil was still a name that inspired. Since the 1958 World Cup in Sweden when Vava, Didi, Garrincha and Pelé had emerged to impress the globe, it had generally been assumed that Brazil were the best. After all, they were the current World Cup holders having triumphed brilliantly in Mexico in 1970. They were a nation with whom Scotland felt an affinity. They had great players, were fanatical about the game, had distinctive music, committed supporters and on a broader front had suffered from having their natural resources pillaged by imperial powers like the English and the Portuguese. They themselves were a loveable people who were much supported by neutrals in the World Cup, for their history had tended not to involve the invasion of anyone else – something that could not be said, for example, of the English, the Spanish and certainly not the Germans!

Scotland had played Brazil three times before, the first being the time at Hampden before the 1966 World Cup when Steve Chalmers had picked up a wonderful pass from Jim Baxter to score a great goal in a 1-1 draw. The other occasions had been honourable 0-1 defeats, but the 1974 Brazil team was weaker than usual, and quite a few people felt that this Scotland team might just be good enough to get the better of them.

The Scottish team selection did not contain either Denis Law or Jimmy Johnstone. The consensus of opinion at the time was that Willie Ormond had got this right. Both men, similar characters in their tremendous natural ability and commitment, were possibly a shade past their best. Denis had played against Zaire and looked tired, and Jimmy did have off-days. On the other hand, in the circumstances of how this game against Brazil turned out, perhaps a mercurial flash of either of these two might just have turned the game for Scotland.

1974 was also a bad year for terrorism. It was no idle threat, for only a couple of years previously at the 1972 Munich Olympics, Palestinian terrorists had massacred Israeli athletes in an incident which shocked the world. There was also at this time an IRA campaign in Britain. This last aspect, although taken seriously by security forces, was treated with a certain amount of levity by the Scottish squad themselves. Jimmy Johnstone, neurotic as always, was afraid of snipers hiding in trees at the training ground, until it was pointed out to him that IRA men were always Celtic supporters, and that as the Scottish squad contained four Celtic men in Johnstone, McGrain, Hay and Dalglish and had one or two others like Bremner and Jordan of a Celtic persuasion, they would be safe. Even Sandy Jardine of Rangers could sleep easy in his bed!

The game at Frankfurt attracted a crowd of 60,000 which included the British Prime Minister Harold Wilson. Wilson, a genuine football fan who supported Huddersfield Town, gave his full backing for the Scottish team, aware that his power base was Scotland and was afraid of any further erosion to the SNP. He knew that as Prime Minister of a minority government he would have to call a General Election in the autumn, and he needed all the support that he could get.

Brazil opened well, and for a long time the Scottish defence was penned back. But this was a good Scottish backline with two Manchester United men Buchan and Holton in the middle, flanked by the Old Firm pair of McGrain and Jardine who took all that the Brazilians could throw at them. Gradually, as the first half wore on, Scotland came into the game with Davie Hay outstanding in midfield and by the end of the first half, the Brazilians were becoming increasingly frustrated and rattled, conceding far more fouls than one would have associated with a Brazilian team.

Half-time that beautiful, warm Tuesday evening in Scotland saw doors opening and neighbours having a walk in the garden talking to one another about the game, glad of a momentary relief in the tension. The mood, however, was upbeat, for it seemed that, incredible as it might be, Scotland were on the verge of beating Brazil. All that it needed was a break, a good shot, a defensive error, a penalty kick – anything that could tip the balance.

Scotland, now confident, pressed forward, but the elusive goal did not come. It was possibly here that Ormond, traditionally conservative in his use of substitutes, made his mistake in not introducing one or other of his ageing maestros to the game. Johnstone or Law could well have produced something unusual, something that might have caught the Brazilians out. The unexpected might well have won the day.

Billy Bremner died in 1997. One wonders how often he played back in his mind that moment half way through the second half of this game when the goalkeeper Leao parried a shot against Billy's shin and the ball rebounded past the post. It happened so quickly that it could not really be held against Bremner, but he clasped his head in his hands, knowing that an inch or two the other way, and the ball would have been in.

He was not the only luckless Scot that night. Several times Joe Jordan got in good headers and both Davie Hay and Peter Lorimer had shots that flashed over the bar. But Brazil held out, even at the cost of several very nasty fouls, with the great Rivelinho lucky not to be sent off for fouling many times after he had been booked. Towards the end, the steam went out of Scotland a little, as the opposing defence was just a little too well organised for them – and the Brazilians also had on their side the quality that everyone needs called luck.

Full-time came with Brazil more delighted to hear the whistle than Scotland. It was a night, however, when Scotland won their spurs on the world stage with everyone more than a little impressed by this tremendous performance. Harold Wilson said so, puffing his pipe and smiling benignly at the interviewers. Noticeably too, some of the English media identified with the Scots more than previously, stressing that most of the Scottish players played for teams like Manchester United and Leeds United, and hoping that 'we' would do well against Yugoslavia on Saturday.

Sadly Yugoslavia had thumped Zaire 9-0, a result which meant that a draw against Scotland would suit them for qualification. It meant that there would be more frustration on Saturday – the game ending 1-1 – while Brazil qualified by beating Zaire 3-0 thanks to a goalkeeping error which was so ludicrous that it defied belief. It was even said that the goalkeeper could not possibly have been bribed to concede such a goal and thus the game, for had he been corrupt he would have surely have been a little more plausible than to lose a goal by making an error like that! Not that it helped either Brazil or Yugoslavia to World Cup success, for Yugoslavia lost their next three games in the second phase, and Brazil, with the consolation of beating Argentina, finished fourth, a disappointment for the winners of 1958, 1962 and 1970. Scotland returned home undefeated and unlucky, and thoroughly deserved the reception that they were given.

38 v ENGLAND 2-1
Wembley; Att: 98,103
4 June 1977

Scotland:	England:
Rough (Partick Thistle)	Clemence (Liverpool)
McGrain (Celtic)	Neal (Liverpool)
Donachie (Manchester City)	Mills (Ipswich Town)
Forsyth (Rangers)	Hughes (Liverpool)
McQueen (Leeds United)	Watson (Manchester City)
Rioch (Everton)	Greenhoff* (Manchester United)
Masson** (Queen's Park Rangers)	Kennedy** (Liverpool)
Dalglish (Celtic)	Talbot (Ipswich Town)
Jordan* (Leeds United)	Channon (Southampton)
Hartford (Manchester City)	Francis (Birmingham City)
Johnston (West Bromwich Albion)	Pearson (Manchester United)

Subs | *Subs*
Macari* (Manchester United) | Cherry* (Leeds United)
Gemmill** (Derby County) | Tueart** (Manchester City)

Referee: Mr Palotai, Hungary

I T WAS ALL happening in London that first weekend of June 1977. It was the weekend of the Queen's Silver Jubilee (she had become Queen in 1952, still retained her looks and her family had not yet disgraced her) and fireworks and all sorts of events were planned. In the racing world, although the Derby was still run in midweek, the Oaks would be run this Saturday and would be won by a horse with the Scottish name of Dunfermline, while the cricket season was in full swing with the touring Australians playing England in one-day internationals. Wisely they scheduled the Saturday game away from London and played at Edgbaston in Birmingham instead. England would beat the Australians that day – they would go on to win the Ashes as well – but there would be little to cheer them on the football field.

For football, there could be little doubt that 4 June would normally be far too late. The domestic season had finished a month before when Celtic beat Rangers 1-0 in a poor Scottish Cup final, and the Home International Championship had only started a week earlier. But Scotland had imaginatively organised a tour of South America later in June, the better to prepare themselves for what they hoped would be a trip to Argentina next year for the 1978 World Cup, and this comparatively late date at Wembley suited them.

Scotland also had a new manager. Willie Ormond had resigned in early May to pursue a career in club management (incredibly, he, a Hibs man, would take over the recently relegated Hearts) and the new manager was the extroverted Ally MacLeod, who had lifted

Aberdeen in recent days. He inherited a strong squad, with fine players, but there was a disturbing lack of talent from the Scottish domestic game which led to an over-reliance on Anglo-Scots, some of whom were destined to let Ally and the country down very badly in the future.

Ally's first game was a feckless goalless draw at Wrexham against Wales, which earned words like 'bore' and 'dull' to describe it. The next game was a far better performance – a good 3-0 defeat of Northern Ireland at Hampden which restored credibility. MacLeod immediately gave that team a vote of confidence by retaining it for the game at Wembley where he would meet the slightly pedestrian England side of Don Revie which had yet to earn the total confidence of its own supporters and journalists. In particular their defeat by Wales in midweek had seen a certain sharpening of knives and rattling of sabres.

Of the 22 players who took the field that day, ten were based in the north-west, and of them, four of the English side were from Liverpool. They would be forgiven if they looked upon this match as 'just another game' as Liverpool had won the English League, the European Cup and been pipped at the post by Manchester United for the English Cup, and their performance that day looked a little jaded, as if they were fed up of football and in need of a rest. In contrast the Scots were frisky, alert and giving the impression to their huge support that they actually *did* want to be there. None of the Scottish team played for Liverpool, and there was a certain feeling that Liverpool had been over-exposed in the media, which therefore prompted a consequent desire to bring them down a little.

The players appeared to a huge cheer with the Scots quite clearly outnumbering the English in numbers and volume of noise in the stands. To the embarrassment of the Establishment this Jubilee weekend, the boos and jeers for the national anthem perhaps indicated that the Queen was not as popular in Scotland as the politicians would have liked to think, but everyone shrugged their shoulders and said that they were entitled to their opinion. Before the day was out, however, the Scots fans would further disgrace themselves in a way which could not be ignored.

Trips to Wembley of late had not been pleasant ones for Scotland since their famous victory of 1967. 1973 had been an unlucky and narrow defeat, but 1969, 1971 and 1975 had seen Scotland outplayed and psychologically battered into believing in English supremacy to an extent that their supporters found disturbing. But Ally MacLeod always felt that it was his job to develop confidence in his squad.

Much talk centred on Celtic's Kenny Dalglish. On his day, he was one of the best players in the world, but for some time he had been less than totally happy at Celtic. Perhaps he was disillusioned with the poverty of the Scottish domestic game at this stage, perhaps he felt that the Celtic Directors lacked ambition, perhaps he found the brooding tyranny of Jock Stein too much – perhaps it was a combination of all three and other factors, but the signals were those of unhappiness and today would be a great opportunity for him to put his goods in the shop window, as it were.

The game started quietly with England finding their man a little better than the Scots but very much employing a defensive 'Safety First' policy at least in the early stages. Scotland's players, most of whom were a little overawed with Wembley and intense TV exposure, took some time to adapt, but after the half hour mark Scotland's midfield, Masson and Hartford in particular began to take command.

Just before half-time Scotland went ahead. Under pressure from Scotland's forwards, Phil Neal handled just outside his penalty box. The free-kick was taken by Richard Hartford (commonly known as Asa) and it was a good one. Dalglish and Jordan were policed but central defender GORDON McQUEEN (in the Scottish tradition of a centre-half coming up for a corner) wasn't and his blond head put Scotland one up. A goal immediately before half-time is a great psychological boost for the scorers and the result was that the teams left the field to a sea of tartan scarves and the chorus of 'Bonnie Scotland, Bonnie Scotland, We'll Support You Evermore' – a cheery ditty, but one which seemed to be short of lyrics.

In the TV box high above Wembley, one of the English commentators rather improbably said: "It's like Loch Lomond down there!" (Naturally, everybody goes to Loch Lomond to sing and wave tartan scarves around, don't they?) and the discussion of the pundits was really rather revealing. Alan Mullery sounded off at length about how bad England were, Revie had got his tactics wrong, the wrong players were playing in the wrong positions etc.

It takes a good man to shout Jock Stein down but Alan did it that day. Jock remained silent, none too upset at earning money for nothing while Alan ranted and raved. Eventually with the players beginning to re-emerge from the tunnel, Alan relented and Tommy Docherty, clearly feeling the need to fight Scotland's corner, turned to Jock and said: "Well, Jock, Scotland are winning 1-0, aren't we?"

The second half saw Scotland continue to impress with good accurate passing and reading of situations so that people were in the right position waiting for the ball. Jordan had gone off with an injury and was replaced by Lou Macari. Lou had enjoyed a good season for Manchester United, particularly in the English Cup final a fortnight earlier, and, having given the impression of being out of favour with Willie Ormond for a spell, was now fighting for his place.

Scotland scored again on the hour mark, and this time it was KENNY DALGLISH. It was not, in all honesty, one of Kenny's better goals – a prod from close range which he didn't hit cleanly first time – but the build up was superb. It came from Willie Johnston, the boy from Cardenden in Fife who had taken on a new lease of life after leaving the sometimes stifling atmosphere of Ibrox for West Bromwich Albion. He embarked upon a superb run down the wing, put in an equally superb cross for Bruce Rioch to knock down and in the resultant melée it was Dalglish who emerged triumphant.

Scotland were now two ahead and coasting. The fans were exultant, the players were enjoying themselves and cans of beer were opened in celebration in countless living rooms back home. There was always at the back of one's mind the Scottish tendency and sometimes even inevitability of self-destruction, but there was little sign of that today as Scotland remained on top and England looked as if they needed their summer holidays. Until the 88th minute, that is, when Trevor Francis, one of England's few successes, charged through and was brought down in a challenge which a tougher referee in the Scottish League would have described as part of the game. However a penalty it was, and the Scottish fans were temporarily stilled.

CHANNON'S conversion of the penalty was not exactly greeted with a sporting cheer by the Scots (the English fans had already gone home, disgusted by their team's lacklustre performance) but it did mean that the remaining two minutes (and a seemingly extraordinarily long allowance for stoppage time) were spent in anxiety with every throw in and boot up the field greeted with cheers. But the whistle did come and Scotland had their deserved victory and the Home International Championship for the second year in a row.

It would have been nice if it had finished there, but sadly it didn't. Over-exuberant Scottish fans invaded the field thanks to inadequate policing and stewarding (the Metropolitan Police clearly being required for other events this Jubilee weekend) and the world saw on its televisions bits of turf being stolen and then the infamous image of Scottish football that year with about 20 long-haired, enthusiastic but misguided youths climbing on the goalposts to celebrate. There soon followed the inevitable crack. Fortunately no-one was hurt, but Scotland as a nation was certainly damaged.

There was nothing really malicious in all this. English newspapers, trying to hide their team's glaring deficiencies, concentrated on the invasion and one would have had the impression that this was some sort of third Jacobite rebellion with the Scots trying to outdo the IRA bombers and even the Luftwaffe in the damage they could do to London. It was not as bad as it was painted, but it was silly, and at least one of the long term causes of the abandonment of this Scotland v England fixture, for in subsequent years, English fans would retaliate – and not only in Scotland, but across the rest of Europe as well. The mid-1970s were the time when hooligans very nearly brought the game to its knees, and this particular event rather tended to overshadow what should have been one of Scotland's greatest moments.

There was a funny side as well. Two Scottish schoolteachers had just watched the game on TV and feeling rather happy with life, talked about people they knew going to the game. "Two of my third year will be there," said one. Then a start and a cry: "Look there they are – that's Sean Higgins on the bar, and Dean Campbell at the bottom of the post". His friend, clearly a fan of Humphrey Bogart, turned and said, "Aint ye proud of them?"

Many years later the same teacher took his pupils one sunny day for a tour round Hampden Park. It being summer, all was quiet apart from the voice of the guide echoing round the eerie stadium, when suddenly a youngster said, "It's like Wembley!" A few funny stares and then his friend asked, "How?"

"Nae goalposts!" came the response.

v CZECHOSLOVAKIA 3-1
Hampden Park; Att: 85,000
21 September 1977

Scotland:	Czechoslovakia:
Rough (Partick Thistle)	Michalik
Jardine (Rangers)	Paurik
McGrain (Celtic)	Capkovic
Forsyth (Rangers)	Dvorak
McQueen (Leeds United)	Gogh
Masson (Queen's Park Rangers)	Dobias**
Rioch (Everton)	Pollak
Hartford (Manchester City)	Moder*
Johnston (West Bromwich Albion)	Gajdusek
Dalglish (Liverpool)	Masny
Jordan (Leeds United)	Nehoda
	Subs
	Knapp*
	Gallis**

Referee: Mr Rion, Belgium

THE ARRIVAL OF the Czechs in September 1977 (they had to come by train because of an air strike) was greeted with tremendous enthusiasm by the Scottish nation. Scotland was on a high with great hopes once again of making it to the finals of the World Cup, this time to be held in the exotic location of Argentina. Once more a tremendous boost had been given by the news that the game would be televised live, and people recalled that tremendous night four years previously when Scotland had defeated the Czechs to reach the finals in West Germany.

The position was different this time, in that Scotland could not qualify by beating Czechoslovakia alone. So far, each of the teams in the three match group had beaten each other. Scotland had put in an abysmal performance in Prague to lose 0-1. They had then needed an own goal to beat Wales at Hampden, but Wales had done Scotland and themselves a great favour by beating Czechoslovakia. So it was still all square, but if Scotland did not beat Czechoslovakia, any hopes of qualification would be very slim indeed.

There can be little doubt that Scotland, more so, one feels, than other nations, are helped by their own crowd. So often Scottish teams who have disappointed abroad have performed brilliantly at home, and it was also true that foreign teams feared coming to Hampden to meet men wearing kilts and drinking beer to excess. Hampden Park was huge and in 1977 had very little accommodation for seating. This was much criticised by those who liked their comfort, but the up side of it all was that it did create a passionate atmosphere. There was truly a world of difference when Scotland played at their intimidating home to when they played abroad.

Scotland now had an ebullient, extroverted manager in Ally MacLeod. Following Willie Ormond's departure, Jock Stein had turned the job down, it was said, but Ally MacLeod who had had a good season with Aberdeen, jumped at the opportunity. Within weeks he had won the Home International Championship including that famous victory at Wembley on the weekend of the Queen's Silver Jubilee, and had taken his men to Argentina for a tour that had seen a draw with Argentina and a defeat of Chile before a (respectable) beating by Brazil. Even a narrow defeat in East Germany in a friendly did not seem to faze the ever-optimistic Ally, and his enthusiasm was infectious and obvious.

The contrast with his opposite number could hardly have been more marked. Josef Venglos was studious, earnest but quiet. Yet his side were the champions of Europe as they had won what was then called the European Nations Cup in 1976, and he had reason to believe that this might be the occasion on which Czechoslovakia could record their first victory on Scottish soil. Venglos complained about his side's unfortunate travel arrangements which had involved travelling up on an overnight train (not a sleeper) from London, but in a very nice, gentle sort of way. One would not have believed that more than 20 years later, this man would become the manager of Celtic.

MacLeod had gone for more than the normal quota of Anglos, for the game in Scotland was undergoing one of its slumps. The Premier Division, which had now been in operation for two years, was manifestly failing in its attempt to make the Scottish game more competitive. That season, for example, Celtic had shocked their fans on the eve of the season by selling Kenny Dalglish to Liverpool. They had then comprehensively failed to spend the money to replace him. As a result everyone already knew that Rangers would win the League, even though a resurgent Aberdeen under Billy McNeill would put up a fight. Hearts had been relegated in 1977 and the year before so had Dundee, blows from which these very fine clubs with long traditions would take a long time to recover, and in the case of Dundee, the recovery would be patchy and partial.

But the BBC kept telling us that the English League was the best in the world, so it made sense for Ally to pick men like Hartford, Rioch, Masson, Jordan and McQueen. Indeed they were all playing well for the moment and were well respected by the Scotland supporters, even though they could not see them very often in the flesh. This team had talent. Most Scotland teams did, and it depended on the manager whether the talent was utilised to the full and moulded together into an effective unit. Ally was telling everyone that he was doing just that.

There were some really exciting players. We knew all about Kenny Dalglish for he had only a month or so previously been with Celtic, but an even pleasanter surprise was produced by Willie Johnston who, now with West Bromwich Albion after he had left Rangers, was now playing some of the best football of his career with the Midlands side. Johnston, though, still had the sad ability to get himself into a great deal of trouble. He had, for example, been sent off in the summer in the friendly with Argentina, although that dismissal was later rescinded. It was perhaps as well that no-one knew what was ahead and how the connection between Johnston, trouble and Argentina would grow even stronger the following summer.

85,000 tickets were sold this autumn night, and televisions were switched on in eager expectation of great entertainment with everyone reminding one another of 1973. By this time, the song 'Flower of Scotland' had been adapted with fervour by everyone in Scotland, not least the Scottish National Party which was clearly making inroads into the established parties. Their slogan: 'It's Scotland's Oil' was a reference to the oil which had been discovered in the North Sea a decade earlier. It was, of course, a spurious argument, for everyone knew that the oil would sadly belong to the oil moguls, but it was effective.

Inflation had been a tremendous problem to successive governments throughout the 1970s as money kept losing value. The Labour Prime Minister was a man called James Callaghan, a transparently likeable and honest fellow who did not really seem cut out for the nasty business of politics, particularly at this time in history when labour disputes occurred with distressing frequency. The Conservatives, on the other hand, had elected in 1975 a lady called Thatcher who looked as if she meant business.

The 1970s have also been described as the 'decade that fashion forgot' with long hair, bell bottom trousers, kipper ties and platform shoes. Women wore trouser suits and open-toed sandals, as if to celebrate their recently acquired equality with men. Scotland had entered the pop world with the Bay City Rollers, and at long last Britain had a winner in her own tennis tournament when Virginia Wade won the Women's Singles in 1977. England also won the Ashes that year against an Australian side reeling from the news that most of them were defecting from establishment cricket in favour of a rogue television-based circus. Fashion was creeping more and more into football. Long, untidy hair characterised players. Team photographs of that era are not flattering.

Multi-channel television had not yet arrived, although one did hear whispers about things called video-recorders. There were still only three channels – two BBC and one STV/Grampian or Borders, depending where you lived. More or less everyone would watch the game in colour now as it had developed slowly over the past decade and thus it was that Scotland got a great view of Alex Cameron of STV being kicked out of the way by a police horse who was clearly not affected by big names. Arthur Montford would be the commentator, so we could be guaranteed sympathetic treatment by a man who was clearly one of us.

It was also clear from the start that the game would be a physical one, but that suited Scotland. In particular it suited Joe Jordan, a giant of a striker who knew exactly how to use his aerial prowess. By half-time Scotland, playing towards the Mount Florida goal, were two up, both involving JOE JORDAN. The big, gap-toothed striker scored the first one from a Willie Johnston corner kick when both he and his Leeds United team-mate Gordon McQueen went up for the ball and the Czech defence were unsure which one to go for. That was in 20 minutes, and then before half-time Johnston sent a ball over, the goalkeeper collided with Jordan in such a way that, if the roles had been reversed, all of Scotland would have appealed for a foul, but the Belgian referee saw nothing wrong. The ball came to ASA HARTFORD who scored to put Scotland two up and looking very comfortable.

Early in the second half, Scotland amazed and delighted their fans by going three ahead. Once again it came from the air with McQueen heading on to Jardine who in turn headed on to DALGLISH who scored. It was a remarkable and unusual goal, but greeted with rapture by the Scotland crowd who now thought that they had an outstanding team here. Scotland were now in total command, with Masson having a great game, passing comfortably and setting up Dalglish and the other forwards. The Czechs were a dispirited bunch and it was hard to believe that they had won the European Nations Cup some 15 months earlier. Josef Venglos was compelled to make two desperate substitutions while Scotland retained their starting eleven. So what did the substitutes' bench do? Being Scotland supporters, they joined in with 'Flower of Scotland'!

But a heart or two may well have missed a beat ten minutes from time when Scotland conceded a shocking goal. Alan Rough of Partick Thistle had had a good game, but was badly at fault when a weak 30 yard effort from MIROSLAV GAJDUSEK managed to elude the rest of the defence and himself. It cast a slight damper on the evening, for this goal might just have been significant if things had gone to goal difference. In addition there was the justified fear of the Scottish death wish which might have led to the loss of another goal and consequent jitters. But Scotland held out and the nation knew that their destiny was in their own hands, for a win against Wales in three weeks time would definitely see them in South America.

MacLeod was more enthusiastic than ever at the end, and had clearly become a big favourite with the Hampden crowd. Venglos moaned about Scotland being too physical, but his team did not lack the raw meat either, and neutral opinion, notably the English Press, were adamant that Scotland deserved to win. They were in fact very impressed.

It was another of these nights that demonstrated (if we had not known this already) just how much football means to the nation of Scotland. Roads and streets were deserted, even in Edinburgh and Glasgow during the hours of the game, but afterwards there was tremendous animation and cheerfulness, and next day going to work was a positive pleasure as everyone beamed at everyone else, and talked in anticipation of the Wales game, whether one had a ticket and whether the game would be on TV, what the team selection would be, and whether Scotland would win.

v **WALES** 2-0
Anfield; Att: 50,800
12 October 1977

Scotland:
Rough (Partick Thistle)
Jardine* (Rangers)
Donachie (Manchester City)
Forsyth (Rangers)
McQueen (Leeds United)
Masson (Queen's Park Rangers)
Hartford (Manchester City)
Macari (Manchester United)
Johnston (West Bromwich Albion)
Dalglish (Liverpool)
Jordan (Leeds United)

Subs
Buchan* (Manchester United)

Referee: Mr Wurtz, France

Wales:
Davies (Everton)
R. Thomas (Derby County)
J. Jones (Liverpool)
Phillips (Aston Villa)
D. Jones (Norwich City)
Sayer* (Cardiff City)
Mahoney (Middlesbrough)
Yorath (Coventry City)
Flynn (Burnley)
M. Thomas (Wrexham)
Toshack (Liverpool)

Subs
Deacy* (PSV Eindhoven)

THE WELSH FA did not realise what they were doing when they transferred this game to England. It was a decision motivated by sheer greed in that Cardiff's Ninian Park had a 10,000 limit, Cardiff Arms Park had no floodlights and Swansea and Wrexham would not have been able to hold a big crowd and therefore would not have yielded enough money. So they decided to move to England. That would have been bad enough, but they actually decided to move to a ground that was on the road to Scotland. Had they moved to Birmingham or Bristol or even London, it would not have been so bad, but Liverpool was on the M6 and not really all that far away from Glasgow. In effect, Wales had sold their ground rights, and the game became, in all but name, a home match for Scotland, such was the size and volume of the Scottish support.

It is probably true to say that the Welsh national game was rugby, especially so in the 1970s, the era of Barry John, JPR Williams, JJ Williams and many others. Welshmen when talking about 'football', often meant rugby. Yet they had had their moments in football as well. They had had a great team in the early 1900s and in the 1930s, and at the World Cup of 1958 they had done the best out of all the British nations. Great players had included Billy Meredith, John Charles, Ivor Allchurch and Derek Tapscott, and the team that they had in 1977 did not lack quality.

The crucial difference between Scotland and Wales was that, historically, a strong Welsh club side did not emerge in the way that Scotland produced Queen's Park in the first instance and then Celtic and Rangers. Nor did it ever produce a strong League of its own.

Cardiff City had won the English Cup in 1927, but apart from that, glorious performances had been few and far between. Wales was a backwater, and the decision that they made to play the game outside of its border was an indication of that status.

It is remarkable looking back on it that Wales 'got away' with that decision to move to Anfield. Czechoslovakia felt aggrieved and saw a British conspiracy to keep them out. That was rubbish, of course, but can you imagine the uproar there would have been if Scotland had decided to eschew Hampden Park, Ibrox, Parkhead and even Tynecastle and Pittodrie in order to play a vital game at, say, Newcastle? Rioting in the streets might have ensued, one feels.

Scotland had already played Wales twice in the calendar year of 1977, two dreadful and easily forgettable games – a 1-0 victory in the World Cup at Hampden where Scotland had needed an own goal to win, and in Ally MacLeod's first game in charge a 0-0 draw in the Home International Championship at Wrexham which had managed to host that game, even though the attendance was on the low side at 14,469.

Since 21 September and that victory over the Czechs the Scottish nation had been on a high. This could often be dangerous, and indeed events next year would show just how dangerous ungrounded Scottish optimism could be. In the autumn of 1977, however, few topics of conversation raised themselves more often than Scotland's chances in the World Cup. Wives and mothers shook their heads resignedly but eventually were caught in the mood of national euphoria. It was like what they said about war time. The rate of suicides and depression dropped rapidly because everyone had a cause to support, something to live for. 'I'm not going to take an overdose this week – I want to see how Scotland do!' seemed to be the attitude and it was a macabre and gruesome fact that quite a few patients suffering from terminal cancer made the supreme effort to keep themselves going for another few weeks. This was not a country which took its football lightly and in this respect, the famous remarks of Bill Shankly that 'Football is not a matter of life and death – it is far more important than that' – although flippant and even offensive to some people – may well sometimes be considered to have a certain validity.

Technically, Scotland were only entitled to the away supporters' allocation. In fact they took over the whole of Anfield, thinking nothing of travelling to Wales, even practising a Welsh accent and saying words like 'bach' and 'boyo' to pass themselves off as Welshmen to buy a ticket. And even if they could not get a ticket, they were quite happy to go to Liverpool that night and watch the game on a pub TV where the atmosphere would be very Scottish – and there would, of course, be loads of drink!

The game was on BBC TV and it was another one of these nights where one could drive a car for miles on a Scottish road without seeing another vehicle, or walk along Princes Street, Edinburgh and meet no-one other than a few Japanese or American tourists wondering where everyone was, until the noise of bustle and animation from pubs would answer their question.

Since the win over Czechoslovakia, Ally MacLeod had been forced to make two changes to his side. Bruce Rioch was out with a leg injury and had to be replaced by Lou Macari, the captain's armband passing to Don Masson, and Willie Donachie of Manchester City came in for Danny McGrain, who had gone down with a foot injury. No-one knew it at the time, but this foot injury was a long term and mysterious one which would have dreadful consequences for Celtic and Scotland. It meant that Danny did not go to Argentina where he was much missed, for his calming and reassuring presence (in short supply in that squad) might have worked wonders in that crazy World Cup atmosphere.

It was perhaps a sad comment on the domestic game in both countries, however, that Wales had only two men who played for a Welsh club – Peter Sayer of Cardiff City and Mickey Thomas of Wrexham, and Scotland had only three players from Scottish clubs – Alan Rough of Partick Thistle, and Sandy Jardine and Tom Forsyth of Rangers. Nick Deacy played for Eindhoven, but everyone else played for English clubs, ironically none too far away from Liverpool!

Bill Shankly would say that he had never seen anything like this night at Anfield – and this was a ground famed for fanatical supporters and its Kop – and it was particularly apposite for Kenny Dalglish. Kenny, the best Scottish player by some distance in the last decade, had been transferred from Celtic to Liverpool a couple of months earlier. He was therefore playing at home. And to be playing on your home ground and to come running out to see your country's flags must have given him a great lift.

Scotland had beaten Czechoslovakia and Wales at home, but lost in Prague. Wales had shocked the world by beating the Czechs at Wrexham (yes, Wrexham, not Liverpool!), so, as a win gave 2 points, Scotland had 4 points, Wales 2 and Czechoslovakia 2. A Welsh victory would give themselves and the Czechs a chance (they still had to play each other in November), a draw would knock out Czechoslovakia but still gave Wales a slight hope, but a win for Scotland meant that they would qualify for Argentina.

The first half, as usually happens in these circumstances, was not a great game of football. There was much excitement and frenzied hysterical football, but little skill. Not only was there such a great deal at stake, but the players, most of whom knew each other from the English League and indeed from the two games that Scotland and Wales had already played against each other that year, were wise to each other. Scotland had a penalty claim turned down and had forced several corners, but against that, Wales had several shots which Alan Rough was glad to see whistle past his post.

At half-time with no lessening of the tension either at the ground or in front of the anxious televisions in stress-filled living rooms and pubs back home, a certain feeling was beginning to manifest itself that Scotland had now to 'do or die', and that a rallying call like the one that Robbie Burns put into the mouth of Robert the Bruce at Bannockburn called 'Scots Wha Hae' was in order. Some pubs did just that, and in spite of a woeful ignorance of the lyrics, there was much clenching of fists and grinding of teeth and quaffing, then recharging of glasses.

The second half saw an upping of the tempo as both sides went for the goal that might send them to South America. On the hour mark, Scottish hearts missed a beat as John Toshack raced clear of the Scotland defence with only Alan Rough to beat. He shot but Rough was equal to the task, turning the ball onto the bar – a nation breathed again. Scotland now were gradually gaining a little territorial advantage, but it was not yet decisive until the incident that still leaves a nasty taste to this day in Welsh mouths whenever the name Scotland is mentioned.

Willie Johnston took a long throw into the Welsh penalty area. Joe Jordan and Davie Jones both went up for it, arms in the air, and the ball was clearly handled. Because the Scottish supporters outnumbered the Welsh by a considerable amount, the cry was 'Penalty', and the referee agreed, pointing to the spot. Even the TV replays were not instantly conclusive, and it took a lot of replaying in slow motion before it appeared that it was Joe Jordan's arm that had touched the ball. The referee would have been justified in saying 'play on', for the contact was in any case hardly deliberate or pre-meditated, but he decided it was a penalty. It was the wrong decision, but it was an honest mistake.

The Welsh protested for what seemed ages, all the while DON MASSON waiting patiently. Eventually, he took the kick and sent the goalkeeper the wrong way as the terracing behind him exploded, and cushions were thrown in the air in living rooms back home. 11 minutes remained but the Welsh team, now clearly demoralised by the crowd by what they perceived as a wrong decision 'earned' by the crowd , had little left. Any sympathy for them had to be tempered by the recollection that the game had become a 'home' game for Scotland, thanks to the cynical desire of the Welsh FA to make money.

If there was a doubt about the first goal, there was glorious certainty about the second which gave Scotland their passport to Argentina. Well within the last five minutes, substitute Martin Buchan sent in a great cross for KENNY DALGLISH to head home from close range at full speed. "Oh yes!" cried Archie McPherson for the BBC, for Scotland had now won the game. Even if the first goal was a refereeing mistake, the second one certainly wasn't.

For the second time in a row, Scotland would be the only British team at the World Cup finals, a point not lost on the delighted nation. It took several days for the celebrations to die down. In fact they were renewed again at the New Year celebrations, for Argentina was seldom far from anyone's lips in these turbulent and momentous days, especially once Ally MacLeod began whipping up a fervour with his predictions of world domination. But if we had known what was going to happen in that distant land in 1978, we might have been less excited. As they say in Scotland: 'It's as weel that ye dinnae ken futs comin!'

v **HOLLAND** 3-2

Mendoza; Att: 35,130

11 June 1978

Scotland:	Holland:
Rough (Partick Thistle)	Jongbloed
Kennedy (Aberdeen)	Suurbier
Donachie (Manchester City)	Rijsbergen**
Buchan (Manchester United)	Poortlviet
Forsyth (Rangers)	Krol
Gemmill (Nottingham Forest)	Jansen
Rioch (Derby County)	Neeskens*
Souness (Liverpool)	R. van de Kerkhof
Hartford (Manchester City)	Rensenbrink
Dalglish (Liverpool)	W. van de Kerkhof
Jordan (Manchester United)	Rep
	Subs
	Boskamp*
	Wildschut**

Referee: Herr Linemayr, Austria

SCOTLAND LAY BROKEN. Never before in the long and lamentable catalogue of Scottish failures had we experienced such a time as this. A dire defeat by Peru and a feckless draw against Iran had reduced the nation to despair. It was Mons Graupius, Flodden, Culloden, the Darien Scheme, the 9-3 in 1961, the 7-2 in 1955 and the 5-1 in 1975 all rolled into one nightmarish package. Small wonder, it was said, that Scotland was suddenly experiencing such a high rate of alcoholism and, yes, suicide.

The reverses were only half of it. Some of the team were in open revolt about the sub-standard nature of the accommodation, Willie Johnston had been sent home for using an illegal substance and the tabloid press gleefully carried stories about drink and women (not all of them substantiated, it had be to be said) on an almost daily basis. Ally MacLeod seemed to be teetering on the verge of a nervous breakdown as the nation became the laughing stock of the world.

Yet it had all been so different the previous autumn when Scotland had qualified for the World Cup with stirring victories against Czechoslovakia and Wales. Throughout the winter we had been told that we were going to win the World Cup – or at the very worst reach the last four – yet the basics were not there. The other teams in the section were not watched or spied upon, and the Home International Championship was a colossal flop with the Hampden crowd rather pathetically shouting "You didnae qualify" to the England team as they beat Scotland 1-0. Incredibly after that, Scotland did a lap of honour when the medieval punishment of being dragged along Sauchiehall Street so that rubbish and excrement could be hurled at them would have been more appropriate.

Added to this, there was Andy Cameron's Scotland World Cup song telling everyone that we would really shake them up when we won the World Cup and reminding everyone yet again that England didnae qualify. Add to that the embarrassing send-off from Hampden before the team left for Argentina, with Gordon McQueen hobbling on the tarmac as he headed to the airport in obvious distress from an injury (there were those who believed the story that he was carried out on a stretcher, but that was thankfully an exaggeration), and you had a calamity waiting to happen.

Now, after the Peru and Iran games, the brutal truth hit Scotland. Sponsors withdrew their support, questions were asked in the House of Commons and relatives of any member of the team were afraid to show their faces in public. The Scottish fans who were in Argentina turned on their team with taunts of 'You only want the money!' and now supported the host nation instead. MacLeod snarled at the Press and TV cameras, and no-one would have been too upset if the players had all decided to follow the disgraced Johnston home.

But there remained the final group game against Holland. The Dutch were one of the favourites for the tournament. They had been the somewhat unfortunate beaten finalists in 1974 with their 'total football' team. Although they were a shade less impressive than four years earlier, they were still a fine side. Incredibly, as Holland could only draw 0-0 with Peru, there existed the possibility (difficult to keep a straight face when one contemplated it) that Scotland could actually qualify if they could defeat Holland by three goals. This was clearly Cloud-Cuckoo Land in the phrase of the Greek comedian Aristophanes of 411 BC or, closer to home, the Never Never land of J.M. Barrie. Although one of the reasons why we play sport is that we are never entirely sure of the eventual outcome, this did seem to be a rather tasteless joke at the expense of a nation which had suffered the horrors of hell in the past week. Possibly, if Scotland decided to put their minds to it, they might get a draw ... but that was all one could realistically hope for.

What gave Scotland a slight chance, but only a slight one, was that the Dutch squad seemed to be every bit as troubled as the Scots one was. They had their problems about not getting enough money, as they thought, and resented the constant comparison between themselves and the team of 1974. Their goalless draw with Peru had been as exciting as it sounded, and their Press both in Argentina and back home in Holland had not been slow to condemn them. Then Ernst Happel, the under-pressure Dutch manager, made the strange statement that he would be quite happy to lose to Scotland as long as it was only by two goals. That way they would still qualify and avoid Brazil in the next round.

At last Ally MacLeod made a realistic team selection. It may be that a delegation of players had approached him with positive ideas and had made a few constructive suggestions which he had acted upon. In particular he gave Graeme Souness his first game of the tour. Souness was never the easiest of men to get on with, but he was a total professional and patriot who would never give less than his best for Scotland, or indeed anyone else he had been chosen for. Don Masson's fall from grace after he missed a crucial penalty against

Peru had been total and permanent, and Kenny Burns, Sandy Jardine and Lou Macari were clearly carrying the can for the Iran fiasco. It was, at least, a business-like and credible Scottish team which took the field at Mendoza to play the Dutch who contained some great players like Johnny Rep, Robbie Rensenbrink and a man called Wim Jansen who would disappear into oblivion (as far as Scotland were concerned) after this game, but who suddenly turned up in 1997 as manager of Celtic.

TV ratings for this game were down, as many Scottish fans, quite deliberately and consciously turned their back on their team and on this lovely Sunday evening played golf, tended to their garden or took the dog for a walk. Those who did so missed Jock Stein before the game in the BBC studio refusing to condemn Ally MacLeod by saying that "whenever the players cross that white line there is nothing the manager can do". They also missed a Scottish performance, which, had it happened in isolation and not in the context of the pre-existing shambles, would have been rated as one of the best of all time.

With the pressure clearly off them, and with everyone giving the impression that they wanted to play, Scotland started well and within the first half hour Bruce Rioch, at long last playing like the captain of Scotland, hit the post. Then Dalglish (who had been described as 'catatonic' in the Iran game) netted, only to have the goal chalked off. It was thrilling Scottish stuff, reminiscent of the way the team had played in some of the qualifying games.

But then Scotland suffered a bad blow when the Austrian referee Herr Linemayr awarded the Dutch a penalty towards the end of the first half when Rep made the most of being sandwiched between Kennedy and Rough. It probably would not have been given as a penalty by a British referee and Archie Gemmill certainly thought so, as he was booked for protesting too strongly. But a penalty it was and RENSENBRINK did the needful. It was absolutely no consolation at all to know that this was the 1,000th goal ever scored in World Cup finals history.

But this Scotland team could fight, and before half-time they were level. The play of Souness had been influential for some time, and it was he who created this one. It was a typical Scottish goal, what was once called a three-card trick where Souness sent a long ball to Jordan who headed the ball down for DALGLISH to score the goal that his fans had been predicting. Scotland left the field at half-time to the cheers of the few Scottish fans in the stadium, the applause of the Argentinian neutrals and the respect of the Dutch. Even those in the TV studio back home acknowledged that this had at last been a Scotland performance worthy of the nation.

Immediately into the second half, Scotland went ahead with a penalty kick after Souness had been barged off the ball in the penalty area following some good work from Dalglish and Rioch. ARCHIE GEMMILL took the ball and confidently stroked it home to put Scotland 2-1 up with virtually all the second half left in which to score the two goals that would yet see the Scots through. And after Dalglish and then Jordan came close with headers, GEMMILL scored the goal that became the one redeeming feature of Scotland's 1978 World Cup.

This goal, a magnificent solo effort, has been shown so many times on television that it seems redundant to describe it. Archie, cutting in from the right flank, jinked past man after man before flicking the ball over the diving goalkeeper. Its effect was electrifying, because it gave Scotland the chance of scoring another to build that crucial three-goal lead. With their tails up, this seemed possible, and Archie McPherson on BBC talked about the "miracle of Mendoza". Husbands who were doing the garden were now summoned in by family members, and the dog walkers, informed by a passing transistor and its suddenly radiant owner, now sprinted for the car hoping to get home in time or at least to listen to the end on the car radio.

For a few minutes the country sprang to life again ... but only for a few minutes because JOHNNY REP soon ran up the other end and scored. Unaccountably he was unchallenged by the Scottish defence, and thus the revival ended with a whimper. The game now fizzled out, but Scotland did at least have the satisfaction of beating the best team in Europe, who would once again finish as runners-up in the World Cup. The game finished 3-2, but it was a bitter victory.

It was also somehow a metaphor for the Scottish nation. "When their boat comes in, they will be waiting at the airport," said a cruel comedian. The team now packed their bags and flew home. They were met not by a hostile stone-throwing mob – the Holland result had at least spared them that – but by something perhaps worse – nobody! A few baggage handlers tried to raise a cheer for them, a couple of spinsters with 'teacher' written all over them told the players they should be ashamed of themselves – and there was little more than that.

The guilty men were pointed out – Masson, Johnston and Macari, for example, never played for Scotland again and MacLeod, although retained for a spell as manager, was predictably sacked and replaced by Jock Stein. It took a long time for Scotland to recover, and there were implications in the wider world outside football.

The Holland game was very annoying. There was something primeval and quintessentially Scottish in the team's ability to beat the best when they were already on their knees, when the result did not matter. It showed the world what Scotland could have done. It was like Bonnie Prince Charlie, who became a hero with the highlanders after he had lost, and after he had led them to disaster. The Holland game only caused more anger at the guilty men, who would never be allowed to forget what had happened.

Gemmill's goal, 'praised not without cause but without end' almost symbolised all this. Here was Scottish talent scoring what was arguably one of the best goals ever in World Cup history – but could they do that when it mattered? Similarly Kenny Dalglish had scored one goal against Holland – once again when the damage had already been done to Scottish hopes. He had no problem scoring goals in important games for Liverpool, like the European Cup final for example. But could he do it for Scotland? No. The Holland game was a very frustrating one. Another glorious failure.

v SPAIN 3-1
Hampden Park; Att: 74,299
15 November 1984

Scotland:
Leighton (Aberdeen)
Nicol (Liverpool)
Albiston (Manchester United)
Miller (Aberdeen)
McLeish (Aberdeen)
Cooper (Rangers)
Souness (Sampdoria)
McStay (Celtic)
Bett (Lokeren)
Dalglish (Liverpool)
Johnston (Celtic)

Spain:
Arconada (Real Sociedad)
Urquiaga (Bilbao)
Camacho (Real Madrid)
Maceda (Gijon)
Goicoechea (Bilbao)
Gordillo (Real Betis)
Munoz (Real Madrid)
Urtubi** (Bilbao)
Senor (Real Zaragoza)
Rincon* (Real Betis)
Alonso (Atletico (Madrid)

Subs
Butragueno* (Barcelona)
Carrasco** (Barcelona)

Referee: Herr Prokop, East Germany

SCOTLAND FANS HAD certain reason to be optimistic as they made their way to Hampden on the clear night of 15 November 1984. Certainly the available tickets had been snapped up quickly enough, for the feeling was that a creditable Scotland side was developing under Jock Stein. Respectability had certainly been restored since the Argentina fiasco of six years ago, but that was not enough. The 1984 European Championships, for example, had passed without any Scottish participation. More was required.

The side had been built around the strong double centre-half pairing from Aberdeen of Willie Miller and Alex McLeish, and beside them were strong players like Davie Cooper, Graeme Souness and the fast developing Paul McStay, a boy who had taken the country by storm since he appeared in a Schoolboys international at Wembley in 1980, and who had scored a wonderful goal in the game against Iceland a month ago.

Up front were the pairing of Kenny Dalglish and Mo Johnston. Dalglish probably caused more arguments in the Tartan Army than anyone else. He had certainly been there for long enough – tonight would be his 96th cap – but he had never won over the hearts and minds of the doubters in the way that he had with his Liverpool fans. In 1978, for example he had won the European Cup with the Reds, famously jumping over the fences to celebrate with the fans, and Scotland supporters had wondered when we were going to see him do this for the national side. Yet he had scored some good goals for Scotland – one against Belgium stood out in the memory – but, his critics argued, not enough. 29 goals in 95 games was by no means an impressive yield.

Yet only a month before this game, your writer had found himself on a train from Leningrad (St. Petersburg) to Moscow in what was then the grimmest of dictatorships called the Soviet Union. A burly Russian looked at me suspiciously, for I was clearly from the decadent capitalist West and might have been a friend of Ronald Reagan or Margaret Thatcher. Worse still, in his eyes, I might have been a German. He asked where I was from. I stammered "Scotland". The Russian smiled and said "Ah, Shotlandia – Boorns, Monstr, Dalgleesh" in a reference to the poet, the creature that lives in Loch Ness and the football player!

And then there was Maurice Johnston, a maverick character, now back in Scotland from Elton John's Watford and with the club that he claimed to love, Celtic. He was less experienced than Dalglish, but sharp and hard working on the field, even though rumours circulated about his extravagant private life. Mo seemed, however, to respond well to the strict leadership of Jock Stein.

The country was in a little turmoil in late 1984. This was the year that George Orwell had predicted would be replete with spies, dictators and Big Brother watching you. That turned out to be none too far from the truth as Britain was involved in a dreadful miners' strike, which the colliers were destined to lose and which more or less finished coal mining in this country. A month previously, at Brighton during the Conservative Party conference, an IRA bomb had come very close to wiping out the British cabinet. Scotland continued to be a country in the wilderness, for it voted Labour, yet was ruled by a Tory Britain. This would have led to riots and revolutions in some countries, but Scotland simply got on with it – and talked about football.

And here were Spain on World Cup business. Spain was a country that had lost a little of its romance and mystery in recent decades because since the early 1960s it had been at the centre of the booming package holiday business for British tourists. Arguably this had sustained the dictatorship of General Franco until his death in 1975. Franco, the victor of the Civil War, had been the last remaining vestige of the axis of evil which had included Hitler and Mussolini, and his dictatorship had been long, vicious and brutal. It was often said that it was only football, particularly the European exploits of teams like Real Madrid and Barcelona which had kept up the spirits of the Spanish people during these dreadful days.

But now Franco was dead and Spain's new leader, King Don Juan Carlos, was sworn in and a fragile democracy established. Just how fragile was indicated in February 1981 when some police and army officers attempted a coup, at one point firing a pistol into the air inside the Cortes building, the home of the Spanish Parliament. But the role of the King had been paramount. He had dissociated himself immediately from this nonsense, ordered the soldiers back to barracks and after a tense day or two, order was restored, and democracy strengthened. Everyone could once again return to their football. Indeed obsession with football was a feature of Spanish life which was most certainly shared with Scotland. Yet Spain's national team had not done as well as it kept promising to do. It had won the European Nations Cup in 1964 (in Madrid itself, beating the USSR to the intense delight of

General Franco who hated communism and on previous occasions had forbidden his teams to play in the Soviet Union), but since then Spain's record in World Cups and European Nations Cups had been distinctly dismal. Until this year of 1984, that is, for they were the beaten finalists in the European Nations Cup in a narrow loss brought about by a goalkeeping error. Many people thought that Spain were the best team in the tournament.

But there had been no victory and their good performance in the summer had to be balanced against many other failures, particularly in the 1982 World Cup, held in Spain itself where they had even managed to lose to Northern Ireland and draw with Honduras. If Scotland considered themselves to be underperformers on the international stage, Spain had even more cause to think that way about themselves.

Other than the fanaticism of the supporters and the impression that no-one ever talked about anything else, Scotland and Spain shared other passions and problems as well. There was, for example, an intense and perpetual internal struggle which did not always work well for the advantage of the nation. In the same way that Rangers fans would frequently boo Celtic players while playing for Scotland, so too would Real Madrid fans abuse the players of Barcelona.

Scotland's record against Spain was not too bad. There had been, for example, a good victory in 1957 at Hampden, an even better one in Madrid in 1963, a goalless draw in 1965 at Hampden and a narrow home defeat in 1974, followed by a respectable draw in Valencia the following February. Scotland's recent form had also been respectable. As well as the win over Iceland in the first game of the World Cup qualifying section, there had been an impressive win over Yugoslavia in a friendly, and it was now well known throughout Europe that Scotland were a difficult team to beat at Hampden, although their away form was less convincing.

As was the custom at the time, there would be no live television coverage. This was a shame for all the tickets had been sold and it would not have affected the attendance. There would be radio commentary and TV highlights later that night, but it remains a shame that the nation was deprived of the opportunity of seeing one of the best Scottish performances against top-class opposition for many years.

Scotland started off playing towards the Mount Florida End, and after surviving a few early scares settled down to play a fine game, refusing to be intimidated by the reputation of the Spaniards, most notably the infamous Andoni Goicoechea who rejoiced in the name of 'El Carnicero' – 'the Butcher' for his ferocious tackles. Once in the summer in the European Nations Cup Finals in France when he himself was injured and the TV cameras panned in to show him receiving treatment from the physiotherapist, one of the TV pundits was heard to remark: "There will be quite a lot of players all round Spain and Europe enjoying this, you know!"

Johnston and Dalglish won the respect and admiration of their fans for their courage in running straight at Goicoechea time and time again, and Graeme Souness, never slow to dish out the meat himself when required, began to exercise a little control over the midfield. Pressure began to mount on the Spanish goalkeeper Luis Arconada, the man who had made the horrendous mistake in the European Nations Cup final, and whose very name lent itself to the chant: "Arconada, You're a ****er, You're a ****er" which now reverberated round the Hampden terracings.

Scotland opened the scoring in the 33rd minute and it was a great tribute to the courage of Mo Johnston, for, during a sustained spell of Scottish pressure, Arconada could only parry a Steve Nicol piledriver, and JOHNSTON dived forward to head the ball home, showing tremendous awareness and athleticism. Before half-time he had once again created pandemonium on the terraces as Jim Bett made space on the right, the referee played advantage when he was fouled, and his cross was met by spring-heeled JOHNSTON, who managed to beat both Arconada and Goicoechea to the ball to head home. Little wonder that Hampden resounded to 'Mo! Mo! Super Mo! Super Maurice Johnston' as the teams left the field at the break.

The Hampden fans had to pinch themselves to see if it were all true. Two-nil up over the strong Spain side, and well on top with every prospect of more goals in the second half from a Scottish team that were enjoying themselves. In particular they were adapting far better than the Spaniards were to the pace that the ball came off the pitch. It being Scotland in November, there had been rain during the day and the ball therefore came off the grass with more of a zip, something which helped Scotland's style of fast, attacking football.

But goalkeeper Jim Leighton did not cope well with one particular bounce in the second half. A free-kick had been conceded and from the resulting cross the infamous GOICOECHEA came up for a header. He nodded the ball down, and it hit the ground in front of the diving Jim Leighton at an unfortunate distance from the Aberdeen keeper, and bounced up over him and into the net. It was the habit of the pundits on BBC and ITV in these days to sneer at Scottish goalkeepers. This incident would not help the cause.

This meant that Scotland might yet be in trouble in this game. But then came the moment in which the DALGLISH lovers came into their own and the Dalglish disparagers had to eat humble pie, or more commonly, say 'I knew he could do it, you know!' 15 minutes remained when Kenny picked up a ball on the right side of the penalty area on the Main Stand side of the ground. He had options to pass, but moved instead across the penalty area, well shadowed but not yet tackled by the Spanish defence, who were clearly waiting for him to pass to someone. With a suddenness which caught everyone – team-mates, opponents, spectators, TV commentators – by surprise, he turned and shot into the top corner. The ball was in the net before Arconada could even dive, and Scotland were 3-1 up. Spain were well beaten.

Scottish commentators went berserk, but the Spanish TV commentator's reaction was perhaps the most revealing. The goal went in, Hampden erupted – but nothing was heard from the Spanish commentator for several seconds before ... "Ah, Dalglish!" It was as if nothing else was needed. At the end, Spanish manager Miguel Munoz was wholesome in his praise of the Scottish performance. He must have reckoned, like all of Scotland did, that if only Scotland could play all their games at home, they would win the World Cup time after time.

v WALES 1-1

Ninian Park, Cardiff; Att: 39,500

10 September 1985

Scotland:	Wales:
Leighton* (Aberdeen)	Southall (Everton)
Gough (Dundee United)	Jones (Huddersfield Town)
Malpas (Dundee United)	Van (Der (Hauwe (Everton)
Miller (Aberdeen)	Phillips (Manchester City)
McLeish (Aberdeen)	Ratcliffe (Everton)
Strachan** (Manchester United)	James* (Queen's Park Rangers)
Nicol (Liverpool)	Jackett (Watford)
Aitken (Celtic)	Nicholas (Luton Town)
Bett (Aberdeen)	Thomas** (Chelsea)
Speedie (Chelsea)	Rush (Liverpool)
Sharp (Everton)	Hughes (Manchester United)
Subs	*Subs*
Rough* (Hibs)	Lovell* (Millwall)
Cooper** (Rangers)	Blackmore** (Manchester United)

Referee: Mr J. Keizer, Holland

'SO FOUL AND fair a day I have not seen' is an oxymoron used in *Macbeth* to describe conflicting emotions. Cardiff on Tuesday 10 September 1985 was just such an occasion. On the one hand, Scotland had earned a play-off for qualification to the 1986 World Cup in Mexico. That, however, paled into insignificance in comparison with the really tragic news of the day; Scotland had lost one of her greatest ever characters in manager Jock Stein.

It would be fair to say that Stein had not enjoyed with Scotland the overwhelming success that he had at Celtic. But he had restored credibility and self-belief to a proud footballing nation that had comprehensively dragged itself through the mud in 1978. Under Stein's wise and restrained leadership, the country had qualified for the World Cup in 1982 and not been totally disgraced; now Stein was determined to see them qualify for the World Cup for the fourth time in a row. Sadly he was to do so at the cost of his own life.

Stein was approaching his 63rd birthday. He was overweight, took football far too seriously (in that respect, he had something in common, perhaps, with the whole Scottish nation) and suffered from assorted other minor health problems, some of them not unrelated to a very bad motor accident that he had been involved in ten years previously. He was a strict, perhaps obsessive teetotaller and, although not a particularly religious man, there was a Calvinistic streak in him. As with most Calvinists, too, there was the occasional fall from grace.

The World Cup qualification group involved Scotland, Spain, Wales and Iceland. Scotland, of course, would not be Scotland if they did not make life difficult for themselves. A defeat in Spain was hardly a disaster, but the defeat to Wales at Hampden was an absolute shocker. This had to be balanced against the autumn of 1984 when Scotland had turned on two fine performances against Iceland when young Paul McStay won his spurs with a great goal and then against Spain a month later when Maurice Johnston and Kenny Dalglish had done the business.

Then in late May Scotland had got away with murder in Iceland when a single goal from Jim Bett had won the game for an under-strength visiting team which had been in grave danger of disgracing the country to an extent unknown since Argentina. Such was the complexity of the group, however, that while a win in Cardiff might qualify Scotland outright for Mexico, a draw would guarantee a play-off against a team from the Oceania zone, Australia as it turned out. It was also odd that of the men who had scored for Scotland so far in this campaign, with the exception of Jim Bett, no-one else took part in this final match against Wales. Scotland's strength lay in their defence where the Aberdeen duo of Miller and McLeish were superb, but the fans were less convinced by the two men up front, whose names suggested that they would be great strikers (namely Sharp and Speedie), but who had as yet had few opportunities to deliver goals in any great quantity.

Wales had been nursing a sense of grievance against Scotland for some time. They had felt cheated at Anfield in 1977 with the Joe Jordan penalty that never was, and also felt financially embarrassed and righteously indignant at Scotland's pulling out of the Home International Championship, which had always been a tidy little earner for the traditionally impecunious Welsh. But this game presented problems in choice of venue. Their decision in 1977 to play the game in England had backfired on them for the Scots had simply taken over Liverpool that night, so they were under political pressure to play the game in Wales. Wrexham was a possibility, but the small ground would mean serious loss of revenue. Cardiff Arms Park, the home of rugby, was a possibility but lacked floodlights, which would have meant a kick-off of 5pm at the latest and TV companies might have lost interest, so they turned to Ninian Park, the home of Cardiff City, a respectable but traditionally underperforming team in the English League. The plain fact of the matter is that Wales prefers rugby to football and at this stage the Welsh FA lacked an appropriate venue for a large football match of this nature.

Once again, the Scots took over. They did not outnumber the Welsh to the extent that they had at Anfield in 1977, but it was clear that even the 'Welsh' areas of the ground had a large Scottish presence in them, and the 'Scottish' end was dangerously packed and seeming to contain more bodies than there had been tickets sold. At one point before the game while the players were warming up, the ball used by the Welsh players disappeared into the Scottish crowd and showed no signs of coming back, no matter how impassioned the pleas of goalkeeper Neville Southall. Neville then approached Jock Stein to use his good offices in getting the ball back. Stein turned to the Scottish crowd and made a gesture indicating that he wanted the ball thrown back to the Welsh. 'Could the Welsh have their ball back please?' The ball returned instantly. The Tartan Army did not argue with Jock Stein.

It was obvious from an early stage that tension would be the order of the day, and that the side which won would be the side which made the fewest mistakes. In addition, the tackling was tough with Welsh centre-forward Mark Hughes clearly set on paying back a few old scores, receiving tit-for-tat retaliation from some of the Scottish defenders. But it was HUGHES who put Wales ahead in the 15th minute when he picked up a pass from Peter Nicholas and drilled home.

For the rest of the first half, Wales were well on top, and the wonder was that they did not score again. James, Rush and Hughes all had reasonable chances but lacked the penetrating touch at the right time, while Scotland's forwards toiled. In midfield, Gordon Strachan ran about like a whippet, winning balls and passing superbly, but there were times when he must have felt that he was playing Wales on his own. In addition to Scotland's other problems, there seemed to be something wrong with goalkeeper Jim Leighton, who was unusually hesitant, indecisive and lacked his usual composure, being seen on more than one occasion to exchange an angry word or two with one of his Aberdeen colleagues, Willie Miller or Alex McLeish.

Half-time brought some relief to Scotland. It would at least give Stein a chance to talk to his men and gee them up, for at 0-1, Scotland were certainly going out. It also gave Jim Leighton a chance to explain his problem. He had lost a contact lens. Such things are notoriously difficult to find, and the short-sighted Jim was struggling. Stein did not hesitate and Alan Rough was ordered to take over in goal. Alan had not played for Scotland since the last World Cup, but this was an emergency ... and in that frenetic atmosphere of the Scotland dressing room, no-one noticed how pale and pinched manager Stein looked.

The second half saw a distinct improvement in Scotland's performance as the Welsh began to buckle. Roy Aitken and Jim Bett came more into the game, as Gordon Strachan, much weakened by exhaustion and rough treatment from Welshmen, was substituted by Davie Cooper. So much now depended on Cooper. Called the 'moody Blue' because of his lack of sympathy or empathy with journalists, he could also be temperamental on the park. Sometimes he could remind the Ibrox faithful of Willie Henderson, Davie Wilson or even Alan Morton with his fine aggressive wing play; other times, the fans were hardly aware that he was on the field.

But tonight he was starting to make a difference as Scotland pressed and tension was cranked up a notch or two. Ten minutes remained when the fates at last smiled on Scotland. A shot from David Speedie hit the arm of David Phillips. It was quite clearly inside the box and was definitely one of the 'sometimes you get them, sometimes you don't' variety, but the huge Scottish support behind that goal was in no doubt and their immediate, unanimous and strident appeal for a penalty may well have influenced Mr Keizer.

In scenes of almost unbearable tension, DAVIE COOPER accepted the gift of the penalty, took the ball, put it on the spot, and placed his shot to Southall's left. The Everton keeper got something on it, but not enough, and the terracing behind that goal exploded like Mount Vesuvius in a mass of tartan favours as everyone jumped on top of one another to celebrate the Scottish goal that might well see them to Mexico.

But ten minutes still remained for something to go wrong. Back home, some Scotland supporters of many years standing had to hide in their garden shed, or flick on to another channel, or go to the toilet – such was the tension. At Ninian Park itself, although Jock had risen from his bench to greet the goal, he now sat back down, leaving all the gesticulations and shouting to his assistant, Aberdeen manager Alex Ferguson. Hardly anyone noticed how quiet Stein had gone, and if they did, they assumed that he was indulging in some private prayer, as everyone does when they need something badly.

And what all Scotland fans needed now was that final whistle. In fact, the players on the field were less stressed, for they sensed that the spirit had been knocked out of the Welsh by the goal and by the huge Tartan Army who now seemed to think that 'We're going to Mexico' somehow rhymed with 'Que sera, sera'! Scotland might even have won the game, had Speedie made a better job of a through ball which was saved by Neville Southall.

At last Mr Keizer signalled full-time, and pandemonium was unleashed on the ground and in living rooms as wives were grabbed and given beery kisses by excited husbands. Even grannie in the corner received a certain amount of amorous attention ... until someone caught sight of a shot on the TV of Jock Stein being carried up the tunnel. It was at first assumed that he had been struck by a missile (a by no means uncommon occurrence in the 1980s) hurled by an irate and frustrated Welsh fan, and that he would soon recover. Or he had simply fainted – after all quite a few fans had been on the point of doing just that during these last tense minutes.

There was a sense of confusion, for although everyone knew that Scotland had now earned a play-off, no-one really knew about Jock Stein. For a good half-hour afterwards, TV reports were unable to confirm that he was all right, and people now began to fear the worst. By the ten o'clock news, it was announced that in the very flush of victory, the Tartan Army had lost its leader.

Jock Stein was cremated on Friday 13 September at Linn Crematorium, Glasgow, the streets lined with fans in Celtic and Scotland scarves. Tribute was paid to him by almost everyone, but two things in particular would have delighted him. One was that none of Saturday's games were postponed – he would have hated to have been responsible for people missing their football! And the other was that Scotland, after a couple of difficult games against Australia, did make it through to Mexico. They won 2-0 in Glasgow and eventually qualified on the morning of 4 December 1985 after earning a draw in Australia. A veteran Scottish fan with clear memories of Hughie Gallacher and Alex James phoned his son to say, "I'll hae to bide alive noo till next summer cos I want tae see them in Mexico!"

Sadly, the man mostly responsible for the national team's resurgence would not be there to see it.

v CIS 3-0

Norkkoping; Att: 14,660

18 June 1992

Scotland:	CIS:
Goram (Rangers)	Kharine
McKimmie (Aberdeen)	Chernisov
Boyd (Celtic)	Tskhadadze
McPherson (Hearts)	O. Kuznetsov
Gough (Rangers)	Onopko
McAllister (Leeds United)	Mikhailichenko
McStay (Celtic)	Aleinikov*
McCall (Rangers)	Dobrovolski
McClair (Manchester United)	Kanchelskis
Gallacher** (Coventry City)	Kiriakov**
McCoist* (Rangers)	Yuran
Subs	*Subs*
McInally* (Dundee United)	D. Kuznetsov*
Nevin** (Everton)	Korneyev**

Referee: Herr Rothlisberger, Switzerland

THE EUROPEAN CHAMPIONSHIP or the European Nations Cup as it was originally called, had never exactly been the favourite tournament of Scotland. The competition had been scorned and ignored in 1960 and 1964. This was annoying, for Scotland had beaten England three times in a row from 1962 to 1964 and would undeniably have done well in a European tournament. Attempts to qualify since then had ranged from the dismal to the abysmal, and Scotland had never been a guest at the top table of this competition. It was odd, for their record in qualifying for the World Cup at the same time was good, but 1968, 1972, 1976, 1980, 1984 and 1988 had been conspicuous by the lack of Scotsmen – apart from the occasional referee or TV pundit.

But, under enthusiastic manager Andy Roxburgh, proud to be seen wearing a tartan scarf even in the dugout on warm nights, Scotland had at last made it to Sweden in 1992 through workmanlike and diligent (rather than breathtakingly spectacular) performances against teams like Romania, Bulgaria and Switzerland in qualifying. Roxburgh, indeed, deserved a great deal of credit because this was on the back of the 1990 World Cup where a defeat to Costa Rica had seriously undermined Scotland's credibility for anything. Also, as Roxburgh himself would admit, there was a serious lack of world class talent at Scotland's disposal.

It was also clear that the days of the massive attendances to support Scotland at home games had now gone. In autumn 1965, for example, on two occasions on a Wednesday night, over 100,000 had attended Hampden to watch Scotland against Poland and Italy –

attendances which had astounded the world – but on 12 September 1990 in the first qualifying match of this European Championship, 12,801 had attended an eerily quiet Hampden Park to see Scotland beat Romania. Credibility was clearly in short supply, as indeed was confidence.

Very much to Scotland's credit however was the appearance on away trips of the Tartan Army, a group of dedicated and peaceful fans whose behaviour, albeit sometimes raucous and drunken, was totally harmless and in stark contrast to that of England's violent, racist and nasty fans. Wherever they went, the Scot fans were loved by the locals who enjoyed seeing their kilts, hearing their music and joining in with their *joie de vivre*. There was even one lovely television shot where a Scots fan invited a Swedish police lady to kiss him on the cheek – and she obliged!

There were only eight teams, drawn into two groups, at the final stages in 1992 and Scotland were perhaps disappointed to avoid England (for they felt that there was a team that they could beat), and they could have been forgiven for being pessimistic as they were put into the group of Germany, Holland and the Commonwealth (sometimes called the Confederation) of Independent States or CIS for short; not to be confused with an insurance company!

The early years of the 1990s were turbulent ones in Eastern Europe, as the communist system of the USSR (dubbed the 'evil empire' by western politicians less than a decade previously) collapsed, for no other reason than that they simply could not kid them on any more, and that the non-Russian parts of the old USSR refused to accept Russian dictatorship. All this meant that the team which had started the qualifying stages of the European Championship of 1992 as the USSR refused to play under that flag, refusing to be called the Union of Soviet Socialist Republics. Some title had to be dreamed up for them and the rather banal one of Commonwealth of Independent States was what appeared. It would be the first and only time that Scotland would ever play a team of that name, for by the next time, they would be called Estonia, Latvia etc, and there would even be a team called quite simply, Russia.

There were other changes as well. There would now be once again a team called Germany rather than East and West Germany, for the Berlin Wall had come down and there was, once again, one united Germany – something which horrified some World War II veterans, although their fears proved groundless. In another separate but connected development, the team which had started the qualifying stages as Yugoslavia found that their country no longer existed but had split up into a collection of states who persisted in fighting brutal and to Western eyes, incomprehensible ethnic and religious wars. Yugoslavia was withdrawn after qualification and replaced by Denmark who thus played in the final stages without having qualified. Rather to the embarrassment of all concerned, for it said a great deal about the qualification process, Denmark won the tournament!

It was generally agreed that Roxburgh's side enjoyed little luck in their first two games. They had started off looking as if they were going to be outplayed by Holland – Rijkaard, Gullit, Bergkamp, Van Basten and all – but rallied to play respectably before going down to a late goal to Dennis Bergkamp. Then, against Germany, a good performance in the first half saw them go in only one goal down before a speculative lob by Stefan Effenberg on the wing took a wicked deflection and beat Andy Goram. Thus Scotland were out, but the irony was that in a poor, defensive minded and unimaginative tournament, they had played as much good football as anyone – and certainly more so than England whose bags were also packed for an early flight home following two appalling goalless draws and a defeat from the host nation Sweden.

Scotland may have been beaten, but the CIS, after grim draws with the other nations, could still qualify. The Scots, however, felt that they now had a chance to show Europe what they could do and to give the travelling fans something to be happy about in this land where beer was an exorbitant price.

Norrkoping, where they had once lost to Paraguay in the World Cup of 1958, did not seem to be a happy hunting ground for Scotland, but the team arrived at the ground to find heavy and persistent rain. At last, Scottish conditions! As every single member of the Scottish team either was currently playing in Scotland or had done so in the past, Roxburgh felt confident that they could adapt to the rain and the heavy ground which reminded everyone of Scotland in November.

It was such an obvious Scottish side as well – seven of the eleven were Mcs! – and they all knew each other and were comfortable with each other's style of play. Playing a 4-3-3 formation with McKimmie, McPherson, Gough and Boyd at the back, then McStay, McAllister and McCall in the middle and McClair, McCoist and Gallacher up front, Scotland took the field with more than a little confidence that they could do well.

Six Rangers players were on the field (Kuznetsov and Mikhailichenko were playing for the CIS), and if one counted Dave McPherson, who was just about to make one of his periodic moves from Hearts to Rangers, there were seven. This was right considering that Rangers had won the Scottish League Championship for the fourth successive year, at the price perhaps of some dull unimaginative football. It was generally agreed, however, that Scotland's best and most creative player was Celtic's Paul McStay. Paul, a quiet unassuming fellow, was rumoured to be about to move from Parkhead and this tournament would give him a chance to shine and impress potential buyers. Paul had the misfortune to play for his beloved Celtic at a time in their history where the club was going nowhere under the guidance of a Board of Directors who lacked ambition and, even more so, lacked common sense. Paul could not have been blamed for wanting to leave, but he did in the end return to Celtic Park. He had also suffered from playing for a fairly mediocre Scotland team to this point, and he had been unable to shine to his full potential there either.

Discerning spectators had noticed his good performances against Holland and Germany, and how fitting it was that it should be McSTAY who put Scotland ahead in the fifth minute of the game. The ball came to him some 25 yards from goal and he drilled it low through a ruck of players to hit the post. But Paul, who had not enjoyed the greatest of luck in his career, for once got a break as he saw the ball rebound off the diving goalkeeper's head and into the net to put Scotland one up.

Ten minutes later Scotland had doubled their advantage. After soaking up sustained pressure, Scotland broke down the left, the ball came to Ally McCoist who touched it back to BRIAN McCLAIR who drove from the edge of the box. The ball took a deflection but might well have been going in anyway, and Scotland were 2-0 up. It was McClair's first international goal after over 20 starts, but it was deserved for the man who had had few problems in scoring for his club sides of Motherwell, Celtic and Manchester United.

This was good stuff and Scotland continued to play like this for the rest of the half, and were given a terrific round of applause from their bedraggled but very happy fans at the break. All that Andy Roxburgh would ask for at half-time would be more of the same.

In fact the CIS, having made two substitutions at half-time, came more into the game in the second half, but their strikers were having an off day and apart from once when Scotland cleared off the line, never seriously threatened the Scottish goal. Roxburgh brought on McInally and Nevin, and it was Nevin who won Scotland a late penalty to put the issue beyond any doubt. It was doubtful decision as Nevin seemed to jump rather high when tackled, and it wasn't clear whether the incident happened inside the penalty box or outside, but the referee had no doubt and GARY McALLISTER made no mistake. Incredibly, he did this to the accompaniment of a lone wet piper behind the goal!

The game finished with the CIS a well beaten side, and it was certainly one of Scotland's better results in the finals of a major tournament. There was something so annoying and predictable about it as well, though, for Scotland had on many occasions only begun to play well after early damage had been done. Minds were cast back to that glorious failure against Holland 14 years previously, although at least on this occasion there was none of the off field machinations to go with it. Never had they been able to start off with a bang and maintain it. If they could cultivate that habit, they could do well.

This team was in need of a Law, Baxter or Dalglish – someone you could point to and say that this fellow was 'world class' (that much over-used cliché). But of course, in football, especially in international football, there is a great deal more to it than that. The team must gel, it must play together and it must be prepared to fight. It must in fact have character. If it has all that, then a team will get somewhere. It will possibly not win the World Cup or the European Nations Cup (Denmark in 1992 and Greece in 2004 being the exceptions), but it will come home with its self-respect intact and will earn the respect and undying admiration of its fans. This team did just that, where other more talented sides in the past did not. More importantly, it did at least give the thousands of fans in Sweden and the millions back home something to cheer about. And that counts for an awful lot.

v **SWITZERLAND** 1-0
Villa Park; Att: 34,926
18 June 1996

Scotland:	Switzerland:
Goram (Rangers)	Pascolo
Burley (Chelsea)	Hottiger
Boyd (Celtic)	Quentin***
Calderwood (Tottenham Hotspur)	Henchoz
Hendry (Blackburn Rovers)	Vega
McCall (Rangers)	Vogel
McAllister (Leeds United)	Sforza
Collins (Celtic)	Koller*
McKinlay* (Celtic)	Bonvin
Durie (Rangers)	Turkyilmaz
McCoist** (Rangers)	Chapuisat**
Subs	*Subs*
Booth* (Aberdeen)	Wicky*
Spencer** (Chelsea)	Fournier**
	Comisetti***

Referee: Mr Krondl, Czech Republic

EURO 96, to be held in England, was a big event for Scotland as well. It was, after all, only the second time that Scotland had qualified for the latter stages of this tournament, and of course, the fact that it was in a neighbouring country made it all the easier for the Tartan Army to attend. In any case, with blanket coverage on TV channels, following the progress of the team was no problem.

'Football's Coming Home' was the theme song of the Euro 96 competition. Football had been started, at least in its organised form, in England, and that was where 'home' was. It was also felt that England would have a great chance of winning the competition just as they had won the World Cup 30 years before in 1966. Certainly a great deal of money had been spent and the organisation was first class, although there existed in the hearts and minds of many Englishmen a real fear that the tournament might be spoiled by the behaviour of their own fans.

The Government was Conservative and had been for 17 years. The strident Thatcher had now given way to the more gentle but dull John Major, a man who liked football but loved cricket and who would famously a year later, on the day after his defeat at the 1997 General Election, resign office to the Queen in the morning and go to the Oval in the afternoon to see Surrey v British Universities. In 1996 he badly needed England to do well to boost his obviously sagging Government, weighed down by its own sleaze and scandals.

Without in any way setting the heather on fire, Scotland had reason to be proud of their qualification for the competition, coming through a tough section that contained Russia, Greece and Finland. Their group for the finals themselves could most charitably have been described as 'a tough test', although we were for the most part spared clichés like 'the group of death'. There is no such thing as an easy draw at that stage of any major international tournament, but this one was given added spice because it contained England. Holland and Switzerland were the other two countries involved, but England, as always, were the important one.

Scotland had not played against England since 1989. The time had been, of course, when Scotland beat England more often than not, but those days were now long gone thanks to a series of pusillanimous performances in the 1970s and 1980s. This was particularly true after the demise of the Home International Championship in the mid-1980s, when Scotland had been bullied by England into deserting Wales and Northern Ireland in favour of more (apparently) lucrative opposition. This had not done Scotland any good, and it was only a matter of time before Scotland v England, the oldest fixture in the world having been first played in 1872, was disgracefully jettisoned.

Scottish fans had missed their biennial trips to Wembley. There had been some great trips, some dreadful ones and some shameful ones of which every fan had his or her own special memory, but they had been much looked forward to and cherished. They had gone now ... or so it had appeared until chance brought them together again. This time however, England were better organised than before and made sure that the stadium had more English fans than Scottish ones, and the spectacle suffered as a result.

It was also a major disappointment for Scotland, and a personal nightmare for Gary McAllister whose penalty miss with the score 1-0 in England's favour cost Scotland so dear. But as Scotland and England had both drawn their first fixtures (in Scotland's case an honourable 0-0 draw against Holland), it meant the Dark Blues still had a chance. They had to beat Switzerland which would give them four points, and then hope that in the other game, Holland v England (who were both on four points), someone would win and thus Scotland might ease through in second place on goal difference. It was, in all truth, a tenuous hope, but Scotland were determined to give their fans something to cheer about.

Manager Craig Brown possibly lacked the flamboyance and in-your-face Scottishness of his immediate predecessor Andy Roxburgh, but he was not without his tactical know-how. It was probably true to say that Scotland did not have as many quality players as other nations had – not surprisingly, given the comparison in population – but then again, it is not always the most talented side that wins tournaments, for other factors come in as well, such as tactics. It was here that Brown scored highly.

But there was one point of issue between himself and the Scottish media and support, and that was why he did not play Ally McCoist. Ally was a larger than life character with his own media career as well as his astonishingly successful Rangers one. He was the sort of fellow that one would want to have in a dressing room, always full of jokes and laughter, and his commitment to the cause, be it Rangers or Scotland, could not be doubted. However he was now however in his mid-30s, and although his career would still have several years to run, he was possibly past his best at least as far as international football was concerned. Rumours abounded about personality clashes between himself and Craig Brown, but no evidence existed of any ill-feeling between the two of them, and McCoist, although disappointed at not being given a greater role, to his credit never gave the journalists anything on which to add an arm and or a leg.

Brown was possibly correct not to field McCoist in the Holland game, his reasoning being that this would be a game that Scotland must not lose and that if this meant they did not score a goal either, then so be it. There was more disappointment expressed and eyebrows raised when McCoist was not in the starting line-up for the England game, although he was brought on halfway through the second half when Scotland were already one down. Sadly it would be another Rangers player, Paul Gascoigne of England who would hit the headlines with his wondrous goal and cheeky celebration.

But for the game at Villa Park, Birmingham on Tuesday 18 June, McCoist was chosen to partner Gordon Durie up front. Goals were required in this game. Scott Booth might have felt entitled to a start as well, for he could certainly score, but it was Tosh McKinlay who took the place of the injured Kevin Gallacher. Apart from that, Brown wisely resisted pressure for more changes, in particular giving Gary McAllister his vote of confidence after the crucial penalty miss. McAllister was, after all, the captain.

Villa Park looked beautiful in the midsummer sunshine, and it was clear that of the 34,926 crowd, more than two thirds were Scottish, with clear evidence of infiltration in the accommodation provided for the Swiss supporters. Switzerland were a team whom Scotland had played 13 times, tending to beat them at home but lose on away soil. They were, like Scotland, a team devoid of superstars but well organised and they worked well for each other. Having drawn with England and then lost to Holland, the Swiss were like Scotland in that they simply had to win to have any chance at all of progressing.

This being the last game in the group, the other game, England v Holland, would kick off at Wembley at exactly the same time. The equipment for the Tartan Army that evening would include a transistor radio with the obligatory headphones, or that most modern of inventions, a mobile phone. Those watching at home knew that news of the scoring of a goal at the other ground would be immediately relayed.

Scotland started well and, with some slick midfield passing, looked the better team but for the first 30 minutes there was no breakthrough until Craig Brown's judgement was proved correct and ALLY McCOIST scored with a fierce drive from the edge of the penalty box. The exuberant McCoist immediately turned and ran to his manager – but there was no 'I told you so!' in all this, merely: 'You asked to do a job, Boss, and I've done it'. Craig Brown was delighted.

This was the score at half-time, and in the other game at Wembley, England were leading Holland 1-0. This meant that because Holland had beaten Switzerland 2-0 – the same score by which Scotland had lost to England, although both Scotland and Holland now had four points, Scotland's goal difference was 1-2 to Holland's 2-1. Therefore, Scotland had to score more goals, and the Tartan Army would have to swallow pride, abandon principles, change the habits of a lifetime, cause their forefathers to turn in their graves – and support England! What must not happen was for Holland to equalise, although if they did and then went ahead, the Tartan Army would want Holland to hammer England into the ground. That would be easier to support! But in the meantime, Scotland could solve their own problems if they could find the net a few more times themselves.

But goals would not come for Scotland against a well marshaled defence which incidentally contained two men who would in later years play for Celtic, Ramon Vega and Stephane Henchoz. Scotland in any case could not afford to give anything away and were much relieved to see the dangerous Stephane Chapuisat substituted at half-time.

The drama affected almost every house in the British Isles with the rare sight of Scotland and England being cheered on equally. With the benefit of satellite television, or with a combination of both television and radio, it was possible to follow both games simultaneously. Thus all Glasgow rose in rare accord to acclaim Sheringham's goal for England, then Edinburgh pubs went crazy as Alan Shearer added another. Holland were losing badly and they were now 2-3 down on goal difference – but that was not yet enough for Scotland – Holland would still qualify on goals scored.

The Scotland players were all completely aware of all this, for the supporters in the crowd were becoming appropriately animated. The players also knew that another Scottish or English goal would solve the problem and put Scotland ahead. There was, of course, nothing that they could do about England, but they did not seem capable of rescuing themselves, as this Swiss defence gave nothing away. Scotland, urged on by the excellent Stuart McCall pressed forward, but few chances came their way, even though Scott Booth was now brought on to give some width to the attack.

Then, just on the hour mark, Villa Park erupted (as did Wembley and indeed all of England and all of Scotland) with the news that Teddy Sheringham had scored again. Holland were now four goals down and Scotland were ahead on goal difference. To what extent this affected Scotland's tactics we cannot be sure, but there must now have been a certain pressure to hold on to the lead and not do anything daft.

This state of affairs continued for 15 minutes until the transistors told Villa Park that Patrick Kluivert had scored what in other circumstances would have been described as a 'late consolation goal' but which now proved vital. Holland's goal difference was now 3-4, and they would go through on goals scored unless Scotland could find the net again. Desperation now being the order of the day, Brown took off the exhausted McCoist and put on the hard working John Spencer, but to no avail.

Full-time came at both grounds with no further scoring, and Scotland were once again out of a major tournament by the slimmest of margins. The fact remained that McCoist's goal against Switzerland was the only one scored by Scotland in the whole tournament, and that was not enough. Football is all about scoring goals, and perhaps McCoist should have been given a start in all three games. Then again, if McAllister had not missed that penalty against England...

v SWEDEN 1-0
Ibrox Stadium; Att: 46,738
10 November 1996

Scotland:
Leighton (Hibs)
McNamara (Celtic)*
Boyd (Celtic)
Calderwood (Tottenham Hotspur)
Hendry (Blackburn Rovers)
Burley (Chelsea)
McKinlay (Blackburn Rovers)
Collins (Monaco)
McKinlay (Celtic)
Jackson (Hibs)**
McGinlay (Bolton Wanderers)***

Subs
Lambert (Borussia Dortmund)*
Gallacher (Blackburn Rovers)**
McCoist (Rangers)***

Referee: Sr. Jose Garcia Aranda, Spain

Sweden:
Ravelli (IFK Goteburg)
Nilsson (Helsinborgs IF)
Sundgren (AIK)
P. Andersson (Borussia Munchengladbach)
Bjorklund (Rangers)
Schwarz (Fiorentina)
Zetterberg*** (Anderlecht)
Thern (ASRoma)
Alexandersson** (IFK Goteburg)
Blomqvist (AC Milan)
Dahlin* (Borussia Munchengladbach)

Subs
K. Andersson* (Bologna)
Larsson** (Feyenoord)
A. Andersson*** (IFK Goteburg)

THE BACKGROUND to this game would have to be described as bizarre. Scotland had been scheduled to play three World Cup qualifiers before this one. In fact they had played only two. They had earned an honourable 0-0 draw in Austria and had won 2-0 in Latvia – but it had been the events of Wednesday 9 October 1996 that had more or less reduced international football to ridicule, and Scotland were the ones who would suffer.

The game against Estonia at the Kadriaorg Stadium in Tallinn had been scheduled to be played in the evening. Scotland objected to the floodlights which did indeed seem to be distinctly sub-standard, and suggested that the game be played in the afternoon in daylight if better floodlights could not be deployed. This was a poor Baltic country still recovering from the repression of the Soviet Union, and no other floodlights were readily available. So it was agreed by FIFA that the game be played in the afternoon in daylight. Initially the Estonians agreed, but then didn't turn up! Scotland were there, the referee and linesmen were there, the TV and Press were there ... but no Estonia. Scotland walked out on to the field, took the kick-off at the centre to show they were willing, the referee blew for full-time and everyone went home!

Naturally Scotland expected to be awarded the points for this farce – indeed it was confidently predicted that Scotland would be awarded a 3-0 victory – but a FIFA Committee, a few days before the Sweden game, under the Chairmanship of Swede

Lennart Johansson ordered a replay in neutral Monaco in February. Scotland now had every right to call 'foul!' on this one, for Mr Johansson should never have been in charge of any decision on this game as Sweden were in the same group. Indeed Sweden were Scotland's next opponents. Mr Johansson was also a man who would later attract adverse criticism from women's groups when he suggested that women wear tighter shorts on the field, and it was generally wondered how he had got to such lofty positions as Vice President of FIFA and President of UEFA. He had also, before the Committee had convened, gone on record as saying that the game would have to be replayed – a clear case of prejudging the issue. Nevertheless, some Swedish supporters arrived in Glasgow for this game singing his praises!

There was also the question of Gary McAllister's suspension. Gary was Scotland's captain, an inspiring one, but a tendency to pick up yellow cards had led to a suspension for the Estonia game, as everyone thought. He did indeed sit in the stand during that non-game, and had reason to believe that he had now served his one match suspension. But in spite of impassioned appeals from Scotland Manager Craig Brown, FIFA ruled that he must sit out the game against Sweden as the Estonia match had not happened.

Sweden had not started the group as well as Scotland. Certainly they had beaten Belarus and Latvia but on the same day as the fiasco in Tallinn, they had lost at home 1-2 to Austria, and it was clear that if they were to qualify for France 98 they would have to get something out of their trip to Glasgow. Scotland, on the other hand, looked quite solid. They had been very unlucky not to get further than the qualifying stages of Euro 96 in England, their draw in Vienna now appeared, in the context of Austria's defeat of Sweden, to be a very good result indeed and there had been a fine 2-0 win in Riga.

The country in general was still reeling from the day six months previously when a gunman had murdered 15 children and one teacher in Dunblane in Stirlingshire. Such things happen, of course, but normally in places like the USA, Scots reckoned, and it was a blow from which Scotland would take a long time to recover. The country was also still recovering from the blows of Thatcherism which had devastated much of the traditional heavy industry. On the football field, mention has been made of the unlucky and honourable defeat in Euro 96 – but it was still a defeat, and there was a real poignancy in the words sung by the Tartan Army: 'when will we see your likes again?'

Domestically, it was Rangers who held sway. They had now won the Scottish League for eight seasons in a row, but were as far behind in Europe as they were ahead in Scotland. Celtic, with their penchant for talented but emotionally insecure foreign players, were at least making a challenge, now that they had got rid of the old Board which had caused so much trouble. In addition, their impressive new stadium was being developed, but the rest of Scotland lagged far behind, sometimes giving the impression that they did not even have the desire to compete with Rangers.

As always the game meant an awful lot to an awful lot of people. The Tartan Army would, of course, be there in strength, adding to their reputation of being silly, drunken and embarrassingly dressed – but there was no harm in them, and their behaviour was always impeccable. In some ways, this game was the country boys' day out to Glasgow. Normally members of the Tartan Army would support teams like St Johnstone or Falkirk or Hamilton and it was a great opportunity for them to see a really big ground.

Agreeably, the game was televised on terrestrial television, allowing everyone to watch. This is as it should be. If Scotland *are* to be the people's team, then the people must surely be allowed to watch them – and for free. The game was to be staged at Ibrox, for Hampden was undergoing one of its prolonged 'repairs' and so was unavailable. As far as the atmosphere was concerned, this was not necessarily a bad thing, for Ibrox, with supporters nearer to the pitch and the players, lent more passion and immediacy to the occasion. Other games would be played at Rugby Park, Pittodrie and Celtic Park, for the SFA were very wary of staging all games at Ibrox, lest they alienate half of the country. Ironically, on this occasion, the only Rangers player wearing Scotland colours was Ally McCoist, who was on the substitutes bench, while Gers central defender Joachim Bjorklund started for Sweden. Celtic provided three players and Hibs two and three came from the unlikely provenance of Blackburn Rovers, then one of the leading lights of English football.

There were two men called McKinlay and one called McGinlay. Billy McKinlay had played for Dundee United but was now with Blackburn, Tosh McKinlay was one of the few men who had played in all three Scottish city 'derbies' for Dundee, Hearts and Celtic, and John McGinlay, who originally came from near Fort William, was a Bolton Wanderers striker.

In the absence of McAllister, Colin Hendry of Blackburn was captain, and behind him was the ever-reliable veteran Jim Leighton, now in his late 30s and earning his 75th cap for Scotland in the twilight of his career with Hibs, after distinguished service for Aberdeen and Manchester United.

Much argument in pubs beforehand centred on Darren Jackson of Hibs. He had previously played for Dundee United, and was one of those players who, when playing in opposition colours, one took an instant dislike to for his perpetual mouthing to the referee, his exaggeration of injuries and his provocative celebrations of goals. He had, however, for Scotland had precious few goals to celebrate – only one, in fact, out of 13 appearances, but it was a good one against Latvia in the last game. It was the opinion of the Tartan Army that he deserved his place – but only just.

Unlike most international matches, this one started with a bang in the crisp autumn sunshine this Sunday afternoon. Sweden had a large support with them, and although there may have been some animosity in the hearts and minds of Scotland supporters about Mr Johansson, the crowd was entirely good natured. Sweden, in fact, were first on the attack, having few reservations about shooting from a distance.

But it was Scotland, playing towards the Broomloan Road End of the ground, who scored first. Darren Jackson dummied a ball beautifully for JOHN McGINLAY to angle his shot home. This was on eight minutes, and Ibrox was much appreciative of a good Scotland move, even though some of the Tartan Army were still assembling, delayed in the traffic jams of the Glasgow motorway. Then, not long after that, Sweden made one of the earliest substitutions in international history when Martin Dahlin, clearly not well or injured, was replaced by Kennet Andersson.

The rest of the first half was far from comfortable for Scotland. The two Colins – Hendry and Calderwood – were immense at the back as wave after wave of Swedish attacks came at them. Once or twice free-kicks were conceded in potentially dangerous positions, but the Swedish shots were inaccurate and half-time came as something of a relief for the hard-pressed Scottish defence and the anxious support. Those fans who expect a Scottish team, playing at home, to be permanently on the attack and ripping the opposition to shreds do not live in the real world. There are times when one has to be able to soak up pressure, particularly when the team is one up.

The second half was all about Jim Leighton. Jim would eventually win 91 caps for Scotland, and although like other goalkeepers, he was capable of a few blunders (his howler against Norway at Hampden in November 1989 which almost deprived Scotland of their place in the 1990 World Cup Finals, still haunts Scottish supporters), he was generally very reliable. Of his 91 games for Scotland, a staggering 45 were clean sheets. He had started off with Aberdeen, winning a host of domestic honours and the European Cup Winners' Cup in 1983 with Alex Ferguson. He then followed Ferguson to Manchester United, where he played for a few seasons, then was dropped for the English Cup final replay against Crystal Palace in 1991 and relationships between the two men were never quite the same again. He moved on to play for Reading, Dundee and was now with Hibs. He would never have a better game than he did that afternoon.

Both Blomqvist and Kennet Andersson had great shots from close in which Leighton managed to claw away, but it was not only that. It was his constant presence and inspiration for the rest of the Scotland defence which won the day – that, and the magnificent play of Hendry in particular, who tackled brilliantly time and time again. All this sat very ill with the Tartan Army, unused to seeing Scotland on the back foot, but gradually as the second half wore on, Jackie McNamara (winning only his second cap) and Craig Burley grew in confidence as Scotland began to come more and more into the game.

When he was substituted by Kevin Gallacher, Darren Jackson earned a standing ovation from a grateful crowd for the sheer amount of work that he had put in, and shortly after that Ally McCoist came on for John McGinlay. It was Brown's policy to ask his strikers to do a great deal of running and to ask them to defend when the opposition had the ball, and these two had virtually run themselves into the ground for the cause. In the meantime, one of Sweden's substitutions passed virtually unnoticed by the Scottish crowd. After all, who in Scotland in 1996 had ever heard of anyone called Henrik Larsson? In the latter stages of the game, Scotland came close with the fresh McCoist doing a great deal of running and hustling, but there was no further score.

The referee's whistle brought a great cheer from the Scottish crowd. It was relief, mainly, and most Scotland fans were glad to admit that Sweden might even have deserved a draw. On the other hand, it was a fine victory and it did a great deal to send Scotland on their way to a place in the 1998 World Cup Finals. And after the kick in the teeth from FIFA over the Estonia fiasco, it was just the fillip that everyone in the country was needing.

v AUSTRIA 2-0
Celtic Park; Att: 43,295
2 April 1997

Scotland:
Leighton (Hibs)
Burley (Chelsea)
Boyd (Celtic)
Calderwood (Tottenham Hotspur)
Hendry (Blackburn Rovers)
McAllister*** (Coventry City)
Lambert (Borussia Dortmund)
Collins (Monaco)
McKinlay (Celtic)
Jackson* (Hibs)
Gallacher** (Blackburn Rovers)

Subs
McGinlay* (Bolton Wanderers)
McCoist** (Rangers)
McStay*** (Celtic)

Austria:
Konsel (Rapid Vienna)
Schopp (Hamburg)
Schottel* (Rapid Vienna)
Pfeffer (Austria Memphis)
Feiersinger (Borussia Dortmund)
Wetl (Porto)
Aigner*** (Casino Salzburg)
Herzog (Werder Bremen)
Heraf (Rapid Vienna)
Stoger** (Rapid Vienna)
Polster (Cologne)

Subs
Casino* (Salzburg)
Vastic** (Sturm Graz)
Ogris*** (Austria Vienna)

Referee: Mr N. Levnikov, Russia

I T IS PROBABLY true to say that Scotland have a somewhat torrid, if surprising, history with Austria on the football field. They are countries with superficial similarities in that they tend, in the eyes and minds of foreigners, to be confused with their larger neighbours England and Germany with whom they share the same language and, to a certain extent, the same culture. There are even historical parallels in the Act of Union of 1707 and the Anschluss of 1938 when the smaller nation was dragged by bribery, skulduggery and threats of violence into a forced union.

Yet when they meet on the football field, any similarity or affinity disappears. Games between Scotland and Austria have often been unpleasant. As far back as 1951, Billy Steel became the first Scottish player to be sent off in an international match. This was in Vienna in May, a matter of six months after Austria had become the first foreign nation to beat Scotland at Hampden in another very unpleasant affair. Then in 1963, English referee Jim Finney was forced to create a piece of infamy by abandoning a game at Hampden after he had sent off two Austrians and general mayhem broke out. Scotland were winning 4-1 at the time.

More recent was the Rapid Vienna affair of 1984, a sad piece of cheating and corruption which had seen Celtic exit from Europe, a business that has still not yet been forgotten or forgiven. By an unfortunate coincidence, this World Cup qualifying game was scheduled for Celtic Park. Hampden was out of commission and it was the SFA's policy to move games around Scotland. Ibrox had hosted the Sweden game, Belarus would go to Pittodrie in September, and on the Saturday immediately before the Austria game, 17,996 had been at Kilmarnock to see Scotland beat Estonia 2-0. It was a fine, competent Scottish perform-ance and a nice riposte to the odd events of the winter when Estonia had failed to turn up for their home game, and had been rewarded with having to play the game in neutral Monaco, where Scotland were distinctly off the boil in a featureless 0-0 draw.

But the game at Kilmarnock had meant that Scotland topped the group with eleven points from five games, as distinct from Austria who had seven points from three. A defeat for Scotland at Celtic Park therefore would mean that Austria would be in a very strong position to win the group, but Scotland were not a bad side at all. Most unusually for a Scotland team, they had yet to concede a goal in their five games played in the section. This was due to goalkeeper Jim Leighton and a fine defence which contained men like Colin Hendry, Colin Calderwood and Tom Boyd. Scotland had already played Austria in Vienna in the first match of the group on 31 August 1996. It had been a goalless draw, and while hardly the most exciting match ever seen by the Tartan Army and those who watched it in pubs back home in Scotland, it was however generally agreed that 0-0 away from home was an excellent result.

Celtic Park in April 1997 was impressive but as yet incomplete. The Jock Stein Stand on the western side of the ground was not yet built, but the rest of the ground was complete and gave an excellent view of the game from all parts. The SFA, worried about poor atten-dances at Scotland games in the 1990s (the team had had a great deal of difficulty in regaining lost credibility after the Costa Rica fiasco on 1990), hit upon a laudable experi-ment of providing cheap admission for youngsters, and the result was that loads of schools, churches and boys' and girls' football teams sent buses to this game. Indeed the pressure of the crowd trying to gain admission at the north west end of the ground beside the cemetery in Janefield Street was more than a little worrying for those in charge of young children.

Craig Brown pulled a surprise when he dropped Paul McStay in favour of Paul Lambert. Considering that the game was to be at Celtic Park, it was a brave decision. McStay would be on the bench and indeed did play for the last couple of minutes. But Brown possibly realised that McStay, whose brief appearance would be his 76th Scottish cap and who had been a huge influence on Scotland ('McStay the mainstay' had frequently appeared as a headline in the *Scottish Daily Express* or the *Daily Record*) was now nearing the end of his career. In this Brown was remarkably prescient. In a few days time, the 32-year-old McStay would be injured at Stark's Park, Kirkcaldy and would never play again.

Paul Lambert would in later years grace Celtic Park, but in April 1997 his greatest moments were yet to come. He had starred for both St Mirren and Motherwell, but he was now with Borussia Dortmund with whom later that season he would win the European Champions League. It had been with Dortmund that Brown had seen him mark the dangerous Austrian playmaker Andreas Herzog of Werder Bremen out of the game. Lambert was chosen that night for no other purpose than to do the same.

Up front, Brown selected the ever willing Darren Jackson and Kevin Gallacher. The forwards had not been exempt from criticism. Rightly were Scotland praised for not losing goals. The problem was that they were not scoring many either. The game in Monaco had seen some feckless finishing, and at Kilmarnock last Saturday, pleased as everyone was with Scotland's performance, it had hardly escaped notice that the two goals were not scored by forwards. One was scored by defender Tom Boyd, and the other was an own goal.

Kevin Gallacher had never been a fixture in the Scotland team. No-one doubted his ability, certainly not those who had watched him at Tannadice Park in his early days. He had started off as a very impressive forward for Dundee United, then had moved to Coventry City in 1989 and Blackburn Rovers in 1993. He had been a star with all three teams, but it was beginning to look as if he was to be one of those players who did not quite make it at international level. Tonight however was to be his opportunity to prove them all wrong.

There was also another factor, an emotional one, and given that the game was at Celtic Park, everyone would be very aware of it. Kevin was the grandson of Patsy Gallacher, generally agreed to be Celtic's greatest ever player. Rumours abounded throughout Kevin's career that he was about to be transferred to Celtic – perhaps for Kevin's sake, it was as well that he wasn't – and there was certainly a massive incentive for him to do well at Parkhead. His grandfather was still a legend there – Patsy couldn't play for Scotland, of course, because he was an Irishman – and how nice it would be for his family if Kevin could produce the goods for Scotland tonight.

It was a fine spring evening, perhaps a touch on the cold side, as Scotland started playing towards the incomplete end of the ground. Very soon it was seen that John Collins and Gary McAllister were taking a grip of the game, and that indeed Paul Lambert was keeping a tight hold over Herzog. Scotland's first goal came half way through the first half after a fine combined move between Gallacher and Jackson. It was Gallacher who first flicked the ball on to Jackson. Darren then avoided the challenge of a defender and ran in on goal. Goal-keeper Michael Konsel came out to narrow the angle and appeared to foul Jackson as he was about to shoot. Screams of 'Penalty' however were rendered irrelevant when the ball broke to KEVIN GALLACHER to score into the empty net and put Scotland 1-0 up.

It was perhaps a scrappy goal, but by no means undeserved on the run of play, and Celtic Park erupted. It was very noticeably a fairly high-pitched howl, rather than the deep-throated cries that one normally associated with football crowds. This was because of the high preponderance of women and children in the crowd, enjoying the comparatively rare spectacle of Scotland scoring.

From now on until half-time, Scotland consolidated their position to such an extent that Jim Leighton was not called upon to make a save. Craig Burley was seldom off the ball, tackling hard, distributing well and cajoling the best out of his team-mates. Scotland had one or two half chances before half-time, but when the Russian referee, resplendent in his silver uniform, pointed to the dressing room, Scotland had cause to feel satisfied by their efforts.

Austria now brought on Walter Kogler for Peter Schotell at the break, and in their first attack of the second half had a strong claim for a penalty when Toni Polster was tackled strongly by Tom Boyd on the edge of box. The referee blew, Scots' hearts leapt into mouths, but the foul was given as a free-kick just outside the area and not as a penalty kick. Scotland had escaped. The set piece was adequately dealt with by the Scottish defence, and it was only when Austria made a second substitution – Ivica Vastic for Peter Stoger that they were able to bring any more pressure to bear on the Scottish rearguard, this time when Vastic forced a brilliant save out of Jim Leighton, who had been seriously unem-ployed for a spell.

By this time, the exhausted Darren Jackson had been replaced by John McGinlay, a change that gingered up the Scottish attack. Jackson had apparently been thinking of withdrawing himself from the squad because of injuries picked up against Estonia, but Brown had persuaded him to stay with the team. He had done a great deal of running, perpetually pulling defenders out of position and creating space for other players.

In the 77th minute of the game, Scotland scored again. This time it was an absolutely superb goal, created in midfield by Paul Lambert who slipped the ball to GALLACHER at the edge of the penalty box. Kevin simply hammered an angled shot high into the roof of the net beyond the reach of Konsel, making a very difficult thing look easy.

There was a sustained explosion of joy at this piece of brilliance with numerous teachers telling their charges 'That's the way to do it', and the TV companies playing the goal back time and time again. It had all looked so simple, and with one stroke Gallacher had silenced his many doubters.

The game was now all over, and Brown brought on McStay and McCoist. McCoist in fact replaced Gallacher, who thoroughly enjoyed his standing ovation as he trotted off.

It was, all in all, a fine night. Two goals scored, the undefeated record and clean sheet run preserved and Scotland now sat seven points ahead of Austria who couldn't catch them even if they won their games in hand. Phil Shaw in the *Independent* the following morning described this game as 'a collective effort, brimming with spirit, skill and tactical awareness' and auguring well for the future. Craig Brown, however, was careful to stress that a great deal of work had yet to be done before Scotland could think of going to France for the World Cup.

As supporters headed back to their coaches and thence their beds, they had every reason to be happy. Indeed the Tartan Army contained so many children that night they might have been called the 'infantry'! They had seen Scotland beat a good European team, and the disappointment of Euro 96 in England now seemed a distant memory. They just knew that Scotland were on their way to the 1998 World Cup finals in France.

v **ENGLAND 1-0** (lost 1-2 on aggregate)

Wembley Stadium; Att: 76,848
17 November 1999

Scotland:
Sullivan (Wimbledon)
Weir (Everton)
Davidson (Blackburn Rovers)
Dailly (Blackburn Rovers)
Hendry (Rangers)
Burley (Celtic)
Ferguson (Rangers)
Collins (Everton)
McCann* (Rangers)
Hutchison (Everton)
Dodds (Dundee United)

Subs
Burchill* (Celtic)

England:
Seaman (Arsenal)
Campbell (Tottenham Hotspur)
Neville (Manchester United)
Southgate (Aston Villa)
Adams (Arsenal)
Beckham (Manchester United)
Ince (Middlesbrough)
Scholes** (Manchester United)
Redknapp (Liverpool)
Owen* (Liverpool)
Shearer (Newcastle United)

Subs
Heskey* (Leicester City)
Parlour** (Arsenal)

Referee: Sr. Pierluigi Collina, Italy

THE BIENNIAL trip to Wembley used to be the greatest event in the Scottish football calendar. It was a feature of the season until the last trip there in 1988, but by then it had been pushed to the absolute end of the season, sometimes on a Wednesday night, and had lost much of its impact. This was due to a combination of hooliganism, player apathy and everyone being more interested in club football, plus the fixture had not been helped by the refusal of the big two British nations to continue the Home International Championship against Wales and Northern Ireland.

One deplored this, but nevertheless moved on. It was left to the European Championships to throw up games between Scotland and England. This happened in 1996 when Scotland played England at Wembley, losing 0-2 on the infamous afternoon of Gary McAllister's missed penalty, and now in 1999, the two British nations were brought together again. Both had finished second in their group sections for qualification for Euro 2000 to be held in the Low Countries, and second placed teams were put into a draw for play-offs. Scotland and England were paired together, with the first game to be played at Hampden on Saturday 13 November and the second at Wembley on Wednesday 17 November 1999.

On paper, it seemed that England had the better team, but their form had not been any too impressive and it was noticeable that many Englishmen who played well for their clubs, did not find it too easy to adapt to the ways of the national side under the guidance of Kevin Keegan. The tabloid press in England had the deserved reputation of being the worst in the world, and it did not hold back on its own team who, they felt, should have qualified automatically instead of being involved in these troublesome play-offs.

Scotland on the other hand were never likely to qualify from their group which contained the very strong Czech Republic team, but a spirited and honest effort in their later fixtures – a draw against Estonia, two wins against Bosnia and a 3-0 win over Lithuania meant that Scotland earned second place. Scotland was thrilled at the idea of playing England again, and emotions about the two-legged game ranged from the absurdly optimistic to the cold realism that men like Beckham, Scholes, Adams and Owen were world class performers. Or were they? Were they not perhaps the product of the biased English media? The two-legged fixture would certainly tell.

The first game at Hampden was a profound disappointment. England scored twice through Paul Scholes in the first half and Scotland never looked like recovering. Scotland were suffering from the loss of Paul Lambert, badly injured in the Old Firm game the week before, and it would have been hard to imagine Scholes scoring twice if Lambert had been on the field to snuff out his threat. Scholes did not add to his popularity in any way by his gesture of running to the Scottish crowd hand cupped to his ear as if to ask where the Hampden Roar was now. Spirited renditions of 'Flower of Scotland' from the crowd could not rouse the home players, any more than could the unpleasant, obscene chants and songs about David Beckham and his wife's alleged sexual practices. They were at least funny, and it was good that a Scottish crowd could retain some sort of a sense of humour in such adversity.

Down 0-2 from Hampden, most Scottish fans now made plans for Wednesday night involving other channels rather than watching the Wembley game which had all the makings of a real trouncing about it. It was not that Scotland had played badly at Hampden, nor that England played well. It was simply that England, clinically and professionally, took their chances, while Scotland, in spite of loads of huff and puff, did not. Craig Brown, already suffering from injuries within the squad, was dealt a further blow when Kevin Gallacher was suspended thanks to the yellow card that he had picked up in the Hampden game. This was unfortunate, but it allowed Brown a chance to give a fifth cap to skilful winger Neil McCann of Rangers, and Brown did, at least in public, remain upbeat about Scotland's chances.

It was almost like old times again when Scotland supporters boarded trains the night before at Waverley Station, Edinburgh and Central Station, Glasgow to go to Wembley. But there were differences. The Tartan Army's allocation of tickets was minuscule, even smaller than in the old days, and this time it would take a brave man to infiltrate the English ranks. It was a midweek fixture as well, it was in the middle of November, traditionally the most miserable month of all and Scotland were already 0-2 down – circumstances that made it difficult to replicate the happy, care-free, euphoric and ridiculously over-optimistic atmosphere of days gone by.

It is, of course, a quintessential Scottish characteristic to throw everything away first, then to come back strongly, almost make it and then complain about how unlucky we all were. It happened in the so called Wars of Independence, it certainly happened in the Jacobite rebellion of 1745/46 and in footballing terms, Argentina 1978 was a collector's item of this foible of Caledonian culture. After blowing things spectacularly with Peru, Iran and a drugs scandal, Scotland fought back and beat Holland – but to no avail. To a lesser extent, this was what happened here.

Kevin Keegan made one major tactical error. Perhaps suffering from over-confidence, the England manager announced his team in advance. He declared that Martin Keown would be replaced by Gareth Southgate. Southgate was a more elegant player than Keown, but lacked the physical power of the Arsenal centre-half. Brown, normally a very cautious manager, now abandoned his normal 3-5-2 formation and pushed an extra man into the attack, that being Don Hutchison of Everton, the idea being that Hutchison would physically get the better of Southgate and would, in the old fashioned Scottish phrase, so often used of men like Jimmy Quinn, 'rummle them up'.

Ironically, Hutchison was an Englishman. He was not even an Anglo-Scot who had been born in Scotland but had played all his career in England. He was a Geordie, born in Gateshead in 1971, but with a Scottish parent, which qualified him to play for Scotland. He had played for a variety of clubs in England and had picked up a certain reputation for being a little indisciplined in his youth, but had now settled down. This was his seventh Scottish cap and he gladly accepted the role given him by Brown with every Scottish defender told not to be shy about the old fashioned route one ball.

Brown also made one other change in his line-up, apart from that enforced upon him by Kevin Gallacher's yellow card. In the first game, Paul Ritchie had played man-to-man on David Beckham. He had done well enough, but for the Wembley game, Brown deployed Callum Davidson, who was more of an attacking full-back who would play off Beckham rather than mark him obsessively as Ritchie had done at Hampden.

From the start it was clear that Scotland were going to have a go. Indeed they had little choice and with the Tartan Army outshouting their English counterparts, they poured forward into the attack. Hutchison's presence in an attacking role was immediately apparent. A great pass from him to McCann might well have led to a goal, but McCann was not sharp enough and the chance went a-begging. Soon after that, Barry Ferguson managed to get a header in on the England goal, but he was just marginally too high. It was as well for England that David Seaman was in great form, otherwise Scotland would have been several up before half-time. England's mega stars reeled, and Scotland fans began to wonder why they had not seen this on Saturday.

England had seemed to have weathered the Scottish storm and even got the ball into the net when Michael Owen scored but the goal was chalked off by ace Italian referee Pierluigi Collina with whom no-one ever dared argue. It was immediately after that when Scotland got the goal that their pressure warranted and their fans craved. McCann, who had played well after his early miss, made space on the left and sent over a cross to the far post for DON HUTCHISON, who rose highest to head home.

The effect was electricfying. The fans in the stadium went wild, and in pubs in Scotland, those supporters who had been trying to pretend to themselves that they were not really all that interested, suddenly became animated, noisy and argumentative over the half-time interval as they relished the prospect of a Scottish onslaught on the England goal in the second half. At the ground itself, the sheer volume of noise from the Scottish fans was much remarked upon.

Scotland did indeed press and press, but they were up against a very well organised defence of Sol Campbell, Tony Adams and others who had had loads of experience against top class attacks. Hutchison was better policed in this half, but Craig Burley and Barry Ferguson took over, creating attack after attack for the Scottish forwards. Ferguson, playing in only his fifth international game, was immense and it was indicative of Burley's role that when he took a blow in the face and had to go off for a few minutes, Craig Brown did not make a substitution, preferring to keep the all-action midfielder in the game.

England had their moments as well in this titanic contest. John Collins had to make a great tackle on Michael Owen as he was about to race clear, and David Beckham shot narrowly past, but it was mainly Scotland, particularly in the closing stages, as they laid siege to the English goal. Within the last ten minutes, Scotland had their best chance when Christian Dailly managed to get his head to a ball but guided it only into the hands of David Seaman. So it was not to be, and England held out for a 2-1 win on aggregate.

Everyone agreed that Scotland had had bad luck. Alan Green on BBC Radio said categorically of Scotland that 'they, not England deserved to got through', and Kevin Keegan himself candidly admitted 'We would be the first to admit that we did not play well. We could not get going. There are lost of excuses to make, maybe it was a bit too much for players psychologically to have a 2-0 lead. It was a poor performance and you have to give credit to Scotland and Craig Brown. They took a chance, they had to and we could not get the ball off them.'

The Scottish Press were unanimous in their praise of the team, but Phil Shaw in The Independent put it very well when he said, 'So in the end Scotland were left with the familiar, despised feeling of having failed gallantly.' Gallant failure had indeed been the hallmark of Scotland throughout the ages. It is often the characteristic of Scotland as a nation, but never has a nation had more cause to be proud of its football team than on the night of 17 November 1999.

So the Tartan Army headed back home again in their trains, cars, coaches and aeroplanes, happy in the knowledge that they had won at Wembley (by no means a common phenomenon as it was a feat which they had last accomplished in 1981) but still with the gnawing realisation that there would be no trip to the Low Countries the following summer. Realistically, they were not likely to win the tournament, but it would have been nice to have been there.

v FRANCE 1-0

Hampden Park; Att: 52,000
7 October 2006

Scotland:
Gordon (Hearts)
Dailly (West (Ham United)
Alexander (Preston North End)
Pressley (Hearts)
Weir (Everton)
Ferguson (Rangers)
Fletcher (Manchester United)
Caldwell (Celtic)
McFadden* (Everton)
Hartley (Hearts)
McCulloch** (Wigan Athletic)

Subs
O'Connor* (Lokomotiv Moscow)
Teale** (Wigan Athletic)

France:
Coupet (Olympique Lyon)
Abidal (Olympique Lyon)
Thuram (Barcelona)
Boumsong (Juventus)
Sagnol (Bayern Munich)
Ribery* (Marseilles)
Vieira (Inter Milan)
Makalele (Chelsea)
Malouda (Olympique Lyon)
Trezeguet** (Juventus)
Henry (Arsenal)

Subs
Wiltord* (Olympique Lyonnais)
Saha** (Manchester United)

Referee: Mr Massino Busacca, Switzerland

SUPPORTING SCOTLAND IN the early years of the 21st century had been grim. Manager Berti Vogts may have been a great player and manager with Germany, but, frankly, he did not understand the small and complex country that is Scotland. Granted, he was unfortunate in that native talent seemed to dry up while the Scottish Premier League clubs themselves turned to foreign players – largely to their own detriment, with the occasional exception like Henrik Larsson or Brian Laudrup. Indeed a great deal of the Scottishness had gone out of the game. Vogts was only one of several foreign managers, and in Edinburgh we had the phenomenon of Heart of Midlothian, a name almost inwoven in the fabric of Scottish football, being more or less entirely taken over by Lithuanians. Fortunately, Scotland is not (in the early years of the new century at least) a particularly xenophobic country, but it was sad to see the whole image of one of Scotland's establishment teams being over by a foreign nation. The history of Hearts in those years is an interesting although not a wholesome one, as their owner kept on promising European glory for the club. Several years down the line, such glory has not yet been forthcoming.

And yet the love of the game remained strong. Although the SPL championship would remain the same two-horse race that it had been for the past 20 years since the heyday of Aberdeen and Dundee United, people kept going to the games (sometimes paying exorbitant prices to do so) and, more importantly, in this new age, watching it on TV. Celtic reached the final of the UEFA Cup in 2003, attracting widespread admiration for their play and for their marvellous supporters in Seville. Football hooliganism in Scotland was almost extinct at a time when it palpably was not so in the wider society, and when it was still prevalent in other countries. Scotland remained the number one nation in Europe for the percentage per head of the population who involved themselves in one way or other with football.

These factors highlighted even more the dreadful performances that the Scottish public had to put up with from their national team against the likes of the Faeroe Islands or Moldova, and Scotland's repeated failure to make it to the finals of any tournament hurt. 2000, 2002, 2004 and 2006 saw no Scottish representation, and for such a proud nation, that was hard to stomach. Vogts did try hard, digging up from obscure teams in England anyone with a tenuous Scottish connection to play for the national side, but he lacked leadership qualities or charisma. Indeed the story is told of the game in the Faeroes in 2002 when Scotland were 0-2 down at half-time and well on their way to becoming the laughing stock of the world, that it was the Old Firm pair of Barry Ferguson and Paul Lambert who took over, kicking the necessary bums and shouting about pride and self-respect in order to salvage a draw, which was still humiliating but not as catastrophic as a defeat would have been.

But times had changed. Scotland's affairs had taken a turn for the better in the appoint-ment of Walter Smith, one time manager of Rangers and a man who certainly did know the Scottish scene. With Tommy Burns and Ally McCoist in his management team, things were looking up, although with Italy and France, the two finalists of the 2006 World Cup in Scotland's group, only a fool would have been sanguine about Scotland qualifying for Euro 2008. As well as the two big guns, there were also Ukraine, Lithuania, Georgia (and none of these three were pushovers) and Scotland's old friends from the Faeroes.

Hope springs eternal, as they always say about the Scottish fan, but realistic assess-ments were that Scotland would not quite make it. But very early on, a change in attitude was detected. In particular, the 'pulling out of the national squad through injury' phenom-enon seemed to lessen. This practice, which had been widespread under Berti Vogts and done with the blatant encouragement of clubs who wished to prevent the injury of a player, is something which causes bewilderment and puzzlement to the Scottish football fan who sees playing for his country as the most important thing in existence, but it was noticeable how seldom it happened now. Wise clubs will realise that a good national team is crucial for the game at all levels, but such altruism is rare among managers.

Scotland's Euro 2008 qualifying campaign began on 2 September 2006. The Faeroes were put to the sword to the tune of 6-0 to exorcise the memories of less strong-minded teams of a few years before. Kris Boyd scored twice and Fletcher, McFadden, Miller and O'Connor once each as the match was won at a canter before 50,059 fans in the high stands of London Road. This game had been played at Celtic Park rather than Hampden because the National Stadium, to its shame, had allowed itself to be hired out for a pop concert that evening. This was a good performance by the Scottish side, and then an even better showing was forthcoming the following Wednesday when Scotland travelled to Lithuania to win 2-1 thanks to goals from Christian Dailly and Kenny Miller. Any away win is a good one, and Scotland, notoriously poor starters in tournaments in previous years, were now top of the group and awaited the arrival of France on 7 October 2006.

France had never really been considered as one of the great footballing nations of the world in the way that Brazil, Germany or Italy were. Indeed Scotland's record against them had been very respectable, but in recent years, perhaps due to the influence of Algerian and Moroccan immigrants, French football had become very strong indeed. Many of their players played for English Premiership clubs like Arsenal and Chelsea, and there was the very recent memory of the 2006 World Cup final where only Zinedine Zidane's moment of madness and a penalty shoot-out had prevented them from becoming World Champions again, following their victory on home soil in 1998.

But Scotland always had this tradition of being very difficult to beat at Hampden, no matter how illustrious the opponents were. They still were blessed with a huge, encouraging, resilient and perpetually well behaved support, and those who could not get tickets would be able to watch the game from their armchairs or, equally likely, with a pint in their hand in the local bar where the atmosphere would rival that of the game itself.

Walter Smith picked what was generally agreed to be the best team available, laudably ignoring factional interests which would demand the inclusion of more people from one particular team. What had been achieved in recent decades (and it reflected well on a succession of Scotland team managers) was unity among the support. So often in the 1960s and previously one had heard, for example, Celtic players being booed by the Rangers support. Anglo-Scots in particular had a hard time if they had displaced a popular Home-Scot. This had thankfully been eliminated, although, sadly, there did remain a few inane chants among the support about the English and the Queen.

The game kicked off at 5pm for television purposes so that as many games as possible throughout Europe could be shown live. The anthems were played – the ever stirring 'Marseillaise' for France with its calls to rid its land of foreign invaders, and 'Flower of Scotland' with a similar message. Opinion remained divided about 'Flower of Scotland'. It had appeared in the 1970s and had been much loved then, but perhaps it had had its day, and something less mournful was required. It mattered not at Hampden that crisp autumn evening. It was given a rousing reception.

The first half which saw France attack the Mount Florida goal was far from comfortable viewing for the Scottish nation. The talented French side exposed one or two weaknesses in the Scottish set-up and had the ball in the net twice – only to be ruled offside. Thierry Henry hit the post, and at the other end Jamie McFadden was ploughing a lonely furrow as Scotland's only attacker. His opportunities were rare, although once he might have done better when he shot straight at the goalkeeper. It was probably true to say that the half-time whistle was heard with a certain amount of relief as the crowd at Hampden turned to their Bovril, those in the pub to their pints and stovies (if the pub was sufficiently enterprising to think of that) and those at home to a cup of tea. 'We're doing no' bad against the second best team in the world' was the general opinion, but it would have been hard to find a Scotsman who would put his hand on his heart and say that Scotland would emerge victorious.

But it was a different Scottish team in the second half. Walter Smith had clearly told them during the break that a Scottish victory was 'on', for they had gloriously taken all that France could throw at them. France would become discouraged and wilt, especially if the Scottish team could persuade the Hampden Roar to come out of abeyance and carry them home.

McFadden, the tireless McFadden, curiously underemployed by his club manager David Moyes at Everton, now came more into his own. He hit one shot that went wide, but now he found that he had more and more Scotsmen up the field helping him. Halfway through the second half, Scotland, now attacking the Mount Florida end of the ground, got a corner on the right. Paul Hartley took it, McFadden ran for it taking a defender with him. He didn't quite reach the ball but instead it fell to GARY CALDWELL who stabbed it home.

Clichés like 'Hampden erupted' didn't quite do justice to the rapture that greeted this goal. A moment or two later, everyone calmed down, however, and realised that there was a job to be done still, and that the second best team in the world still had more than 20 minutes to earn themselves a draw. McFadden was now withdrawn and replaced by Garry O'Connor, one time of Hibs but now with Lokomotiv Moscow. The emphasis now being on protecting the lead, a 'fresh pair of legs' was required to do the solitary running up front.

It was now that a certain street wisdom could be seen in the Scottish side, as experienced players like Barry Ferguson and Darren Fletcher took the heat out of the match. Yet the Tartan Army had all seen men like Makalele, Henry and Vieira turn games for their clubs in the English Premiership and no-one could relax. The prize was so huge – top of the group and ahead of France – and coming ever more tantalisingly close as the minutes ticked away.

A great deal depended on Craig Gordon of Hearts in the Scotland goal, but he was up to the task, not least because he knew when to come out of his goal and how to dominate the penalty area. Indeed the final whistle sounded with the ball in Gordon's arms, and the way that he reacted was imitated by the whole nation. It was a superb victory, making up for the myriad disappointments in recent years and an indication to Europe that Scotland was now back in contention for qualification for big tournaments.

The team had to travel to the Ukraine on Wednesday night. That would be another story, but for the time being, Saturday 7 October 2006 was declared party time throughout the land. The much maligned and sneered-at Scotland had defeated the World Cup runners-up!

v **FRANCE** 1-0

Parc Des Princes, Paris; Att: 42,000
12 September 2007

Scotland:	France:
Gordon (Sunderland)	Landreau (Paris St.Germain)
Hutton (Rangers)	Abidal** (Barcelona)
Alexander (Burnley)	Vieira* (Inter Milan)
McManus (Celtic)	Makelele (Chelsea)
Weir (Rangers)	Malouda (Chelsea)
Ferguson (Rangers)	Thuram (Barcelona)
Fletcher* (Manchester United)	Escude (Sevilla)
McCulloch (Rangers)	Trezeguet (Juventus)
McFadden** (Everton)	Diarra (Arsenal)
Brown (Celtic)	Ribery (Bayern Munich)
Hartley (Celtic)	Anelka (Chelsea)
Subs	*Subs*
Pearson* (Derby County)	Nasri* (Marseilles)
O'Connor** (Birmingham City)	Benzema** (Olympique Lyonnais)

Referee: Mr Damir Skomina, Slovenia

NOT FOR MANY decades has it been possible to consider Scotland as the best footballing nation in the world. It was certainly true of the early 1880s, possibly the Edwardian years, certainly the 1920s and perhaps the 1930s. But the 1950s produced the 0-7 defeat from Uruguay from which Scotland and her self esteem never really recovered, and although many people thought that the team of the mid 1960s would have done well in the England World Cup of 1966, the fact is that they did not qualify. The last time that we have been respectably placed in World ratings was 1974. Since Argentina in 1978, the tale had been one of sorry mediocrity – and perhaps worse than that!

Yet what Argentina did prove was that Scotland *wanted* to be the best in the world. Perhaps we were so accustomed to centuries of doing what the English said and decades of what the Americans dictated, that we could not rouse ourselves out of our self-imposed slave mentality (which manifested itself in players acting like slaves to drink and bad behaviour, falling out with the manager or moaning about accommodation) to do so.

But no nation on earth is more interested in football than Scotland. Per capita of the population, Scotland leaves other nations standing with its utter devotion to the game. And this is why teams like Forfar Athletic, Annan Athletic and Linlithgow Rose are so important. They keep people talking about football, and as long as our obsession with the game continues, there is no reason why we cannot believe that some day we may yet again rise to the top. We need three things – natural talent, attitude and good management.

There is little we can do about the first one, but the other two are certainly within our grasp and compass.

There are the odd occasions when Scotland can turn up trumps with these attributes. Such a day was 12 September 2007 when Scotland rocked Europe by beating the World Cup runners-up France – in Paris! Scotland will always be hard to beat at Hampden, as they had proved in defeating this same, difficult opposition the previous autumn, but a really good team has to be able to turn up trumps away from home as well. This is exactly what Scotland, with the correct attitude, achieved on that never to be forgotten night in September 2007.

When Scotland found themselves in the same World Cup Qualifying Group as Italy, France, Ukraine, Georgia, Lithuania and the Faeroes, cause for pessimism was justified. Little wonder that Walter Smith and Ally McCoist, after giving Scotland a good start, ran away back to Rangers, leaving the job to Alex McLeish. Scotland had, in spite of a predictable defeat in Italy, remained in contention. On 8 September they had delighted Hampden with a win over Lithuania – a particular source of joy to everyone in Scotland other than the lovers of Hearts who had for the past few years in scenes reminiscent of the film *The Invasion of the Body Snatchers* been taken over by men from the Baltic. But the trip to France would be difficult, if not impossible.

The game would attract a huge invasion of the Tartan Army, many of whom had no tickets but were justifiably confident of getting in anyway, but there was also the benefit that the game would be on terrestrial BBC TV, meaning everyone would see it. The home games tended to be on Sky Sports, which was a shame because many people, including politicians made the point, 'Why does everyone talk about the national team, if not everyone can see them?' But away games were available to everyone, and it would be one of these nights where everything stopped at a given time so that the nation could watch Scotland.

Politically, Scotland was in a curious position in 2007. The Scottish Parliament was run by the SNP, but with no effective majority, while the British Parliament was controlled by Labour, whose leader and therefore Prime Minister was Gordon Brown from Kirkcaldy, as Scottish as one is likely to be and the son of a Presbyterian Minister. Both parties slagged each other off *ad nauseam*, but they both generally wanted the same thing, and the country was, fairly obviously, booming with the bad old Thatcher days of unemployment and lack of government spending a thing of the past.

And what about France? It seems a curious thing to say about the World Cup runners-up, but France was a far more culturally diverse nation than Scotland, as far as football was concerned. Rugby, horse racing and other sports often gave the impression of being more important, and the standard of the French domestic *Ligue Un* had never reached the dizzy heights of comparable countries like Spain, Italy, Germany and England. The stereotypical image of the French man as a chap with a beret on a bicycle selling onions while eating snails at the same time, and finding it difficult to satisfy his sexually demanding wife had clearly gone but he had not yet been replaced by a football player. French players tended to play abroad. Arsenal, for example, often gave the impression of having been invaded by

Napoleon's conquering armies in the same way that Lithuania had taken over Hearts. The difference, of course, was that Arsenal had done it far more successfully, securing trophies galore under professorial French manager Arsène Wenger. Most good French players played in Italy's Serie A, La Liga of Spain or the English Premier League, although perhaps recalling the difficult past with the 'Bosch' or the 'Allemagnes', comparatively few played in the Bundesliga.

But national pride was at stake in the Euro Qualifiers – although not as intensely as in Scotland. Scottish fans turned up, bought tickets and sat blatantly in the French section, recalling memories of Mary Queen of Scots and the Auld Alliance by singing 'We hate England more than you!' The stadium was far from full at 42,000, French fans not supporting their team as they should have done, and perhaps proving that France, for all its success in recent years, is still not a football-loving nation. Scots fans, if not outnumbering the French, made up a sizeable proportion of the crowd and made most of the noise. They might have felt entitled to shiver in apprehension at the sight of so many household names – Makelele, Trezeguet, Vieira and Anelka – but there was always hope.

Scotland's players were lower key than that, but Barry Ferguson, Jamie McFadden, Davie Weir and Paul Hartley had all proved their value at that level, and in Craig Gordon, once of Hearts but now of Sunderland, they probably had the best goalkeeper around. Early indications were that he was in for a busy night. Statistics indicated that the teams had met on 14 occasions, there had never been a draw and both teams had won seven each.

But what Scotland did not lack was commitment. This was in stark contrast to their previous visit to the same ground in March 2002, the first game of the nightmarish Berti Vogts years, when the team simply collapsed in face of a French onslaught and ended up lucky to get away with a 0-5 defeat in one of Scottish football's more embarrassing nights. The 2007 team, well disciplined by Alex McLeish and Roy Aitken, simply did not believe that there was an immutable law that Scotland must lose football matches, and buckled down to their task admirably. They rode their luck on quite a few occasions, but backed up by their magnificent Tartan Army clearly outshouting the French, sustained a solid defence in the first 30 minutes and by the end of the first half were beginning themselves to cause a few problems.

Playing in white with a light blue saltire on the top, Scotland played a 1-4-1-4-1 formation with Craig Gordon, Paul Hartley and Jamie McFadden being the 1s, as it were. Hartley in front of the back four was particularly outstanding in that first half, never shirking a tackle and frequently being seen with the ball, encouraging and inspiring Scotland.

Half-time brought a little relief. A draw would not be the hugest disaster in the world for Scotland's qualification hopes, and television pundits praised the team, although warning that more pressure was to come. Indeed it did come, but once again Craig Gordon showed why Sunderland had paid £8 million for him with saves at point-blank range from Malouda, Ribery and Anelka. Gradually some of the sting went out of France's play as they became discouraged. It was then that Scotland and Jamie McFadden struck.

Opinions divided over McFadden. He had started off at Motherwell under Terry Butcher, then moved to Everton where his career had stalled to the extent that he could not always be guaranteed a place. The previous season, for example, he had started only six Premier League games for the Goodison men, and scored a grand total of three domestic goals. Yet he was charismatic, he could score for Scotland – he had netted on Saturday against the Lithuanians, and one remembered with affection his great strike against Holland at Hampden in the 2003 play-offs – and he loved playing for his national team.

Tonight was to be his finest hour. 65 minutes of the game had gone, and 'Faddie' was virtually on his own up front, with everyone else back helping the over-stretched defence. A hopeful clearance from Gordon found him about 35 yards from the goal and with four Frenchmen and a goalkeeper between him and the goal. But then again, football (in spite of what any number of coaches and technical directors will tell you) remains a simple game, and the object is simply to get the ball between the sticks and under the bar. McFADDEN did just that, catching everyone by surprise with a scorching, swirling left-footed drive which found the top corner, leaving keeper Landreau clutching thin air. It was so good and so unexpected that it even took the Tartan Army a few seconds to realise the enormity of what he had done.

Bedlam erupted all over the nation, but the sobering thought was that there remained 25 minutes to hold out against the team which was still rated the second best in the world. Professionalism, however, now reigned. A few brief moments of celebration, then back to the task in hand. Fletcher was already off injured and had been replaced by the excellent Stephen Pearson, and towards the end McLeish brought on Garry O'Connor in place of McFadden, whose place in Scottish folklore was now guaranteed by that goal.

The last few minutes were tight, but tempered with the knowledge that even a draw would be a good result. As it was, the Slovenian referee blew for full-time with Scotland still ahead, and Sauchiehall Street in Glasgow and Princes Street in Edinburgh lit up with an explosion of patriotic fervour rarely seen, with even the politicians the next morning hailing what Alex McLeish would call "Scotland's best victory for years".

History, of course, tells that Scotland did not quite make it to Euro 2008 and that the old guard of Italy and France did. That was a huge pity, and both teams eventually disappointed their supporters in the Finals, but this game was a lesson to Scotland. Scotland have been taught too many 'lessons' in the past after underrating countries like Costa Rica and the Faeroes and finding egg on their face, but this was a more positive lesson of how a proficient, committed Scottish team with the correct attitude can get the better of a technically far superior team.

Scotland as a nation deserves far better than some of the grizzly horrors of results that it has got over the years and this book at least goes some way to redressing the balance in that it focusses on the ups more than the downs of its footballers. There remains no nation on earth with greater and more passionate love of its national team, and one can only survey the debris of games like Uruguay in 1954, Peru and Iran in 1978, Costa Rica in 1990 and the Faeroes in 2002 and say 'It disnae need tae be like that!' This result against France in 2007 proves that.

BIBLIOGRAPHY

The Encyclopaedia of Scottish Football – David Potter and Phil.H.Jones
(Know The Score Books)

Scotland: The Complete International Football Record – Richard Keir
(Breedon Books)

The Roar Of The Crowd – David Ross
(Argyll Publishing)

Scottish International Football Miscellany – Brian Belton
(Pennant Press)

Wizards and Bravehearts – David Potter
(Tempus Publishing)

A Scottish Soccer Internationalists' Who's Who 1872-1986 – Douglas Lamming
(Hutton Press)

England v Scotland: The Auld Enemy – Dean Hayes
(Sport in Word)

Scotland: The Team, 1872-1987 – Andrew Ward
(Breedon Books)

Scotland's Quest For The World Cup: A Complete Record – Clive Leatherdale
(John Donald Publishers)

The Scottish Football Book (all years) – Hugh Taylor
(Stanley Paul Press)